THE FALLACIES OF STATES' RIGHTS

THE FALLACIES

OF

STATES' RIGHTS

SOTIRIOS A. BARBER

HARVARD UNIVERSITY PRESS
Cambridge, Massachusetts and London, England
2013

Library of Congress Cataloging-in-Publication Data

Barber, Sotirios A.
The fallacies of states' rights / Sotirios A. Barber.
p.   cm.
Includes bibliographical references and index.
ISBN 978-0-674-06667-0 (alk. paper)
1. Federal government—United States.   2. States' rights (American politics)
3. United States—Politics and government—Philosophy.   I. Title.

JK311.B36   2012
320.473'049—dc23   2012012910

For Karen

CONTENTS

THE FALLACIES OF STATES' RIGHTS

INTRODUCTION:
AMERICA'S OLDEST CONSTITUTIONAL DEBATE

The states' rights debate is America's oldest constitutional debate. Every issue in the campaign to ratify the Constitution was connected to the question of the future of the states in the proposed federal union. Resistance to national power in the name of states' rights brought the nation close to civil war on two occasions before firing started on Fort Sumter in 1861. Fearing that the Civil War Amendments to the Constitution would "fetter and degrade the State governments," the Supreme Court nullified all but the amendments' minimal promise for generations after the war. The scope of national power relative to the states was a major part of the conflicts of the Progressive Era and the New Deal. Expressing concern for the states' traditional control of the public schools, the Supreme Court abandoned the promise of equal educational opportunity less than two decades after the desegregation decision in 1954. Claims of "states' rights" have played an important role in opposition to the Court's decisions on school prayer, the treatment of criminal defendants, abortion, and gay rights. "States' rights" was a battle cry of the strategy that transformed the Republican Party from the party of Lincoln to the party of Reagan. A dramatic if limited return to states' rights was the signature achievement of the Rehnquist Court. At this writing states' rights is the battle cry against the Patient Protection and Affordable Care Act of 2010 ("Obamacare"). And though it has no real connection to states' rights, something called "competitive federalism" is part of the present campaign of corporate forces to deregulate the nation's economic life.

Yet in most of these cases observers could wonder whether states' rights was the most important issue. Did Thomas Jefferson and Alexander Hamilton disagree mostly over states rights or over the merits of an urban-industrial order? Was the Civil War fought for states' rights or for slavery?

1

Do pro-life forces oppose *Roe v. Wade* for taking an issue from the states or for legalizing abortion? Are opponents of the federal minimum wage indifferent to state minimum wages? Would critics of "Obamacare" remain silent if the states enacted similar measures? Behind these questions is a larger question of whether anything general can be said about what is really at stake in the federalism debate. If there is a bigger issue behind the federalism debate, what might it be? And if the federalism debate is a mask or a proxy for other issues, is anyone really interested in federalism or states' rights?

Whatever the American Constitution says about federalism it says indirectly. "Federalism" does not appear in the text of the Constitution, and though the document does refer to "the States," "the several States," and, of course, "the United States," *federalism* refers not to the mere existence of the states but to a relationship between the state governments and the national government. The closest the Constitution comes to describing this relationship is the Supremacy Clause of Article VI, which I shall discuss momentarily, and the Tenth Amendment. This amendment concerns "the powers not delegated to the United States by the Constitution, nor prohibited by it to the States"; these powers are "reserved to the States respectively, or to the People." Americans tend to read this language as apportioning responsibilities between two spheres of government, not unlike parents parceling duties between their children. The task of courts in federalism cases is usually described as drawing the line between the powers of the nation and of the states—drawing the line to maintain "the federal balance" intended by the founding fathers.[1]

This widespread view of American federalism is a mistake. The Constitution does not divide responsibilities between levels of government; it does not say, for example, that interstate commerce belongs to Congress, and education belongs to the states. With a few exceptions, like the limited powers to set voter qualifications and name members of the Electoral College, the Constitution delegates power only to one government. It delegates powers to Congress while *reserving* other powers to the states, reserving them without naming them. Delegating some and reserving other powers may seem little different from parceling powers between two governments. But the difference is a big one, and judges who deny the difference, including a majority of the present Supreme Court, are taking chances with the nation's future.

Should We Value Federalism?

Federalism is a relationship between layers of government, and, appropriately, the correct understanding of federalism is a layered problem. As one approaches the bottom layer one talks less about constitutional law than about ideas like reason, action, the nature of values like justice, and how Americans see themselves—whether they now see themselves or ever saw themselves as Americans or as New Yorkers, for example, or as both. But since federalism is most immediately a legal concept, our inquiry should begin with the Constitution, which begins with a preamble. The Preamble refers to "We the People of the United States," an entity that aspires "to form a more perfect Union." Beyond this reference to "Union," the Preamble lists substantive goods—good things, like "the common defence," "the general Welfare," and "the Blessings of Liberty." Much will be said about these preambular words and phrases in this book, and I start with a matter of the utmost importance: the Preamble does not describe governmental institutions; it describes desirable social states of affairs. True, "Union" could refer to a political institution (an electorate or a citizenry) as well as a condition of society (how people see themselves in relation to others). But with the possible exception of "Union," the Preamble mentions no ideas relating to the arrangement of governmental offices and powers. "Federalism," "separation of powers," "democracy"—no such term appears in the Preamble. The Preamble therefore suggests that the mere maintenance of constitutional institutions, including federalism, is not an end for which the Constitution was established.[2]

A neglected passage of *The Federalist* tells why this might be so. In No. 45 James Madison says that "the public good, the real welfare of the great body of the people is the supreme object to be pursued; and . . . no form of government whatever, has any other value, than as it may be fitted for the attainment of this object." This is the message of the American Revolution, Madison claims, and he applies it even to the constitution whose ratification he is arguing for. "Were the plan of the [Constitutional] Convention adverse to the public happiness," he says, "my voice would be, reject the plan. Were the Union itself inconsistent with the public happiness, it would be, abolish the Union. In like manner as far as the sovereignty of the States cannot be reconciled to the happiness of the people, the voice of every good citizen must be, let the former be sacrificed to the latter."[3]

This passage makes sense. Who would establish a government just to watch it operate? Democracies, federal systems, and systems that separate powers may be thought essential to self government, which is a good thing. But federated democracies that separate powers have been known to offend the principles of self government and erode its social and economic preconditions. Though representative governments with separated powers at both the state and national levels ruled the nation for almost a century prior to the Civil War, slavery flourished during that period. And under the Articles of Confederation, populist opposition to taxes threatened national defense by leaving the Revolutionary War debt unpaid, while populist economic policies in the states undermined the confidence of investors and threatened the developing national market. Federalism and separated powers did nothing to relieve these problems. Citizens value the separation of powers and other institutional forms, of course, but they do so assuming that they will secure goods like liberty, fairness, security, and plenty. Madison's view of the ends of government is just common sense. By emphasizing substantive goods as the ends of government, the Preamble manifests this commonsense view of the relationship between substantive goods and governmental institutions: the latter are means to the former; constitutional government is chiefly a means for pursuing good things. Thinking about constitutional questions should therefore follow the ordinary ways people think about pursuing good things. These ordinary ways of thought make up the patterns and principles of practical reason.

Common Sense, States Rights, and the True Constitutional Federalism

If constitutional thinking were governed by practical reason, constitutional power would appear to be a good thing, as it does in the first paper of *The Federalist*, where Alexander Hamilton claims, surprisingly to the modern ear, that liberty and strong government are on the same side.[4] Constitutional power would seem a good thing because it authorizes the pursuit of good things. Congress's power "To coin money [and] regulate the Value thereof" is a good thing because it authorizes the pursuit of a useful and stable currency. Where constitutional thinking reflects ordinary practical reason, grants of constitutional power are grants of discretion, not restraints on discretion, for there is no telling what means might be necessary to secure a stable currency and other ends of constitutional

4

power. People who see constitutional institutions and powers as means to good things will appreciate what Alexander Hamilton calls two "axioms as simple as they are universal": that "*means* ought to be proportional" to ends, and that "persons, from whose agency the attainment of any *end* is to be expected, ought to possess the *means* by which it is to be attained" (23:147, 149).

Adding these axioms to other propositions, we can see that limiting the powers of the national government in behalf of the states makes little practical sense. The first of these other propositions is that it is impossible to predict what problems the nation will face—impossible to predict "the extent and variety of national exigencies," as Hamilton puts it in *The Federalist* (23:149). The second, more controversial, proposition is that national ends are more important than conflicting state ends—more important as a matter of constitutional logic, and more important to "the People of the United States."

That some ends are more important than others is implicit in the Supremacy Clause of Article VI, which provides that "This Constitution, and the Laws of the United States which shall be made in pursuance thereof . . . shall be the supreme Law of the land; and the Judges in every State shall be bound thereby, any Thing in the Constitution or Laws of any State to the Contrary notwithstanding." The Supremacy Clause thus requires that when powers conflict, national powers override state powers. And since powers are granted to pursue certain ends, "superior powers" implies "superior ends." If, for example, the Constitution makes the national government responsible for promoting the security and prosperity of all the American people (as I argue in Chapter 2), the Supremacy Clause implies that the Constitution favors national security and prosperity over any potentially conflicting ends whose pursuit is reserved to the states. An observer who sees the Constitution chiefly as a means to ends will thus conclude with Chief Justice John Marshall, the nation's most celebrated jurist, that the big question in clashes of state and federal power is not locating the line that will maintain some "federal balance." The big question is whether the national government is doing what it is supposed to do. If the national government is trying to secure the nation from foreign attack, or trying to promote job growth, or trying to ensure equal treatment and opportunity for the nation's people—if the government is pursuing ends that a reasonable reading of the Constitution authorizes—then clashes with the states are constitutionally irrelevant.

Consider some examples. If Congress were concerned with the impact of drunk teenage drivers on the price of auto insurance, someone who thought about constitutional questions the way Marshall did would let Congress withhold federal highway subsidies from states that failed to set the drinking age at twenty-one. Indeed, a Marshallian would agree that Congress could enact a national drinking age of twenty-one if that seemed a reasonable way to lower insurance rates. True, a national drinking age would displace fifty policies in an area that the states have historically regulated. But the Constitution says neither that the states alone shall set the drinking age nor that Congress shall never interfere in areas that the states have historically controlled. Another example would be a congressional mandate that Americans purchase private health insurance. If this mandate addressed a national economic problem, in a reasonable way, and if the states could impose such a mandate because it offended no personal "liberty to contract" or other protected individual right, Congress could enact it. In both of these examples Congress would be doing what it is supposed to do—promoting national prosperity—and when Congress is doing what it is supposed to do, clashes with the states are irrelevant. This is "Marshallian federalism"—state-federal relations in the manner that Marshall thought about them—and I claim that Marshallian federalism, not states' rights federalism, is the true constitutional federalism.

Proving this claim is a challenge, however, and a rather complex one. It requires more than citing the authority of John Marshall or any other historical figure. It also requires more than common sense about the relationship between means and ends and the need for discretion in changing circumstances. Though Marshallian federalism does have constitutional language and common sense on its side, it faces serious objections of different kinds from different political directions. These objections could begin by challenging my right to the term "Marshallian federalism." The uncompromising nationalist view of federalism that I have sketched above derives from *McCulloch v. Maryland,* an 1819 Supreme Court case widely regarded as John Marshall's most carefully reasoned opinion. But Marshall said things elsewhere that clash with what he said in *McCulloch.* So taking *McCulloch* as the authoritative statement of Marshall's position will invite objections. I might have avoided this difficulty by choosing another name, like "national federalism." But we shall see that Marshallian federalism is but one form of national federalism. I have elected "Marshallian federalism" for reasons connected to general principles of constitutional interpretation. Since this book is on federalism, I keep principles of inter-pretation in the background. But I can sketch the reasons for my choice of names and refer readers elsewhere for the elaboration of those reasons.[5]

A law cannot guide conduct—cannot function as a law—if its message is mixed. You can't tell someone to stand up and sit down at the same time. Readers who take a writer (like Marshall) to speak for the law must there-fore shape his inconsistencies to fit his principal thrust. This prescription applies to any legal authority, including the sovereign people for whom the Constitution speaks. Madison makes the point in No. 40 of *The Feder-alist*. Here he invokes a "rule[ ] of construction dictated by plain reason," that "every part of . . . [a legal] expression ought, if possible, to be allowed some meaning, and be made to conspire to some common end" (40:259–260). I shall follow this rule when discussing Marshall's opinions in cases other than *McCulloch*, and readers can decide for themselves whether I am entitled to use Marshall's name as I do. I use Marshall's name and rely on his argument in *McCulloch* to underscore a point: there is nothing novel or "ahistorical" about the theory of federalism I defend in this book. It fits comfortably within a reasonable interpretation of the American founding, and it enjoys the decisive advantage of being the only view of our subject that makes sense.

Limited Government in What Sense?
Marshall's critics have claimed from the beginning and still claim that *McCulloch* abandons the idea of limited national power, and on one view of what "limited power" means Marshall's critics are right. Readers can see this from my example of a national drinking age. A government can be limited in several ways, however. It can have a limited number of aims. It can be limited by the procedures through which it pursues its aims. And it can be limited in the means it may choose. The Constitution limits the national government in all these ways. The Preamble and the enumera-tion of powers in Article I and elsewhere indicate limited aims. Congress can regulate commerce, coin money, and declare war; there is no men-tion of power to promote highway safety, literacy, childbirth (as opposed to abortion), or sexual morality. Provisions for lawmaking, elections, appoint-ments, and amendments limit the ways the government pursues its aims. And the constitutional rights of individuals prohibit some means to those aims. Congress would violate these three kinds of limits simultaneously if it authorized the Southern Baptist Convention to decide whether the

United States should be a Christian commonwealth. The federalism debate is not simply a debate over "limited government," therefore, for the national government would remain limited in important ways even if there were no states. The federalism debate is a debate about specific kinds of limits, namely (1) whether the national government should conceive its ends narrowly, to minimize conflict with the states, and (2) whether the powers of the states constitute limits on the means available to the nation when it is pursuing its authorized aims.

The debate over these two questions (the breadth of national ends and limits on national means in behalf of the states) is a debate between three versions of American federalism: Marshallian federalism, states' rights federalism, and process federalism. Marshallian and states' rights federalism join in opposition to process federalism. Process federalism holds that beyond the constitutional rights of individuals and the procedures for electing public officials and making laws, the national government can do whatever it wants. Thus, a process federalist would say, were it not for the First Amendment Congress could establish a national religion even without explicit power to do so. Marshallian federalism and process federalism jointly oppose the claim of states' righters that the reserved powers of the states limit national power just as the First Amendment limits national power. States' righters claim, for example, that states' rights preclude a power in Congress to make people buy health insurance, just as the First Amendment precludes a power in Congress to establish a religion. Combining the above questions and answers, we get Figure 1.

Marshallian federalism thus shares a conclusion with each of its contenders while they disagree with each other across the board. To prove their case Marshallians would have to show that though the Constitution limits the national government to certain ends, the national government

Figure 1

Affirms limited national aims	Denies limited national aims	Claims states' rights against the nation	Denies states' rights against the nation
Marshallian federalism			Marshallian federalism
States' rights federalism	Process federalism	States' rights federalism	Process federalism

can disregard the states when it is pursuing those ends. The Marshallian argument against states' rights federalism can begin and almost end with a simple observation: states' righters need an argument. A states' rights reading of the Constitution is not unreasonable. At least before all the evidence is in, one can read both the Constitution and the American founding to allow a state to nullify (on its own or through the federal courts) an otherwise authorized congressional act. On occasion, after all, major American statesmen and constitutional theorists have read the Constitution just that way. This list includes Thomas Jefferson, James Madison, and John C. Calhoun. But few will contend (and none successfully) that, in reason and justice, there is no other way to read the Constitution. Neither Jefferson, nor Madison, nor Calhoun managed to be a consistent states' righter, as we shall see. They proved by example that the Constitution can be read in different ways. States' righters therefore need an argument; they need an argument why everyone should read the Constitution their way.

Because, in making the needed argument, states' righters will be addressing parties on all sides of the debate, they must appeal to some value that the whole nation, including nationalists, can accept as a reason for the states' rights interpretation of the Constitution. Such an appeal would invoke a good that both sides accepted and that would serve as a standard for the conduct of each. This standard would be applied by a representative of both sides, which, perforce, would be an agent of the nation as a whole. Yet the existence of a controlling national standard whose application rests with an agent of the nation is precisely what states' writers deny. So states' righters need an argument, yet the very forum in which they make the argument—a national forum—excludes the kind of argument they need.[6]

Consider an example. "Liberty" exemplifies the kind of standard that states' righters need; they would claim that their reading of the Constitution enhances liberty. This has been the principal states' rights reason throughout American history, especially since the Civil War discredited reasons flowing from the mutual obligations of contracting parties (discussed in Chapter 5). But liberty is not the same as particular opinions about liberty, and one cannot offer what one admits to be a mere version of liberty as a reason for the other party in a debate to change its mind. Let me be clear: The expectations of debating parties enable the states' righter to claim that "states' rights enhance liberty." But these same expectations exclude the claim that "states' rights enhance John's conception of liberty" or "our Southern conception of liberty" or any particular conception of liberty. Claims of this last variety may be true—states' rights may well enhance John's conception or any other particular conception of liberty. But these claims cannot count as reasons for changing anyone's mind. That John values states' rights is no reason Jane should.

Yet in an actual debate, a particular person or faction will say "states' rights enhance liberty," and the other side will construe this claim in terms of what it believes to be the speaker's conception of liberty. If John C. Calhoun says "states' rights enhance liberty," the other side will construe his claim in light of his known theory that liberty requires race-based slavery. Calhoun will say "states' rights enhance liberty"; the other side will hear him say "slavery enhances liberty." So proposing in the course of a debate that "states' rights enhance liberty" implicitly commits the speaker to defend his view of liberty as the true understanding of liberty or the best understanding in light of the available evidence. He will have to do more than merely assert a personal, local, or historical view of liberty. He will have to defend his conception of liberty to an agent that represents both sides, which can only be an agent of the nation. Thus, as we shall see in Chapter 5, Calhoun did more than assert his conception of liberty or claim that states' rights enhance liberty. He tried to persuade the nation that the dominant view of liberty was wrong and that his view was right—that is, that liberty itself really necessitated slavery. And the reason he did this lay in the usual understanding of what counts as a reason in any debate, including debate in a national forum.

To see how ordinary expectations of practical reason defeat states' rights, assume a national debate about the virtues of a racially integrated society. Imagine a states' righter proposing that liberty is served best if each state answers the race question its way and each individual resides where he or she pleases. Our states' righter would thus conceive of liberty as freedom of racial association. Suppose he persuades Congress and the Supreme Court about the meaning of liberty. Put aside all complicating questions and factors, like competing values, the composition of the government and the armed forces, the policies governing federal enclaves and territories, and whether attitudes would remain sufficiently diverse to ensure adequate populations for the different kinds of states. Assume only two races, "black" and "white," and that each American belongs to one or the other, with no problem telling people apart. Each American would then have a choice of residence among three of four options: states that exclude whites, states that exclude blacks, mixed but segregated states, and integrated states. Our states' righter thinks that this situation enhances the liberty of individual Americans, and we accept this position for argument's sake.

This position would give no state a right to nullify or obstruct the nation's decision, taken in liberty's name, to divide itself into four groups of states. Since this decision would entail a nationally guaranteed right of every individual to relocate to one of three kinds of states, no state could deny its citizens a right to emigrate or prospective citizens of the appropriate colors a right to immigrate. Nor could any group of states decide to change its character. If the segregated states became integrated, the options of segregationists would be diminished in number, which would mean less liberty, an impermissible result in liberty's name. If integrated states became segregated, individuals who sought associations across racial lines would lose their freedom of association altogether, another result that liberty would not allow. And since states might want to change their character, security for liberty would require the nation to ensure that they did not do so. The value that justified states' rights would thus restrain the states. This is why defending states' rights is a self-defeating enterprise.

One Nation or Many?

Marshallians will also have to contend with the states' rights view of who or what made the Constitution. Did the framers speak for one national community, thirteen separate political communities that were determined to stay that way, or something in between? Readers might think that the Civil War settled this issue, and it did to some extent. But the war failed to silence talk of "state sovereignty," "nullification," and even "secession." Three generations after the war, segregationist states could still threaten to nullify the Supreme Court's decision in *Brown v. Board of Education* (1954). For ten years starting in 1995, states' righters on the Rehnquist Court struck down numerous national laws in their campaign to restore the "separate and independent existence" of the states as "sovereign" entities. At this writing somewhere between three and five members of the Roberts Court, all Republicans, see continuing constitutional relevance to a position rejected by the founder of their party: that the Constitution was founded by an act of thirteen separate peoples, "not the . . . people of the Nation as a whole." Current proposals in statehouses throughout the country would "nullify" national laws that regulate controlled substances, firearms, agricultural production, air pollution, mine safety, and even legal tender. And a recent candidate for the Republican presidential nomination, Governor Rick Perry of Texas, the nation's second-most populous state, claims that his state can lawfully secede from the union in protest of national policies. Though substantive policy disagreements fuel this states' rights revival, the constitutional claims of states' righters deserve a response.

A Marshallian answer to the states' right theory of the founding can begin with the same observation that begins the Marshallian answer to the states' rights understanding of "limited government": states' righters need an argument. While no one doubts that members of the founding generation saw themselves as Virginians, New Yorkers, and so forth, one can doubt that any saw themselves as no more than citizens of their states. Consider the personal history of John C. Calhoun, the nation's leading states' rights theorist. Calhoun held that the Constitution was a union of states and that individual Americans owed political allegiance solely to their states, not the nation. Yet Calhoun took the oath as vice president of the United States twice, and he considered running for president twice. He served in the president's cabinet twice, as secretary of war and as secretary of state. And he died in the nation's capital as a sitting U.S. senator, having previously served in the U.S. House of Representatives. These facts justify doubt that Calhoun saw himself as a Carolinian only, instead of a Caroline-American. How much of the same can be said of other occasional states' righters like Jefferson and Madison, one the author of the Declaration of Independence, the other a coauthor of *The Federalist* and the "father of the Constitution," and both holders of the highest national office? What evidence is there that they saw themselves as Virginians instead of Virginia-Americans?

What evidence is there that the people who lived in the states saw themselves as members solely of communities defined by geographical lines, as opposed to people with mixed political identities, like Virginia-Americans and New York–Americans? Do we know of any member of the founding generation with such a parochial view of himself? If we did, could we call such a person typical of his generation? Had the people of America seen themselves solely as citizens of their respective states, what sense could we make of the guarantee of Article IV of the Articles of Confederation that "the people of each state shall have free ingress and regress to and from any other state, and shall enjoy therein all the privileges of trade and commerce, subject to the same duties, impositions and restrictions as the inhabitants thereof respectively"? Given the undeniable ambiguities of the nation's history and of the personal histories of its major figures, states' righters need an argument. They need to show why we all should read an ambiguous historical record their way.

To succeed, states' righters must show some good that would result to the nation from viewing the founding their way. Ultimately they must show that the typical American would be better off seeing herself as a citizen of one state, not as a citizen of the United States with a right to relocate to another state. This formulation of what states' righters must show is not intended to be an insuperable hurdle. Though the states' righters cannot make a *constitutional* argument, they may be able to make a *political* argument. Indeed, I shall argue in Chapter 3 that the nation must be open to a states' rights argument. But, to recall *The Federalist* No. 45 and take a slight liberty with Madison's words, states' righters can make their showing only when "the Union itself [has proved] inconsistent with the public happiness" and the time has come to "abolish the Union." This conclusion would no longer be part of a traditional states' rights argument, however. As the idea of powers reserved to the states makes sense only if some powers are delegated to the nation, states' rights makes sense only if there is a nation from whose power the states are exempt. The argument that proves states' rights thus turns out to be the argument that would destroy states' rights. So when I say the nation must be open to a states' rights argument, I mean the nation must be open to its own dissolution. We shall see in Chapter 3 that the nation's openness to its dissolution is both a legacy of the American Revolution and the key to an understanding of the Constitution's ultimate end.

Is the Constitution Committed to a Specific Way of Life?

The federalism debate today is a two-way contest with states' rights on one side and what is seen as a monolithic nationalism on the other. This situation is one in which the weakest position intellectually has become the strongest position politically and the debate that the nation deserves is not taking place. If common sense influenced the agenda, states' rights would be tabled and the Marshallians would be left to contend against their fellow nationalists, the process federalists. Process federalism is the only form of federalism that opposes the idea that the enumeration of national powers implies limited ends. For several reasons, as we shall see, Marshallians may find it hard to disagree with the process federalist—hard to argue for limited national ends. One reason is that "limited national ends" that are also superior ends implies that the Constitution subordinates some ends to others and is therefore committed to a specific way of life. This prospect clashes with the belief that a right to "the pursuit of Happiness" is a right to live more or less as one pleases and that the Constitution "is made for people of fundamentally differing views."[7] In fact, Americans cannot live as they please; they have never enjoyed nor could they have enjoyed more than a "reasonable" array of life choices, and a reasonable set of options is a restricted set. To see that reasonable options hardly means unlimited options, ask members of the Fundamentalist Church of Jesus Christ of Latter-day Saints, The Creativity Movement, Earth First!, Christian Identity, the Nuwaubian Nation of Moors, or the Communist Party U.S.A. As a logical matter, where an agent (like "the People") grants powers to pursue only some ends (like national security and prosperity), and where the agent makes power to pursue these ends superior to all other powers (like the states' reserved powers), the agent implies that some ends outweigh others.

As uncontroversial as this conclusion may seem in the abstract, it represents a risky way of thinking about the Constitution. Indeed, this way of thinking jeopardizes the Constitution's own aspiration to "domestic Tranquility." Few readers will be disturbed by a conclusion that excludes the aspirations of the groups listed above. But many would be disturbed by the view of prominent Marshallians that the Constitution subordinates religion to secular aims.[8] Though believers can deny this conclusion, some acknowledge it, and a few have condemned the Constitution as godless and even satanic—a "pact with the Devil," the abolitionists said. Surely, judges should not exacerbate this kind of conflict. Even judges who agree that the Constitution subordinates religion can feel they should avoid saying so if they can. To see how they might avoid it, imagine Congress authorizing gay marriages in the armed forces and mandating that the states recognize these marriages. The intensity of religious hostility to same-sex unions would move some states to challenge this mandate as an incursion on the states' traditional power over family law. In response, federal judges need not hold that religiously based opposition to gay marriage clashes with the Constitution's subordination of religion to national security, which includes military morale as Congress sees it. Judges could hold instead that Congress's power to defend the nation trumps contrary state policies no matter what motivates them. Or judges could hold that victory for a religiously motivated claim would violate that governmental neutrality toward religion that is essential to religious freedom itself. In rejecting the states' rights challenge judges could thus employ either an openly secularist rationale, or a national defense argument, or a religious freedom argument.

True believers could accept the openly secularist rationale only under duress, for they would see it elevating national security over living as God commands. Alert believers would also reject the second and third rationales. That Congress prevails no matter what motivates the states assumes that the nation trumps the states even when the states act as God wills. And neutrality regarding religion implicitly denies religious truth. Neutrality between truth and falsity, unthinkable as a general matter, makes sense only when some higher good can come of it. But since no good could be higher than God's approval, those who insist on neutrality among religious beliefs imply either that all beliefs about God are true, or that none is true, or that the truth of none can be known—things no true believer could accept. So the argument concerned with the rights of believers and the argument concerned with institutional order would be as offensive to alert believers as the argument that openly subordinated religion. Yet two of the arguments disclose their offenses only to people who dig for them. They offend religion only implicitly; they avoid subordinating religion in a forthright and unmistakable manner. So the case for Congress's gay marriage policy that cites institutional principles (federal supremacy in pursuit of national security) and the case that claims to be based on liberty of conscience are less likely than the ends-oriented argument to offend the nation's religious communities.

We can thus see why constitutionalists would promote respect for rights and institutions ("our democracy," "our federalism") and avoid cultivating an appreciation for constitutional ends that depreciates other ends. An emphasis on rights and institutions enables a government to pretend to be "neutral" among ends. This feigned politics of neutrality—call it the "new politics"—might keep the peace and enable people to withdraw into their "private" lives without feeling that they are lesser persons or bad citizens for it.[9] Marshall himself subscribed to this new politics, as did other leaders of the founding generation, including the authors of *The Federalist*.[10] This is a problem for Marshallian federalism, which emphasizes public purposes like national defense and prosperity. The problem is how Marshall's ends-oriented view of federalism can fit within a larger constitutional philosophy that deemphasizes constitutional ends in favor of institutional forms and private rights. And the answer is that it cannot—that an ends-oriented approach to federalism implies an ends-oriented constitutionalism across the board, which in turn implies a particular way of life, including the kinds of people who are attracted to that particular way of life. This way of life would honor certain rights—to property, for example, and religious freedom. But it also denies rights that untold millions of people throughout human history have held of the utmost importance—like the right to live in a community that uses the criminal law for religious ends.

Marshall's approach to federalism should define his constitutionalism generally because an ends-oriented constitutionalism makes more sense than the constitutionalism of rights and institutions. Maintaining constitutional institutions as such cannot be a constitutional end because constitutional institutions are human establishments and no one would establish a constitution solely or chiefly for the pleasure of watching it function. Nor would a reasonable person establish a government for the sole or chief purpose of restraining its power. The chief purpose of constitution making as a rational enterprise can only be some substantive good like happiness, security, prosperity, or liberty—liberty, that is, mostly from third parties, not from government, and therefore liberty that all can share under government. For the Constitution to make sense, maintaining institutions and securing constitutional rights are best seen not as fundamental constitutional commitments but as strategies for pursuing constitutional ends.[11]

If Marshall's constitutionalism is to make sense, therefore, its two parts must fit together in a certain way; the part that emphasizes institutions and private rights must be subordinated to the part that emphasizes public purposes. In practice this would require a public-spirited leadership community whose task it was to "refine and enlarge" popular preferences, leading the people away from their momentary inclinations and toward their true interests. This would be an elitist way of combining an emphasis on rights with an emphasis on ends. But its elitism would not make it un-American. It was the approach of the Federalist Party, to which Marshall belonged, and it was also the approach of the New Deal. The Federalist Party disappeared by 1820, felled by the Jeffersonian revolt of the 1790s, and the New Deal and its successors fell to the Reagan revolt of the 1980s.

Marshallian federalism thus seems an anachronism, and this fact demands attention. It does not compel capitulation, however, for no one can guarantee the success of the nation's present antigovernment populism.

Union and Real Values

Another challenge to Marshallian federalism flows from disagreements about the nature of the Preamble's ends. Do expressions like "Justice," "Liberty," and "the general Welfare" refer to anything beyond the opinions of individuals, groups, or communities? Was liberty compatible with slavery just because Calhoun said so? Would liberty be compatible with slavery if everyone everywhere believed it, including persons held as slaves? What words like *liberty* signify is connected to the question whether the American population constitutes one community. When I touched on this question above I denied that states' righters could give a reason why everyone should view a mixed history and an ambiguous constitution as they do. They could succeed, I claimed, only if they could show all sides that their view enhances a good like liberty, the real thing or its best approximation, not just someone's view of liberty, since the real thing or its approximation is the only thing that all sides could agree was a reason for interpreting the Constitution the states' rights way.

But are states' righters obligated to give a reason? They will find it hard either to decline or to accept such an obligation. If they decline it either they concede that they have no reason for their interpretation or they assert that they need no reason because their interpretation is true beyond question. Asserting the latter would force them to describe the nationalist position as flowing from either incorrigible ignorance, fanatical closure to self-evident truth, or ulterior desire to subvert the Constitution. Either view of nationalism would cancel any obligation states' righters might have to justify their position. States' righters therefore face either capitulation or self-protective silence, incivility, or violence. If states' righters do choose to debate, they lose the debate, for they cannot debate without exchanging reasons, and the practice of exchanging reasons assumes what states' righters implicitly deny: that Americans are united in a common good or in the quest for a common good.

If states' righters offer liberty as their reason for their position they must refer to liberty itself—the one true understanding of liberty, not this or that local or partial or partisan conception of liberty—for, we have seen, the latter cannot serve as a reason. (Calhoun's view of liberty, as such, cannot be a reason for everyone to interpret the Constitution Calhoun's way.) And by offering liberty in debate—by the act of doing so—they assume that the debate is a truth-seeking process and that each side is more interested in the truth than in standing by its original position. Broaden the debate to embrace all of the Preamble's ends, and you have participants aspiring together to formulate one true and comprehensive notion of the good society. These individuals will reside in different parts of the country, but they will assume they and their children can move to a better place without losing their sense of who they are. Indeed, they will assume that their capacity and their right to better themselves in all senses are integral to who they are.

States' righters thus deny what any effort to justify their position assumes: that there is one best conception of the good society; that good-faith participants in the debate aspire to approximate it; and that exchanging reasons is the way to do that. William Rehnquist was the leading states' righter of his era, and he openly rejected these beliefs. Rehnquist maintained that there was no truth about ideas like justice and well-being and no basis for political morality beyond whatever just happened to be enacted into law.[12] This makes Rehnquist's popularity with the Religious Right one of the great ironies of the nation's political history. But states' righters are not the only moral skeptics in the debate; process federalists turn out to be skeptics too, and they too should lose the debate (at least the theoretical debate) because they cannot help but assume knowledge of the common good that their stated position denies. True Marshallians (that is, Marshallians who accept the full implications of an emphasis on constitutional ends) will support constitutional institutions and selected private rights as part of a strategy for pursuing the common good, which Marshall and The Federalist conceived largely as material security and prosperity.

By contrast, as we shall see in Chapter 7, process constitutionalists are rights oriented; they will inevitably substitute private rights for public purposes. They will see no good beyond private goods and processes that serve private goods. Marshallian constitutionalists will eventually move beyond merely private goods; they will see why individuals might want to identify themselves as part of the preambular "We" that declares the cooperative pursuit of justice and other public purposes "the supreme Law of the Land." Marshallian federalism sees reason as public reasonableness in pursuit of public purposes. Process federalism associates reason with self-serving calculation, of voters seeking private gain and politicians seeking votes. Marshall and *The Federalist* saw good government as educating people, turning them from their unreflective inclinations to their true interests. This essentially educative understanding of good government assumes that the community can produce and recognize political leaders who mean it when they proclaim devotion more to the community's best interest than to their private interests. Process constitutionalism makes no such assumption; it assumes no more than politicians who can achieve the electoral support they need to stay in office. For the process constitutionalist good government does not educate people, it coordinates people; it keeps them from colliding with each other as they go about their private pursuits.

Why Marshallian Federalism

The contest between Marshallian federalism and process federalism will turn ultimately on three sets of issues. First, whether process constitutionalism can justify (that is, cite a public good served by) its preference for representative democracy over other processes of decision and its preference for some rights (like freedom from racial discrimination) over others (like freedom of racist association). This question answers itself: to cite a public good as the reason for preferring one process or one right over others is to suppose that the public good is prior to processes and rights, something no process constitutionalist can admit without ceasing to be a process constitutionalist. As a theoretical matter, therefore, process federalism may prove as indefensible as states' rights federalism. The second set of issues is about whether there is a real difference between the two forms of nationalism. This complex question will occupy us in Chapter 7, which acknowledges the prospect that thinking about constitutional questions as Marshall did may well culminate in process federalism. The final issue between Marshallian and process federalism involves the practical prospects for public-spirited and competent leadership in a mass democracy. No one can deny that in today's America this prospect is a pipe dream. This woeful fact is bad news for Marshallian federalism.

Yet all may not be lost, for the process theorist himself implicitly recognizes more to reason than self-serving calculation. Like everyone else, he cannot help assuming the possibility of public-spirited, competent, and widely trusted civic leadership. When the process constitutionalist submits his position to a debate over how Americans should view their institutions, he assumes that his readers can see his submission as other than an act of self-serving calculation. He assumes his readers can see him as telling the truth as he sees it, not stroking their prejudices. He assumes his readers need someone to help them discover the truth and that they can recognize this need and turn to him as such a person. He assumes that his audience is at least open to the possibility that he is trustworthy—that he aspires to truth and possesses the personal qualities that make a person trustworthy. Unlike the members of Plato's guardian class, our process constitutionalist was not bred and raised in some special way that makes him much different from the rest of us. So if he can be trustworthy and regarded as such, possibilities he assumes in the very act of submitting his position to public approval, he cannot deny these possibilities for others, including elected politicians and the electorate at large.

Yet the process theorist can concede the theoretical possibilities and still deny the real-life probabilities. He can legitimately ask with a pessimistic air whether a consumer society is likely to produce and support a public-spirited elite whose members approach their disagreements in a civil and scientific spirit. Here is another question that all but answers itself, and the answer is more bad news for Marshall's constitutionalism. The Marshallian need not give up, however; for bad news also awaits his competitors.

The Future of Constitutional Federalism

The Marshallian's competitors are the process constitutionalists and states' rights constitutionalists. Albeit in different ways, the latter two emphasize constitutional institutions and rights over constitutional powers and ends. Constitutional practice in the United States has emphasized institutions and rights over constitutional ends at least since the closing years of Reconstruction, when the Court revived states' rights to rationalize the nation's refusal to redeem the implicit promise of the Civil War Amendments: full membership for black Americans in American life. Essential to a constitutionalism of ends was Marshall's promise in *McCulloch* that the Court would strike down attempts by Congress to pursue unauthorized ends under pretense of authorized ends. By all accounts the Court had reneged on this promise for two generations before Rehnquist launched his states' rights campaign in *National League of Cities v. Usery* (1976). A progressive majority of the Court regained control and overruled *Usery* in *Garcia v. San Antonio Metropolitan Authority* (1985). A slim majority in

20

Garcia formally adopted process federalism when it held that the Court would no longer review state claims against national power that did not allege that the latter had abridged the states' rights to participate in the processes of national decision. But Rehnquist and his allies regained control less than a decade later and renewed the states' rights revival for which Rehnquist will be most remembered. Throughout all of this the Court has emphasized constitutional institutions and rights, not constitutional ends. And though one cannot blame the Court for the nation's current political pathologies, the current situation calls for revisiting the issues between a constitutionalism of institutions and rights and a constitutionalism of ends. One of these issues concerns the risks of emphasizing constitutional ends. The emphasis on rights and institutions has simply failed to avoid the clash of ends—the clash of different visions of what the nation should be.

A related reason for reconsidering an emphasis on constitutional ends involves Madison's view of what constitutional government is chiefly about. Recalling Madison's observation in *The Federalist* No. 45, we can say that a theory of federalism works only if it contributes to "the real welfare of the great body of the people" (45:309). Because one element of a people's welfare is its capacity for reasonable progress toward reasonable goals, a people's well-being requires confidence in its government.[13] By this measure also, it is far from clear that a constitutionalism of rights and institutions works. Major research organizations report a drop of around 30 percent in the public's overall approval of the national government in the past twenty-five years. Important students of American institutions of different political persuasions—thinkers like Ronald Dworkin, Richard Posner, William Galston, Michael Sandel, Robert George, Sanford Levinson, David Brooks, Walter Murphy, Stephen Macedo, Alan Wolfe, Thomas Mann, Norman Ornstein, Paul Krugman, and Sheldon Wolin—have openly questioned the ability of the American system to maintain a healthy politics and a competent government. One can no longer reject a constitutionalism of ends on the theory that a constitutionalism of rights and institutions works.

Another reason to reconsider a constitutionalism of ends lies in what process federalism and states' rights federalism have jointly prepared the way for. The Court announced process federalism in *Garcia* in 1986, only to abandon it in *New York v. United States* in 1992. Six years is an exceptionally short life for a major constitutional doctrine, and the question is how to explain *Garcia*'s early demise. One possibility is that replacing Marshallian federalism with process federalism, was replacing a sense of fallibility in pursuit of presumably real goods with the belief that what's "good" is whatever anyone wants, no matter what that might be. Because this kind of skepticism can support no workable system, what's good will eventually become whatever the community's dominant force says is good. This may seem to be an argument for states' rights federalism. You may think that because there is no one right way to treat women or no one right answer to the morality of homosexuality or no one correct theory of equal opportunity, there can be no point in submitting different opinions about these matters to a central political process whose ultimate justification rests on its capacity to free public opinion from local prejudices and reconcile it to what is right for the nation as a whole. In view of Rehnquist's moral skepticism, this could be what he had in mind. But a lot depends on context, and appearances can deceive. If all conceptions of justice really are arbitrary, there can be no reason for not imposing one view of justice nationwide. And this seems precisely what Rehnquist's revival of state sovereignty has prepared the way for. In other words, the states' rights revival may have little to do with reviving states' rights. The real aim of the states' rights revival may be its predictable consequence: subordinating government—state and national—to "The Market." And not the local market, mind you; not even the national market, but the Global Market.

We shall see in Chapter 4 that something like this is afoot in America today. A Trojan horse falsely named a kind of "federalism" is rolling in ready to drop the new regime that sits in its innards. The owners of this false federalism are economic libertarians who call it "competitive federalism" or "fiscal federalism." Where old-fashioned states' righters sought to strengthen the states by weakening Congress, these new "federalists" would weaken Congress not to strengthen the states but to enhance corporate power over both the nation and the states.[14] As it happens, therefore, the states' rights federalism that Rehnquist resurrected and expanded turns out to be an instrument of the Reagan doctrine that America's problem is too much government—too much government at all levels. By this is meant too much electorally accountable government—not what political scientists call "private government." This appearance of a new kind of "federalism" demonstrates the wisdom of Walter Berns, who said some fifty years ago that the federalism debate was never really about states' rights; it was and remains a debate about what the nation ought to be.[15] This leaves us with a question about the difference between Marshallian nationalism and the new corporate nationalism and internationalism called "competitive federalism." We shall see that the difference involves different kinds of elites, different conceptions of reason, different attitudes toward self and others, and, above all, the distinction between real and apparent goods.

1

WHY THE STATES CAN'T CHECK NATIONAL POWER

The Immediate Problem

This book comes at a time when the nation waits to see if the Roberts Court will resume the campaign for states' rights that William Rehnquist launched in the mid-1970s. This campaign was Rehnquist's contribution to an outlook on politics that regards government as a necessary evil. This outlook is well represented in popular opinion, the nation's statehouses, and the current federal judiciary. It is also represented in legal academe. At present, this antigovernment outlook stands behind an attack on the Patient Protection and Affordable Care Act of 2010 (ACA or "Obamacare"). The leading argument against the ACA is a states' rights argument.

In January 2011, a federal judge in Florida declared the ACA unconstitutional. The judge was Roger Vinson, a senior member of the Northern District of Florida. The ACA was void, the judge declared, because its key provision offended "our federalist system," which he conceived as a "system of dual sovereignty."[1] In reaching his decision Judge Vinson seemed unaware of what James Madison held to be a principle of the American Revolution, that "the public good, the real welfare of the great body of the people is the supreme object to be pursued; and . . . no form of Government whatever, has any other value, than as it may be fitted for the attainment of this object." When Madison said "no form of Government whatever," he meant more than "forms" in the broad sense, like democracy and monarchy; he also meant institutional arrangements, like separation of powers and, on this occasion, federalism. Thus he went on to say that if the Constitution and the union should prove to be "inconsistent with the public happiness," he would reject the Constitution and abolish the union. "In like manner," he added, if "the sovereignty of the States cannot be reconciled to the happiness of the people, the voice of every good citizen must be, let the former be sacrificed to the latter."[2]

Americans generally see physical and mental health as integral to their welfare, and the Preamble of the American Constitution says that "the general Welfare" is part of what the Constitution seeks to promote. When Congress passed the ACA in 2010, about one in six Americans lacked health insurance, and Americans have long seen this situation as a national problem. A Congress in which progressive Democrats were in the minority addressed this problem in a manner agreeable to a politically powerful constituency: corporations that sell health insurance policies for profit. Congress devised a system in which the insurance companies could afford to cover high-risk clients at costs that clients could afford to pay. The key to this plan was the ACA's "individual mandate," a requirement that everyone, high and low risk alike, purchase insurance so that the companies could afford to insure high-risk individuals. It was this section of the ACA that Judge Vinson found offensive to "our federalist system," and since he saw this part of the act as pivotal to the rest, Judge Vinson declared the entire act unconstitutional.

To see the ultimate implication of Judge Vinson's treatment of the ACA, we should first note his failure to suggest that buying insurance was like deciding how to vote or whom to marry or what religion to join. The judge steered clear of any suggestion that the Constitution secured an individual's freedom to decide whether to have health insurance or a person's liberty to contract for it. Judge Vinson treated the issue before him as a federalism matter, not a civil rights matter—a matter of states' rights, not individual rights. Nor did Judge Vinson imply that Congress had made a national mountain of a local molehill. In fact, he acknowledged "myriad problems in our health care system," and he openly regretted striking down the ACA at a time of "virtually unanimous agreement that health care reform is needed in this country."[3] Rather than claim that health care was something left to the states, he repeatedly referred to health care as a national problem, and noting that one-sixth of the national economy was devoted to health care, he said that "without doubt, Congress has the power to reform and regulate this market."[4] Nor did Judge Vinson question the motive behind the ACA; he assumed the act was what it was advertised to be: a response to the nation's health care problem. Nor did he suggest that the ACA was unreasonable in the sense of poorly calculated to achieve affordable health care for more people.[5]

Judge Vinson thus struck down the ACA despite his recognition that it addressed a big problem for the economic well-being of the American population, that the problem it addressed fell within problems that Congress could lawfully address, that the law aimed at what it said it aimed at, that it was reasonably calculated to achieve its desired result, and that it violated no individual's federal constitutional right. The ACA's sole defect was its offense to states' rights. Judge Vinson held that in its pursuit of the nation's economic well-being Congress cannot employ means that offend "our federalist system." He also said that there were constitutional ways to accomplish Congress's aims, even though he failed to mention ways acceptable to constituencies like the insurance companies whose approval was politically necessary to enact any such program.[6]

Judge Vinson apparently believes, therefore, that "our federalist system" is important enough to burden or perhaps even prevent Congress's pursuit of an unquestioned element of the general welfare. Judge Vinson would surely object to this description of what he believes. He would say either that he is following the Constitution, not his personal beliefs, or that a judge sworn to uphold the Constitution must conceive the nation's well-being in terms of what the Constitution permits. But Judge Vinson recognizes the present health care system as a national problem independently of what he says the Constitution permits. This leaves us with the suggestion that states' rights are important enough to the Constitution (or were important enough to the founding fathers) to compel the nation's people to live with an inadequate health care system. And since what applies to health care applies to other elements of the general welfare, Judge Vinson suggests that states' rights are important enough to compromise Congress's pursuit of the general welfare and, therewith, to force a lower standing of living on the American people.[7]

Who was Judge Vinson speaking for? If James Madison spoke for the framers when he explained why people adopt constitutions and what makes them valuable, we can at least doubt that the framers would have held states' rights to be more important than the people's well-being. So Judge Vinson cannot say that, without question, the founding generation thought states' rights important enough to burden pursuit of the general welfare. Nor can Judge Vinson say that the language of the Constitution must be read his way, for the Constitution says nothing about "federalism," much less "dual sovereignty." The Constitution does allude to sovereignty at one point when it declares itself "the supreme Law of the Land."

But this declaration in Article VI can hardly put states' rights in competition with the general welfare because the very same sentence of Article VI claims supremacy also for "Laws of the United States made in Pursuance of" the Constitution, "any Thing in the Constitution or Laws of any State to the Contrary notwithstanding."

True, we don't have to interpret Article VI as I am interpreting it here. Judge Vinson could say that laws pursuant to the Constitution are, among other things, laws that respect state sovereignty—that since the Constitution fails to mention anything like "health care," Congress can enact the ACA only if it is a "necessary and proper" means to regulating commerce, and a national law that disregards state sovereignty is not a "proper" constitutional law.[8] On Judge Vinson's reading of the Necessary and Proper Clause, the Supremacy Clause of Article VI turns out to mean that national laws pursuant to the Constitution are supreme over state constitutions and laws as long as national laws do not conflict with state constitutions and laws, "any Thing in the Constitution or Laws of any State to the Contrary notwithstanding." This states' rights version of Article VI makes no sense at all, but if we allowed it for the sake of argument, the most we could say for Judge Vinson is that he had a choice between two readings of the Supremacy Clause: a nationalist reading and a states' rights reading. The nationalist reading would permit Congress to overrule state policies when Congress is pursuing authorized ends, which Judge Vinson admitted Congress was doing in this case. The states' rights reading would hold consistency with state policies to be an overriding national end. Our question then would be what reason Judge Vinson could give for his interpretation. Why should everyone believe with Judge Vinson that states' rights are important enough to burden or even cripple Congress's pursuit of the general welfare?

Instead of answering this question, Judge Vinson begs it. He indicates that if we do not read the Constitution his way, there will be no limit to national power, especially the national commerce power, under which Congress enacted the ACA. But the question of why we should read the Constitution as Judge Vinson does is equivalent to the question why we should understand limited national power as he does. The idea of "limited government" per se is not at issue. No one questions limits in behalf of individual rights and limits in the form of procedures for passing laws, electing representatives, appointing officials, and amending the Constitution. No one questions or should question a general requirement, enforced by the courts under several constitutional provisions, that all laws, state as well as national, should meet some minimal standard of reasonableness, as Judge Vinson admits the ACA does. The question is why we should read the Constitution to impose additional limits. Why must Congress address admitted national problems in ways that avoid conflicts with what the states claim they have a right to do? We know what is good about an adequate health care system. We know what is good about security, plenty, tranquility, opportunity, and other elements of the general welfare. What's so good about states' rights?

This book seeks an answer to this question—What's so good about states' rights?—and finds not only that there is none but that there cannot be one. The chief obstacle to showing this is a widespread and entrenched belief about a feature of the Constitution that favors Judge Vinson's decision. I call this belief the federalism axiom. According to this axiom, the states' reserved powers limit the nation's delegated powers—that is, the national government cannot lawfully do what it could do if it were the only government. If the national government were the only government it could establish public educational systems, for example, for Congress could do this in a manner consistent with other constitutional principles, like the separation of powers, democracy, and security for individual rights. But since the national government is not the only government, and since its list of authorized powers contains virtually nothing about education, the national government cannot establish and operate the nation's public schools, even though it can prevent the states from operating them in ways that violate individual rights. If the states were to stop operating schools altogether, according to this view of federalism, the nation still could not establish and operate public schools, no matter what the consequences for national security and prosperity. Judge Vinson thinks in terms of this axiom when he gives his one and only argument for striking down the ACA: If Congress can force people to buy health insurance, there's no limit to what Congress can do. Yet, axiomatically, there must be a limit to what Congress can do. Therefore, Congress cannot force people to buy insurance.

To show the fallacy of Judge Vinson's thinking I will have to show that the federalism axiom is but one version of what it means to say that Congress's powers are limited, and that this is the one version for which nothing favorable can be said. The first step in showing the federalism axiom is indefensible is to outline alternative understandings of what "limited national power" and therewith "federalism," mean. I shall then show the federalism axiom cannot be treated axiomatically because it conflicts with other constitutional principles for which axiomatic status has been claimed, like the idea that Madison treats as an axiom in *Federalist* 40: government is made for people, people are not made for government, and the people's welfare therefore takes priority over any and all governmental forms, including "federalism." Conflicts like this force interpreters of the Constitution to choose among principles, and a responsible choice must be backed by reasons. Our question then becomes why we should choose one version of American federalism over others. It turns out, however, that each understanding of American federalism has its problems. As I outline the different models of federalism in this chapter, I will preview how later chapters resolve these problems. The one question that this chapter does try to settle is whether the Constitution permits the states to use armed force against the national government.

Readers may think—I trust that they do!—that the answer to this last question is so obvious that proving it is a waste of time. But if we could put armed force against the nation altogether beyond constitutional possibilities, we could have a kind of rule of the game to invoke when exploring other questions. We shall see how this rule of the game defeats two dogmas of states' rights federalism, dogmas of great influence on the way Americans think about federalism. The first of these dogmas is that the American system is one of "dual sovereignty." The second holds that the states enjoy some kind of "check" on national power. We shall see that these dogmas must be false, for both will be shown to imply a result that's constitutionally off-limits: armed force by the states against the nation.

Three Models

"Federalism" signifies a state of affairs in which the functions of government are shared by a central government and the governments of member provinces, states, and/or local governments. In this descriptive sense of federalism, the system of government in the United States is a federal system. But calling the United States a federal system need mean no more than the Constitution provides two layers of government. The word *federalism* alone doesn't settle the question of what should happen when the policies of those governments conflict. The nation would still have two layers of government and therewith a federal system if the policies of one government were supreme in cases of conflict. Judge Vinson himself takes this for granted, for he doesn't see overruling the ACA in the name of states' rights as compromising "our federalist system." If the national government were entirely subordinate to the states—if each state had a veto over national policy and the national government could act only as permitted by a solid national consensus (as might be expected, for example, in case of foreign attack) we would still have what many have called a "federal system."

We need more, therefore, than a mere description of the United States as "a federal system." We need a theory of "juridical federalism," a principle for judges to use in cases of conflict between the layers of government. This principle would guide judges trying to adjudicate claims that one level of government had gone beyond its authority and encroached upon the other. This book seeks a true account of this principle: What does the Constitution indicate about how judges should resolve cases of state-federal conflict? What is the true constitutional federalism? The most common understanding of juridical federalism in America has long been dominated by a spatial metaphor, the "two spheres" metaphor. This understanding of juridical federalism assumes that the powers of government are divided between a national sphere and a state sphere; that a line of some sort separates the two spheres; that this line restrains each level of government; and that the problem that judges face is where to draw the line, both in principle and in concrete cases.[9] If we accepted this understanding of federalism, as most Americans do, we would have to conclude, as we shall see, that federalism is not a genuine principle of the American Constitution.

But we do not have to accept the two-spheres model. Even though the two-spheres model has dominated American constitutional thinking, the nation's history reveals more than one understanding of federalism. In fact, constitutional discussion over the years discloses three models: states' rights or dual federalism, which is the two-spheres model just described, and two varieties of national federalism. I call the first kind of national federalism Marshallian federalism, after Chief Justice John Marshall's opinion in *McCulloch v. Maryland* (1819), which remains the most celebrated of the Supreme Court's pronouncements on juridical federalism, notwithstanding its covert subversion by the Rehnquist Court in the 1990s. I call the second kind of national federalism process federalism or, sometimes, *Garcia* federalism, after the Court's opinion in *Garcia v. San*

Antonio Metropolitan Transit Authority (1986), an opinion that tried, and ultimately failed, to reverse the movement away from Marshallian federalism that Rehnquist skillfully engineered in the 1976 case of *National League of Cities v. Usery*.[10]

Though no major figure of American political history has consistently supported states' rights or dual federalism, it was the occasional federalism of Thomas Jefferson, James Madison, John C. Calhoun, Roger Brooke Taney, and, of course, William Rehnquist. Marshallian federalism was the federalism of Alexander Hamilton, Daniel Webster, Abraham Lincoln, Harlan Fiske Stone, William Brennan, and scholars like Martin Diamond, Walter Berns, and Herbert Storing. Process federalism was the federalism of Justice Harry Blackmun and scholars like Herbert Wechsler, Jesse Choper, and John Hart Ely. States' rights federalism is the familiar two-spheres conception of federalism; it takes seriously the idea of a line between the spheres. Marshallian federalism recognizes no such line, at least none that restrains the nation. If we must speak of a line, a Marshallian would say, it restrains only the states; the national government may freely disregard policies and practices of the states as long as it is pursuing national security, national prosperity, and other authorized national ends. Process or *Garcia* federalism holds that state policies and practices constitute no subject-matter restraints on national power—that as long as the states are represented in Congress and other institutions for determining national policy, as the Constitution provides, the national government can do what it wants to do vis-à-vis the states.

These models overlap in some respects. Marshallian federalism does not deny an axiom of dual federalism (an ambiguous axiom, as we shall see), that the national government is one of limited powers. Dual federalism, in turn, takes two forms, one of which can be construed as a weak form of Marshallian federalism. And process federalism will prove to be either a diminished form of national federalism or the perfected form of national federalism. This chapter outlines these models, discusses some of their implications, and sets up a debate between them whose unfolding will occupy the remaining chapters. This debate reaches three main conclusions: First, no coherent account of what the Constitution says or originally meant can justify states' rights federalism or avoid a choice between the two forms of national federalism. Second, Marshallian federalism deserves to win the intellectual debate with *Garcia* federalism because Marshallian federalism belongs to a superior understanding of the Constitution as a whole. And third, notwithstanding the superiority of Marshallian federalism, *Garcia* federalism may be the best that the nation can hope for.

The most defensible view of the Constitution as a whole is an ends-oriented or positive understanding of the Constitution. Positive constitutionalism holds that constitution makers establish governments chiefly to do good things for people. Negative constitutionalism holds that constitutions seek chiefly to restrain governments from doing bad things to people. Positive constitutionalism emphasizes constitutional powers, like the commerce power, over constitutional rights because constitutional powers are authorizations to act, and it is only through action that government can pursue the public goods listed in the Constitution's Preamble. Negative constitutionalism emphasizes constitutional rights over constitutional powers and conceives constitutional rights as restraints on government's power to pursue good things. Positive constitutionalists include Alexander Hamilton, the early James Madison, John Marshall, Abraham Lincoln, Franklin Roosevelt, and signers of the Declaration of Independence and the constitutional proposal that the Constitutional Convention submitted to the Continental Congress in September 1787.

At times I refer to the ends-oriented or positive view of the Constitution as a "welfare" view of the Constitution. I borrow this term from Madison's statement in *The Federalist* No. 45 that "the real welfare of the great body of the people is the supreme object to be pursued; and that no form of Government whatever, has any other value than as it may be fitted for the attainment of this object" (45:309). I have defended this welfare understanding of the Constitution at length in other works, and I repeat the main arguments in abbreviated form here. Yet I recognize that a concern for constitutional rights can have, and should have, a crucial place within a larger emphasis on constitutional ends. But this will depend on whether people who devote most of their energy to private pursuits can recognize the greater importance of the public interest and seek leaders who they sincerely believe are more patriotic than self-seeking and partisan. In other words, I acknowledge that a constitutional consciousness that emphasizes rights can be functional to the pursuit of constitutional ends, but only if those asserting constitutional rights accept the leadership of those devoted to pursuing constitutional ends. This, of course, is a most unlikely state of affairs. Madison claimed in *The Federalist* that this leader-follower pattern actually materialized at the nation's founding (49:340–341), and it may have.

But no one expects it to happen again. No one expects Americans generally to recognize that they may be wrong about what is in the long-term interest of their children and that they should therefore seek out candidates for office who seem more interested in the truth than in partisanship or flattery. In the course of defending Marshallian federalism I indicate how the federalism debate implicates larger issues of constitutional design, success, and failure.

States' Rights Federalism

Because conventional opinion has always favored the states' rights or dual federalist understanding of the nature of juridical federalism, our discussion begins with the states' rights model. This model is the familiar two-spheres model. It maintains that the national and state governments each have their proper concerns—national defense a responsibility of the nation and education a responsibility of the states, for example—and that each government has a constitutional obligation to avoid or at least minimize encroachment on the sphere of the other. For dual federalism, the juridical problems concern the "line" that separates the two spheres. The first of these problems is finding a rule or principle for locating the line. Two basic answers to this problem have emerged. One answer describes the line in terms of the Constitution's famous "enumeration of powers," which occurs mainly in Article I, Section 8. The other answer looks past the enumerated specifics to what Lincoln called "the principle of generality and locality": the national government handles matters of general concern, and the states handle state and local matters.[11] Dual federalists favor the first answer. They draw the line, or claim to, by consulting the specific powers enumerated and such "implied powers" as Congress must exercise if it is to avoid nullifying the grant of specific powers, all of which they conceive narrowly. Thus, dual federalists strongly deny that the commerce power and related powers add up to a general power to pursue the nation's economic health. But a narrow conception of enumerated powers is not enough for dual federalist aims, for even the narrowest conception of national powers could erase the alleged line between the powers of the nation and the states.

Consider a power that no one doubts is exclusively within the national sphere, like the power to declare war and, implicitly, to wage and win wars. This war-making power would leave the government free to wage war successfully by all but expressly exempted means, like imposing cruel and unusual punishments (at least on civilians) or forcing people to attend religious services. And the means requisite to winning a war would be determined solely by unpredictable developments that no prior categories of action could cover. Hamilton emphasizes this point in a famous passage of *The Federalist* (23:147). Powers of national defense "ought to exist without limitation," he says, "*[b]ecause it is impossible to foresee or define the extent and variety of national exigencies, or the corresponding extent & variety of the means which may be necessary to satisfy them*" (his emphasis). Winning a war might thus require all manner of national encroachments on traditional state responsibilities. The endless list of possible examples includes banning taverns, brothels, and casinos within short traveling distances of military bases; training recruits in math, science, and computing, as needed for high-tech weaponry; building roads, canals, and railroads that are useful for military purposes; funding scientific research that might have military applications; educating or paying the states to educate potential recruits in foreign languages, customs, and religions, as needed to cultivate skills and attitudes for consolidating the occupation of captured territory; and mandating the racial integration of schools, businesses, and public institutions as prerequisite to racially harmonious fighting forces. Contingencies could justify all these measures, even under this narrowest conception of national objectives: waging and winning wars. This is why one can see one form of states' rights federalism (defining national power narrowly) as a weak form of national federalism.

Eventually, therefore, the dual federalist must employ a strategy other than narrowly conceiving national powers. This other strategy is to claim that the states have rights that exempt them from Congress's acknowledged power. Thus, under Rehnquist's leadership, a plurality of the Supreme Court held in *National League of Cities v. Usery* (1976) that even though the Constitution gave Congress power to regulate the hours and wages of the nation's workforce, state governments were largely exempt from such legislation as a matter of constitutional right because power over the working conditions of state employees in "essential governmental functions" was implicit in a constitutionally mandated state sovereignty.[12] Failing to admit the fact, maybe to keep Justice Blackmun's vote, Rehnquist sought to overrule the defining proposition of Marshallian federalism: that states' rights constitute no limit on national power. We shall see in Chapter 6 that a nationalist majority reasserted itself in 1986, a decade after *Usery*, to arrest the states' rights movement that Rehnquist tried to launch in that case.

By 1992, however, the composition of the Court had changed. Rehnquist was now chief justice, new appointees sat on the Court, and a states' rights block of five justices resumed Rehnquist's campaign. This was hardly an inevitable development, but it did respond to the logic of the federalism axiom. This axiom describes the national government as one of "limited powers," and the dominant interpretation of "limited powers" is a negative one—that some classes of acts are prohibited to the national government. Though these prohibited classes of acts are not specified, dual federalists believe they know them by inference from what the Constitution does specify, mostly in Article I, Section 8. Suppose, for example, that Congress and the national government had been established to pursue but one end, national security. A dual federalist would take this fact to imply that Congress could pursue no aims in education, public morality, and race relations, even as means to national security.

By contrast, a Marshallian would construe the "limited' in "limited government" as "dedicated to"—dedicated to national security, in our present example. A Marshallian would say that national security is something that the government has a duty to pursue and that when it is pursuing this end it can freely disregard the policies and practices of the states. A Marshallian therefore would deny that Congress can never do anything in fields like education, public morality, and race relations. Rehnquist realized that carried to its limits, this Marshallian view made a nullity of the idea that the Constitution reserved powers to the states—"reserved" in the sense of set aside for the states to govern without interference from the national government—which is the way he, along with most students of the Constitution and the general public have interpreted the Tenth Amendment.

To salvage something of the federalism axiom, as he understood it, Rehnquist therefore had to undermine Marshall's opinion in *McCulloch*, and he did so in a less than candid way probably because he dared not risk open conflict with a case as prestigious as *McCulloch*. As we shall see, Rehnquist's Revolution made a sputtering start in the mid-1970s, stalled in the mid-1980s, and resumed and advanced in several directions in the mid-1990s. It stalled again in 2005 as two members of the states' rights block broke with the Chief Justice and Justices Clarence Thomas and Sandra Day O'Connor to uphold application of the Federal Controlled

Substances Act to the possession of home-grown marijuana for medical purposes as permitted under California law.[13]

The Rehnquist Revolution is now on hold as the nation awaits the judgment of the Roberts Court on the constitutionality of the ACA ("Obamacare").[14] The issue in this case can be phrased in terms of the alternative forms of dual federalism, one concerning the scope of a congressional power (Does the power to regulate commerce include the power to force people to purchase insurance policies?), the other concerning states' rights exemptions from an admitted congressional power (Can the states alone compel their residents to purchase insurance policies?). Answers to these questions can take one or more of three forms: historical, textual, and moral, all of which I will discuss in due course.

Two problems of states' rights federalism warrant mention at this point; the first involves the states' rights theory of the Constitution's origin and basic normative character; the second concerns an acceptable sense in which the state governments might "check" the exercise of national power. Dual federalists see the Constitution as a *contract* between the states—more precisely, between the peoples of the several states *as separate sovereign communities*. Dual federalists claim that the original parties to this contract sought to establish a common government to pursue the few common interests of the separate contracting parties (and such communities as might later join the compact) and otherwise to restrain the common government from encroaching on the prerogatives of the states.[15] By this account of the founding, the Constitution was designed for a negative function, and dual federalists list federalism with the separation of powers and judicially protected individual rights as the Constitution's principal restraints on national power in behalf of liberty. One question raised by the contract theory is what kind of theory it might be. We shall see in Chapter 5 that if it is a report of how people understand themselves, no one would accept it today and it is a most implausible account of how members of the founding generation understood themselves. At best, the contract theory simply exceeds the historical evidence. We shall see further that if our evidence comes from the personal histories of leading states' righters, including John C. Calhoun, the nineteenth century's best-known elaborator of the contract theory, that theory is simply false.

Our second problem at this point is the manner in which the states might check national power. Chapter 4 will show that one answer to this question is the power of nullification that Thomas Jefferson defended in the Kentucky Resolutions of November 10, 1798: the power of each state to declare an offending national law "void and of no force . . . within its own Territory." Madison and Calhoun advanced similar theories. But we shall also see that prestigious states' righters like Calhoun at midcareer and James Madison at the end of his career compromised their versions of nullification. Calhoun effectively denied the right of free states to nullify the Fugitive Slave Act, and Madison retreated from his earlier support for nullification (or, in Madison's case, "interposition") when he came to see it as a step toward disunion. Thanks to the Civil War and notwithstanding recent attempts of some state legislatures to nullify the ACA, I assume that this particular states' rights check is no longer on the table of serious discussion.

If states have no power to nullify national laws they may have other powers to check national policy. These other possibilities involve the states' powers to tax national instrumentalities and even to form state militias for potential use against national authority. Use of the states' taxing powers as a check on national policy was an issue in *McCulloch*; I comment briefly on this issue below, and I return to it in Chapters 2 and 3. The power to form militias bears on our question because no less a nationalist than Alexander Hamilton suggested in *The Federalist* that the states can deploy their militias as checks against "[p]rojects of usurpation" by the national authorities (28:178–179). This has proved to be more than a theoretical possibility, of course. State-supported armed checks against national authority have been threatened or actually attempted a number of times before and after the Civil War, the opening act of which was an artillery assault by cadets of the South Carolina Military Academy. More recent assertion of such power included Governor Orville Faubus using the Arkansas National Guard to block court-ordered racial integration of Little Rock's Central High School in September 1957, and Alabama's Governor George Wallace "standing in the school-house door" with helmeted state troopers to block court-ordered integration of the University of Alabama at Tuscaloosa in June 1963.

Gary Wills reports that eighteenth-century authorities considered rights to make war and peace and enforce laws at home as essential attributes of sovereignty. These attributes imply powers to raise, support, and deploy one's own armed forces.[16] Hamilton says in *The Federalist* that "by the COERTION of the magistracy, or by the COERTION of arms," coercive sanctions are "essential to the idea of a law," and that the former applies against individuals, and the latter applies "against bodies politic, or communities or States" (15:95). Combining the observations of Hamilton and Wills, we could say that the states' power to use the militia as a check on abuses of national authority would be evidence for the contract theory of the Constitution. A states' power to use its militia against what it declared to be usurpations of the national government would also justify references to "state sovereignty" and therewith "dual sovereignty."

But Hamilton saw use of state militias against national authority not as a constitutional right but as a natural right—"that original right of self-defense which is paramount to all positive forms of government" (28:178). The *constitutional* uses of the state militias are entirely unconnected to a right of any state to do its own thing, for the *constitutional* uses of a state's militia are completely circumscribed by national authorities.[17] Thus, by Article I, Section 8, the power to organize and arm the state militias belongs to Congress, not the states. By the same article, the states appoint the officers of the militias and train the militias, but Congress sets the rules for training them. By the same article, Congress has power to call state militias into national service "to execute the laws of the Union, suppress insurrections, and repel invasions." Without Congress's consent, moreover, "No state shall . . . keep troops or ships of war in times of peace, enter into an agreement or compact with another state, or with a foreign power, or engage in war, unless actually invaded" (Art. I, Sec. 10). And in 1869 the Supreme Court held that the Southern Rebellion—a massive attempt to check national power militarily—exceeded any constitutional right of the states.[18]

None of this proves that a military check enjoys utterly no constitutional connection, for the Constitution has a pre- or extragovernmental aspect that reflects a principle of the Declaration of Independence: a people's right "to alter or to abolish" governments "that become destructive of the[] Ends" for which "Governments are instituted." The Constitution is explicitly an expression of "the People," not of any government created by the people, and however they might be formally organized and controlled, the state militias can be seen as the safeguard of separate political communities against a tyrannical central government. This safeguard, moreover, could be constitutionally recognized even if its actual use would be unlawful or extralawful. Joseph Story, commenting on the Second Amendment, called the militia "the natural defence of a free country against sudden foreign invasions, domestic insurrections, and domestic usurpations of power by rulers." Story added that the right of "citizens" to bear

arms "has justly been considered, as the palladium of the liberties of a republic; since it offers a strong moral check against the usurpation and arbitrary power of rulers."[19] Story thus suggested that the militia-as-threat
against national power is constitutional even if the militia-in-use against
national power may not be.

Borrowing from *Federalist* No. 40 and James Fleming's recent reflec-
tions on constitutional emergencies, we might explain Story's suggestion
by the aid of a distinction between constitution*al* action and constitutional*ist* action. The thesis would be that constitutional prescriptions presuppose a certain state of affairs; this state of affairs may not always obtain (in
some emergencies, for example); and in situations for which the rules fail
to provide, political leadership (which materializes where one finds it) can
work either to change the rules or restore the conditions under which the
rules can again work. Following the rules would be constitution*al* conduct; acting outside the rules to restore their conditions would be constitutional*ist* conduct. Lincoln's presidency would be the exemplar of constitutionalist conduct.[20]

Broader issues of constitutional emergencies—their nature, constitutionalist responses to them, and their ultimate implications for institutional
design—belong to a different discussion than the present one.[21] Here we
can assume that a military check against national authority cannot be a
constitution*al* possibility even though it could be a constitutional*ist* possibility. Because the states cannot constitutionally use armed force as a
check against national policy, we can conclude that the states cannot constitutionally oppose national policy in any way that would depend on armed
force. Examples of prohibited policies would include a state tax designed
to defeat national policy and state laws barring the collection of national
taxes. Armed force would be needed to collect taxes from an unwilling
government and to resist tax collection from a determined government,
and Congress's power over the militias leaves the states with power to do
neither. Unconstitutional state measures thus include the tax Maryland
levied on transactions of the Baltimore branch of the Second National
Bank, an issue litigated in *McCulloch*, and South Carolina's attempt in
1832 to stop collections within its borders under the tariffs of 1828 and 1832.

Beyond taxing national instrumentalities and warring against national
authority, alternative checks available to the states involve courts. States
could ask courts to declare that the national government had exceeded its
lawful authority at the expense of the states. But whose courts? If the

United States were a party in a case involving a state, the order of a state court against the United States would be enforceable ultimately by the chief executive of the state employing military force against the United States. To avoid this inadmissible result, direct conflicts between state and national governments would have to be settled by federal judges, for, as noted, Congress's power to call state militias into national service does admit military force against a state, or if not a state as such, against those of its officials engaged in "insurrections" against the "laws of the Union" (Art. I, Sec. 8, par. 15). This might still leave one broad kind of federalism case to be settled by state courts: the case in which a nonfederal party claims injury by a state acting contrary to the Constitution or national policy. This genus has many species, some of which Chapter 5 discusses in connection with the Eleventh Amendment. But Sections 1 and 2 of Article III do two things that vitiate state courts as agents for checking national policy. They authorize Congress to establish inferior courts, and they extend the "judicial Power" of the United States "to all Cases, in Law and Equity, arising under this Constitution, the Laws of the United States, and Treaties made, or which shall be made, under their Authority." If, by declining to establish lower federal courts, Congress should leave state courts with jurisdiction over federal questions at the trial and lower appellate levels, the federal branch of state judicial power would still be left to Congress's discretion, and state court decisions would or could be reviewable by the Supreme Court as Congress might provide under its power to regulate the Supreme Court's appellate jurisdiction (Art. II, Sec. 2, par. 2). State courts as enforcers of the national Constitution and laws would thus be a matter of national policy, not constitutional right.

Of course, federal courts could always find and enforce states' rights against national policy as they did selectively in the decade before the Civil War *(Dred Scott)*, from the 1880s to the mid-1930s *(The Civil Rights Cases, Hammer v. Dagenhart, Carter v. Carter Coal Co.)*, and from 1976 *(Usery)* to the present—over a third of the nation's history to date. Yet some radical states' righters (like Robert Barnwell Rhett and maybe Jefferson, but not, as we shall see, Madison and Calhoun) claimed that the Constitution left *ultimate* decision in federal conflicts to each individual state, not the federal judiciary or three-quarters of the states in convention, both of which would be national agencies. Chapter 4 shows that, at least before the Civil War, all renowned states' righters, moderates like Madison and extremists like Rhett, correctly saw that states' rights protected by any national agency are the contingent expressions of national policy, not genuine exemptions from national power.[22]

Article V, which provides for constitutional amendments, may contain the final possibility for a states' rights check on national power. Indeed, the first use of such power after the founding period, the Eleventh Amendment, established the states' immunity from certain lawsuits, which immunity had been historically claimed as a prerogative of sovereign powers. A major part of the federalism revival of the Rehnquist Court was to reassert and extend the concept of "state sovereign immunity" from lawsuits. Chapter 6 comments on this development. Chapter 4 shows how Madison and Calhoun each connected his version of nullification to the role of the states in the amending power—compromising their states' rights credentials in the process. But the point for now is that a right to amend, and thus to check by amendment, is not enjoyed by individual states acting alone; it is not a right of the *several* states to do their own separate thing, go their own separate way in any particular whatever. Any right that might derive from Article V can be no more than a right to be a part or to take part, not a right to act apart. A right under Article V would therefore be a process right, a right to participate in the amending process. This would be a right to function as a national agent because the amending process is a national process.

Lacking good historical and textual arguments for their claim that the states enjoy a measure of sovereignty in a system of dual sovereignty, dual federalists have turned to moral arguments, by which I mean arguments grounded in some form of goodness or rightness. They do this by citing goods, like democracy and liberty, allegedly furthered by states' rights. Richard Epstein, Randy Barnett, and Michael Greve are some of the important constitutional theorists making such claims in recent years. Chapter 4 surveys these claims and concurs with a substantial body of academic opinion that none of these claims works or can work. The reason none can succeed is that the goods cited in behalf of states' rights can only constitute national standards that the states can fail to meet. If, for example, democracy works best in small units and enhanced opportunity for citizen participation is the reason for honoring a state's rights, the states would not be free to determine the meaning of democratic participation. Without some sense of what participatory rights should be nationwide, the

Court might have allowed Texas to treat the Democratic Party of that state as a private club that could lawfully exclude blacks from voting in the members-only Democratic primary on the theory that blacks could vote in the general election of what was then virtually a one-party state.[23] The Court rejected the "white primary" system of Texas and other Southern states because a racist idea of democracy was officially contrary to that of the nation as a whole.[24]

In sum: What justifies a right limits it. National standards alone can justify states' rights. National standards therefore limit states' rights. And states' rights limited by national standards are not states' rights. States' rights federalism is therefore a bogus constitutional concept. What makes it so is the inability to defend it by any argument: historical, textual, or moral. Chapter 4 will show this in greater detail.

Marshallian Federalism

The Marshallian model is the first of two kinds of nationalism. This model derives from John Marshall's opinion in *McCulloch v. Maryland*. If dual federalism (the two-spheres view) is the conventional view of federalism, national federalism is a one-way federalism, and nationalists who trouble to preserve the term "federalism" at all must explain how what seems a dual idea can be rendered as a one-way affair. What makes national federalism one-way federalism is Marshall's holding in *McCulloch* that (1) Congress can incorporate a bank with branches in the states despite lack of explicit constitutional authorization, and (2) Maryland cannot tax the bank despite lack of explicit constitutional prohibition. As a dual federalist might put it, Marshall holds that the states must respect what Congress is free to ignore: the line separating state from national power; hence, one-way federalism.

What could be the best known passage in American public law reads: "Let the end be legitimate, let it be within the scope of the constitution, and all means which are appropriate, which are plainly adopted to that end, which are not prohibited, but consist with the letter and spirit of the constitution, are constitutional."[25] This sentence is the upshot of a lengthy argument with institutional and cultural implications that Marshall either failed to appreciate or declined to acknowledge. Chapter 3 will reveal these implications to include a powerful national government dominated by a political elite that pursues public purposes like economic security and plenty over religious righteousness, and virtues like industry over virtues like piety. A major failing of nationalists over the years has been their unwillingness to acknowledge and defend the broader cultural implications of their legal position. But no one can miss a point plain upon the surface of Marshall's opinion in *McCulloch*: Marshall's test for the constitutionality of national policy omits the reserved powers of the states. Ask first whether Congress is doing the kind of thing the Constitution authorizes, says Marshall; ask next whether the Constitution prohibits the particular measure in question; no need to ask whether the particular measure trenches on the reserved powers of the states. So the nation can encroach upon the states' powers and still act constitutionally. More, under appropriate circumstances, Congress can do things not expressly authorized, and the states cannot use their otherwise unquestioned powers as a check. One-way federalism, indeed.

Marshall justified his controversial test with a comprehensive argument that disagreed with Maryland's argument *almost* point by point: The Constitution, said Marshall, was not a compact among the sovereign states, as Maryland claimed; it was a charter of government authorized by the American people as one cultural entity.[26] The charter's aim was the good of the whole people, which Marshall understood chiefly in bourgeois or Lockean fashion as national security and material prosperity.[27] And since these goods were the controlling political goods (an implication of constitutional supremacy, as Chapter 2 explains), courts faithful to this charter—a charter of positive benefits to the people—should construe the charter's terms in ways that facilitated pursuit of the people's good.[28]

A point of agreement between Marshall and the dual federalist, at least ostensibly on Marshall's part, was that the national government was a government of limited powers. Marshall spoke as if this proposition were an axiom. "We admit," he said, "as all must admit, that the powers of the government are limited, and that its limits are not to be transcended." "But," he added immediately, "sound construction of the constitution must allow to the national legislature that discretion, with respect to the means by which the powers it confers are to be carried into execution, which will enable that body to perform the high duties assigned to it, in the manner most beneficial to the people."[29] And his critics (including Madison and Jefferson) could not see and still cannot see how to reconcile a theory of limited powers vis-à-vis the states with a theory of means unlimited by the states' reserved powers.[30] National federalism's big problem is thus its apparent conflict with the axiom that "the powers of the [national] government are limited."

The key to resolving this conflict is to recognize that the axiom is ambiguous. It can mean that admitted national power is less than complete or "plenary"—for example, that because education belongs to the states Congress cannot establish schools of any sort even if Congress thinks them necessary to train military, bureaucratic, and diplomatic personnel. Or the federal axiom can mean that though the ends of the national government are few, they are the controlling elements of the people's happiness, and as long as Congress pursues them in good faith, it can disregard the reserved powers of the states. Thus Congress, in good-faith pursuit of national defense (a recognized good and a crucial element of the people's well-being), could respond to Sputnik with the National Defense Education Act of 1958, or Congress could impose requirements on the nation's schools as needed to meet foreign economic competition or even to change racial attitudes that damage the nation's image in economically and strategically valuable areas of the world.

These last possibilities—Congress actively working for a smarter workforce and against racism—suffice to excuse critics who see Marshall's theory of unlimited means as tantamount to unlimited national power. Under the right circumstances, any and every area of social life could become subjects of concern to policy makers working for ends like national security and prosperity. As Chapter 2 will show, this does not mean that at any given moment Congress can do whatever its majority might want vis-à-vis the states. But it does mean no categorical limits on Congress's power—no prior limits in terms of categories like "education," "public health," or "public morality." The completeness of national power to pursue national ends may thus conflict with the axiom of limited national power, depending on one's understanding of the axiom, and Madison could have been right when he said that the founding generation would not have ratified the Constitution on Marshall's understanding of unlimited means.[31]

In Marshall's defense, however, critics should not beg the question of what "limited national powers" means. Nor should critics underestimate the complexity of propositions regarding what the founding generation would have done. A theory of unlimited means to limited ends would still require legislation honestly motivated by the ends that the legislature invokes, and in *McCulloch* Marshall himself promised (vainly, as it turned out, though tellingly for constitutional theory) that the Court would void pretextual uses of national power.[32] Accordingly, if Congress says that national security is what motivates its push for more scientists and engineers, a reviewing court must either notice or be presented with facts that make it reasonable to believe that schools historically under state and local control are failing to produce the talent needed for national defense. Congress has often failed this test of good faith. One can doubt, for example, that anything a historian, a sociologist, or a journalist might describe as a commercial motivation was behind either the Mann Act or the Partial-Birth Abortion Ban Act, notwithstanding their enactment with the Court's approval under the Commerce Clause.[33] Balanced against the fact that the courts often ignore Marshall's promise against pretexts are claims that a no-pretext rule was unworkable from the beginning. Those who eschew analysis of congressional motives point out that in another of Marshall's famous opinions, *Fletcher v. Peck* (1820), Marshall rejected judges' asking whether legislators are properly motivated. So Marshall's promise against pretexts turns out to be a complicated matter, to which I return several times in this book.

Equally difficult is the question of what the founding generation would have done had it known the Constitution implied Marshall's theory of plenary national power. This question turns on the proper approach to constitutional interpretation. When Madison said the founding generation would have rejected the Constitution had it known it would be construed as Marshall construed it, he spoke as if constitutional meaning lay in the concrete expectations of the founding generation, an interpretive approach presently known as "concrete originalism." Writers like Ronald Dworkin and Michael S. Moore have proved to all within argument's reach that concrete originalism is unworkable for reasons that involve language meaning, the expectations of good-faith inquiry, the ambiguities of history, and the claims that the framers made for themselves.[34] The leading difficulty of concrete originalism is its implicit departure from the assumptions of everyday political discourse, including constitutional discourse. People who take constitutions as normative for political life assume that nonmoral words like *commerce* and moral words like *justice* and the varieties of justice like due process and equal protection actually refer to real practices and properties, like practices of a commercial nature and properties like fairness. People who take these notions seriously assume that both their definitions and examples of them can be wrong, just as their definitions and examples of *frog* can be wrong (have some not mistaken toads for frogs?) and that if people are truly interested in regulating commerce without depriving people of due process, they will replace worse definitions and examples of commerce and due process with better ones, which they can do by exploring what separates economic from other kinds of behavior, why anyone would want to regulate economic behavior, and why due process might be worth more than the time and money saved by kangaroo courts and lynchings.

Moore elaborates the point by reflecting on our ordinary beliefs about life and death. He observes that transplant surgeons who would obey the rule against removing the organs of live donors will abandon a definition of death as heart stoppage when experience teaches them that stopped hearts can be revived. And they will do so without feeling that the meaning of "death" has changed from heart stoppage to, say, brain death. The abstract rule "don't transplant from live donors" remains the same even if we apply it differently in light of better understandings of death.[35] Dworkin proved early in the interpretive debate that the moral authority of the framers depends on taking them at their word. So, if the framers said they were interested in fairness, they had to mean the concept or general idea of fairness, not their mere definitions and examples at the time, which experience and/or debate could always show to be wrong. Should the framers have meant not fairness but their view of fairness, Dworkin argued, they would have made the imposition of their opinions "the heart of the matter," despite the Preamble's claim that their interest lay in the well-being of their posterity.[36] The framers' view of well-being would be unquestionably consistent with their posterity's well-being only if the framers were infallible, a possibility the framers themselves implicitly denied by adopting Article V, whose amending procedures assume not only the framers' fallibility but the fallibility of the constituent authority, namely, "We the People.[37] Though Madison spoke as an originalist when criticizing Marshall, he adopted what we would now call a Dworkinian approach to legal interpretation in *The Federalist* when he denied that the Constitutional Convention had been faithless to its charge from the Confederation Congress (40:259).[38] The Constitution's amendability will figure large in this book's final argument for Marshallian federalism.

Accept the presuppositions of ordinary political discourse, in any event, and you can be confident the framers would have rejected Marshall's understanding of "limited government" only if you can be confident that a different understanding better served what the framers, on reflection, would have considered the common good. After all, the framers admitted their fallibility, and no one who counts as a framer ever said in public that he was interested in anything less than a true understanding of the common good. Marshall apparently believed that right-thinking people would accept a Lockean version of the common good, a version distinguishable from a civic republican version, and that the Lockean version could comfortably fit the relevant historical material and constitutional provisions.[39] The soundness of Marshall's interpretive approach hardly guarantees the truth of Locke's version of the common good; nor does it end the debate on how we should conceive and whether we should value the framers' intentions. But it does show that Marshall's imputation to the framers was a responsible one and that either rejecting or affirming it would involve complex moral, semantic, and social scientific arguments.

Process Federalism

We have seen that states' rights or dual federalism can restrain national power in two ways: by denying that national power is plenary and/or by defining national ends narrowly to avoid encroaching on the reserved powers of the states. We have seen that Marshallian federalism conceives national ends broadly and as goods integral to the general welfare. Marshallian federalism insists that national power is plenary and denies that the states can use their powers to check the pursuit of national ends. Marshallian federalism thus assumes a theory of nationally authorized ends. This theory would both specify the content of national ends and justify the sacrifices in other goods that the pursuit of national ends involves. This theory might hold, for example, that national security, national prosperity, and equal economic and political opportunity for all responsible adults are more important to the people's true happiness than membership in racially and religiously exclusive communities. Defending the possibility of such a theory and then developing it would be formidable philosophic and social-scientific undertakings. Process federalism is a species of national federalism that would avoid these burdens.

The substantive authorizations of Article I, Section 8 and the Civil War Amendments mean little to process federalism; its focus is not substance but *process*, the processes of national policy making. The Constitution outlines the institutional core of this process and identifies who participates in it, the recruitment of these participants, and the terms of their tenure. Process federalism assumes (with Marshall, as we shall see) that national decisions in which a state's congressional delegation has participated represent the state's true interests better than the state's government does. The process federalist therefore will not review states' rights claims about the scope of national power.If the processes of national representation and decision are working as the Constitution specifies, Congress can do what it wants vis-à-vis the states, regardless of the substantive ends pursued.[40]

Process federalism has an ambiguous relationship to Marshallian federalism; it could be either a corruption of Marshallian federalism or its perfected form. Process federalism is treated here as a separate model because its emergence in the late twentieth century represented an academic value skepticism that was foreign to the constitutionalism of John Marshall.[41] The latter embodied the belief that Lockean liberalism was the true political morality and that the task of political leadership was to make the public sensible of that moral fact. Process federalism implicitly denies moral truth and assumes that the absence of moral truth supports democracy. The familiar claim is that the nonexistence of an objective good recommends that each responsible adult be left to decide ultimate questions of the good life for himself, and that democracy aggregates and represents in law those preferences that comport with this tenet. The problem with this argument is equally familiar: skepticism supports no conclusion— scientific skepticism supports no scientific conclusion; moral skepticism supports no normative conclusion. Without a presumed objective good, a conception of harm is meaningless and representing so-called harmless preferences cannot be good. Democracy derives support not from skepticism but from the belief (and ultimately therefore an argument) that justice is good, people are morally equal, and that the moral equality of persons makes it unjust for any one to rule another without the other's consent. Once this dependence of process on moral substance (propositions regarding goodness, justice, equality, liberty) is appreciated, process federalism faces collapse, which it can avoid only by connecting itself to some substantive good. Chapter 6 will show that process federalism must eventually claim that the aggregation of private preferences, reflective or not, just *is* the political good. We shall see that this proposition is either false or untenable.

Process federalism can then defend itself only by switching to offense. It will claim, in skeptical fashion, that Marshallian federalism is equally untenable, since all political stances must be grounded in commitments that reason cannot defend. It will claim further that it is actually the perfected form of Marshallian federalism since the latter is ultimately committed to nothing more than a process. The case for Marshallian federalism will prove to depend on whether the Constitution envisions a substantive state of affairs that is beyond reason's power to reject and whether that state of affairs is the good served by Marshallian federalism. The answers to these questions will favor Marshallian federalism.

2

JOHN MARSHALL AND A CONSTITUTION FOR
NATIONAL SECURITY AND PROSPERITY

A theory of juridical federalism would tell judges and others what questions to ask to determine if the national government had exceeded its constitutional authority vis-à-vis the states. Such a theory, I contend, should direct judges to ask only two questions: (1) whether a challenged congressional act is reasonably calculated to achieve an authorized national end (like national security); and (2) whether, despite its justifying purpose, the act trenches on some protected individual right (like freedom of the press). Some would argue for a third question, regarding prerogatives reserved to the states. And others would ask only whether the act abridges some individual right and, very rarely, whether it disrupts some process of national decision involving the states. Each set of questions reflects a different model of federalism.

Chapter 1 sketched three models of juridical federalism: Marshallian federalism, states' rights federalism, and process federalism. Marshallian federalism presupposes a national community that predates the Constitution; it holds the national government responsible for facilitating or securing that community's controlling values (conceived mainly as national security, national prosperity, public order, and specified forms of fairness), and it denies that individual states can lawfully avoid the burdens of pursuing these values. States' rights federalism, or dual federalism, implicitly denies the existence of a national community of values, except for national security. Dual federalism sees the Constitution as a mere contract among separate political communities, and to protect the interests of those separate communities, it either conceives most national responsibilities narrowly or recognizes states' rights exemptions from national powers. Process federalism holds that national power is constitutionally unlimited as long as the states (that is, voters in the states) are represented in the processes of staffing the national government, forming national policies, and amending the national constitution. Unlike process federalism (a federalism of process), national federalism and dual federalism are federalisms of substance: they involve theories of substantive ends. The ends of Marshallian federalism include national security, national prosperity, equal opportunity, and a secular and rationalist political culture. States' rights federalism is ostensibly concerned with goods like democratic participation and social experimentation. But because the ends of states' rights federalism appear only when asserted against national power, and because the ends of national power are broadly liberal, the ends of states' rights federalism are broadly antiliberal; hence the historical association of states' rights with ends like religious salvation and racial purity. This chapter and the next take a closer look at Marshallian federalism; Chapters 4 and 5 do the same for states' rights federalism.

John Marshall's opinion in *McCulloch v. Maryland* (1819) remains the leading statement of national federalism.[1] Though Marshall failed to confront the full implications of his position either in *McCulloch* or elsewhere, *McCulloch* displays the essential premises of a national vision with as much clarity and as little equivocation as one could reasonably expect from a democratic statesman addressing a divisive public question. The most striking feature of the *McCulloch* opinion is its pervasive instrumentalism: the view that government and law are chiefly about means to desired ends, essentially the people's happiness. Marshall's instrumentalism stretches from his theory of the Constitution's origin (who established the Constitution and why) to his views of the nature of governmental powers, the questions judges should ask in federalism cases, and who bears the burden of persuasion in such cases. Credit also goes to Marshall's critics, however, for they exposed the further implications of Marshall's instrumentalism, and these implications are indeed unsettling to the conventional ear. Critics charged that Marshall would sacrifice both federalism and republicanism and put the country on a path to both unitary (or "consolidated") government and government by a moneyed elite. Under two pen names, Marshall took to the popular press to deny these charges. As we shall see in Chapter 3, however, he might better have demurred. Marshall's critics were right in important respects, and the public might well have accepted elements of each charge. This is especially true since, as Chapter 4 shows, Marshall's critics spoke for a negative constitutionalism (the Constitution as essentially a restraint on government) that was and remains untenable.

John Marshall's Nationalism

Marshall's opinion in *McCulloch* is widely known, its key passages among the most quoted in the constitutional literature. A nationalist tract, the opinion defends doctrines of implied national powers, liberal construction of national power, and national legislative supremacy. The opinion answers two legal questions: whether Congress can constitutionally incorporate a bank with branches in the states and whether a state can constitutionally tax transactions of the branch national bank. Marshall answers yes to the first question despite acknowledging that Article I fails to mention either banks or acts of incorporation. For the Court, Marshall holds that Congress has power to incorporate a bank with branches in the states even though the list of Congress's powers mentions neither banks nor corporations and the Tenth Amendment says powers not delegated to the nation are reserved to the states. Marshall answers no to the second question despite acknowledging that the states' power to tax is broad and, with minor exceptions, concurrent with Congress's taxing power. He defends these answers with arguments concerning the identity of the constituent sovereign (the people of the whole nation); the instrumental nature of congressional power; the nonrestrictive nature of both the Necessary and Proper Clause of Article I and the Tenth Amendment, and what I am calling the one-way nature of American federalism.

Making a special point of the case's importance to "the great operations of the government," Marshall opens with a crucial claim: if state-federal legislative conflict or even more serious conflict is to be avoided, "by this tribunal alone can the decision be made" (401). This claim is crucial because it would force the states to submit their claims against the nation to an agency of the nation. If Marshall is right, a state cannot decide the scope of its power vis-à-vis the nation or the scope of the nation's power vis-à-vis the states. Marshall's claim for his court appears as a mere assertion because it comes at the beginning of the opinion, before the arguments that support it. Yet an argument for national *judicial* supremacy would be the same as an argument for national *legislative* supremacy—essentially, that the national government is the government of the nation's people and that it represents the most important interests of the nation's people, including the people of Maryland. Marshall devotes the greater part of the *McCulloch* opinion to this argument for national supremacy, and since national supremacy implies the supremacy of the nation's judiciary, Marshall's argument for national legislative supremacy saves him from the charge of begging the question of who decides state-federal conflicts.

But Marshall never suggests that the nation can do whatever it might want with respect to the states. Congress can override state policies, he holds, but only when pursuing nationally authorized ends. Though Marshall claims supremacy for the nation's judicial and legislative powers, he also promises something for those concerned with limits on constitutional ends: The Supreme Court will not leave the question of national ends to Congress; it will continue to referee state-federal conflicts, and "[s]hould Congress, under the pretext of executing its powers, pass laws for the accomplishment of objects not entrusted to the government[,] it would become the painful duty of this tribunal, should a case requiring such a decision come before it, to say that such an act is not the law of the land" (424). Marshall thus implies that the states have at least one judicially enforceable right against Congress, namely, a right against pretexts. The full implications of Marshall's promise must await Chapter 3, but for now we can see that Marshall assumes two possibilities: Congress pursuing constitutionally authorized ends, as it is supposed to, and Congress pursuing constitutionally unauthorized ends. He promises that the states can ask courts to remedy harms to the states' interests that result from unauthorized congressional acts. He denies that the states have rights against Congress when Congress pursues constitutionally authorized ends.

Clearly, Marshall's promise against pretexts is far from innocuous, as examples in our own time show. Citing Marshall's promise to void pretexts, physicians and other affected private parties could claim rights under a no-pretext rule against Congress's criminalizing late-term abortions. The Commerce Clause does not authorize morals legislation, and observers could reasonably hold that the Partial-Birth Abortion Ban Act of 2003, enacted under the Commerce Clause, served a moral purpose, not a commercial or economic purpose.[2] One could reasonably (though more contentiously) say the same for the Violence Against Women Act of 1994, voided in part by the Rehnquist Court on states' rights grounds in 2000.[3] Yet Marshall's theory would permit Congress to set a minimum wage for the nation's workforce, as the Court did in *United States v. Darby Lumber Co.*,[4] thirty-five years before the Court reversed field and granted a states' rights exemption from the Fair Labor Standards Act in *National League of Cities v. Usery*—a decision the Court overruled nine years later in *Garcia v. San Antonio Metropolitan Transit Authority*.[5] Nor would judges persuaded by *McCulloch* define national power narrowly to avoid encroaching on the states, as the Court has done in many cases, including *Dred Scott v. Sanford*[6] and *Hammer v. Dagenhart*,[7] for defining national power narrowly to preserve some antecedent conception of state prerogatives (to permit slavery in *Dred Scott* and child labor in *Hammer*) is practically equivalent to declaring a states' rights exemption from otherwise acknowledged congressional power.

To repeat: everything in *McCulloch* turns on Marshall's instrumentalism—that is, his overriding concern for realizing good things like national security and national prosperity. The Constitution's formal character for Marshall was that of *means* to *ends*—that of a corporate charter or an enabling act that establishes a government to pursue purposes or ends, like national security and prosperity, whose meaning and value preexist the government. This was a *positive* constitution to be distinguished from a *negative* constitution or constitutional enactment like Magna Carta. Though a positive constitution may guarantee specified exemptions from the power of government, as the Constitution does in its first eight amendments, the overarching and controlling function of a positive constitution is establishing a government to pursue desirable social conditions, like security and prosperity. By contrast, the chief purpose of a negative constitution is governmental in nature, specifically, to restrain governments in behalf of rights (of persons, communities, corporations, "markets") to be left alone by the governments. The U.S. Constitution combines positive and negative functions, but Marshall joined *The Federalist* in viewing the Constitution as fundamentally a positive instrument of collective aspirations.[8]

Marshall's positive constitutionalism is evident in his disposition of the bank controversy. The following premises ground his conclusion that the Constitution gives Congress authority to establish a bank with branches in the states.

1. Congress's powers were delegated to it by the people of the nation, not the state governments, and "are to be exercised directly on them [the people], and for their benefit" (404–405).
2. "[T]he government of the Union, though limited in its powers, is supreme within its sphere of action . . . represents all . . . acts for all . . . [and] must necessarily bind its component parts," namely, the states (405).

3. Because the powers of Congress are granted for the sake of certain ends or benefits, courts should construe those powers in a liberal manner, a manner that facilitates pursuit of those ends or benefits (413–416).

Marshall then follows with the famous summary of his instrumentalism: "Let the end be legitimate, let it be within the scope of the constitution, and all the means which are appropriate, which are plainly adopted to that end, which are not prohibited, but consist with the letter and spirit of the constitution, are constitutional" (421).

For Marshall in *McCulloch*, both the *meaning* and the *scope* of national powers flow from the ends or purposes for which the powers were granted. Because he attaches greater importance to these national purposes than to conflicting state purposes, his view of the relationship between nation and state presupposed a substantive theory of paramount policy objectives. For Marshall the Constitution was not an instrument for aggregating and expressing popular preferences, regardless of their content. He did not believe the Constitution was "made for people with fundamentally different views," as Justice Holmes was to claim in *Lochner v. New York* (1905).[9] Marshall saw the Constitution dedicated to the ends of Lockean or bourgeois liberalism, ends like security, social peace, liberty conceived largely as the right to acquire and enjoy property, and freedom from sectarian imposition. As Marshall conceives these ends in *McCulloch*, they are limited in number but "great" and "vast," not at all modest either in scope or weight.[10]

In *McCulloch*, Marshall reads the list of authorizations in Article I, Section 8 as more than a mere aggregate of narrow specifics. From clauses dealing with military matters and foreign affairs Marshall derives power over "all the [nation's] external relations." This is a comprehensive power, a power much more than the sum of its textually explicit parts. This finding of power over "all the external relations" is an act of induction that reasons from a list of specific grants of power to a broad public good that explains why people delegated the powers in the first place. This broad public good is then taken to imply other powers. Thus, the expressed Article I powers to declare war, raise and maintain armies and navies, regulate their conduct, and call the state militias into national service—all make sense only if you assume that national defense is a public good for which the national government is responsible. And if you add the Supremacy Clause to the mix, national defense becomes a public good of overriding importance. National defense is one of the Constitution's "important objects," and "from the nature of the objects themselves," the "minor ingredients which compose those objects" are "deduced."[11] So Marshall concludes that Congress can govern "all the [nation's] external relations," and, in tune with Marshall's reasoning about national security, others deduced that Congress could establish military academies despite the Constitution's failure to mention any such power and despite the states' ability to establish academies for training the nation's military leaders—an ability arguably recognized by Article I, Section 8, par. 16, which "reserve[es] to the States respectively . . . the Authority of training the Militia according to the discipline prescribed by Congress." These others include none other than Thomas Jefferson, the "father of West Point," who opposed a national military academy on states' rights grounds in the early 1790s and changed his mind in 1800.[12]

If the issues involved no more than power over "all the external relations" and ancillary institutions like the military academies, Marshall's broad construction of national power would seem imperative. Why grant power over foreign and military affairs if not for national security, and why grant only some powers requisite to that end? Dual federalists rarely question this way of thinking about national power over foreign affairs. Yet, in view of the Supremacy Clause, plenary power for national security would imply a ranking of values that could raise many problems for dual federalism. For example, truly plenary power to defend the nation would enable Congress to override a state's opposition to the conscription of its citizens to serve in a racially integrated army that provided abortion services, admitted open homosexuals, and was presently in combat against deeply religious nations. Power to defend the nation that was both plenary and supreme would imply that national security as Congress conceives it would outweigh conflicting conceptions of racial integrity, humanity, sexual morality, and religious truth as these goods might be conceived by dominant forces in some states. Taking all relevant constitutional provisions into account, plenary and supreme power to defend the nation could eventually shape the nation's religious and moral beliefs to fit the perceived needs of a national security establishment.

A dual federalist might try to avoid this result by distinguishing more urgent from more important ends and denying that the powers of Congress envision the most important ends. She might say that Congress's authorized ends override state ends only because Congress's ends are more urgent, not because they are more important. Survival might be more urgent than living as one pleases, but this would hardly prove life more important than liberty. So, on the theory that national ends are merely more urgent, Congress could override a state's racial, moral, or other policies on national security grounds only when and to the extent that failing to do so would mean palpable risks to national security. Congress, our dual federalist continues, could not order the racial integration of public accommodations in civilian areas adjacent to military bases without a showing that segregation off base is a major cause of racial problems on base and that forced integration off base will probably work to ameliorate racial tensions on base. Also, at the outer limit of what dual federalism requires, Congress may have to show that national defense is impossible without a racially integrated military.

This answer—the greater importance of state ends notwithstanding the greater urgency of national ends—was implicit in all the classic states' rights theories before the Civil War, beginning with Jefferson's theory in the Kentucky Resolutions. Maryland's counsel employed it against the bank in *McCulloch*. Maryland claimed that since a branch national bank in Baltimore encroached on the state's reserved power to govern its financial system, Congress could establish the branch bank only if there were no other way to fulfill Congress's responsibilities, narrowly conceived to avoid clashes with the states—no other place to deposit national tax revenues collected locally, for example, or no other depository from which to pay federal troops serving locally. Marshall argued that Maryland's position was unworkable since virtually no measure Congress might use would be the only way it could avoid doing nothing at all, and that Maryland's test would effectively give the states a veto over national policy and return Congress to its impotence under the Articles of Confederation.[13]

The fallacy of Maryland's test was evident by what it implied: a presumption in behalf of the states in federalism cases. This presumption would flow from the greater importance in people's lives of ends reserved to the states, like the prosperity of their people, not the people of the nation as a whole. This in turn would imply people who saw themselves as no more than state citizens, not individuals able to think critically about their situations and leave home to better themselves. People of the sort that Maryland assumed would have reserved their right to nullify national laws. And in fact Maryland claimed an equivalent right in *McCulloch*: the right to tax the branch national bank in Baltimore out of existence. Jefferson saw the nullificationist implications of states' rights as early 1798, the date of the Kentucky Resolutions. Jefferson may not have appreciated the opposite implication of the Constitution's placement of state militias under national control. That fact alone makes nullification constitutionally impermissible, for it empowers the nation to repress insurrections while leaving the states no way to enforce declarations against national authorities. And since a constitutional doctrine that presupposes nullification is off limits, Maryland's test of "necessary and proper" federal law was unconstitutional.

Giving a liberal construction to the Necessary and Proper Clause, the *McCulloch* opinion goes on to say that once a court decides that Congress is doing the kind of thing that it is authorized to do, the degree of necessity that a measure must meet is a legislative matter, not a judicial matter, and that for constitutional purposes, therefore, "necessary" means merely useful or convenient, so long as reasonably calculated to advance an authorized end.[14] Marshall concluded this precisely because he held that the national government was as much an agent of the people of Maryland as was the legislature of that state and that the happiness of the people of Maryland, along with everyone else, depended more on national security and prosperity than on ends whose pursuit might conflict with these ends. Marshall saw national powers as "great powers," not modest powers, "over no inconsiderable portion of the industry of the nation . . . on the due execution of which the happiness and prosperity of the nation vitally depends" (415–416).

Yet Marshall declined to go as far with power over domestic matters as he did with power over foreign and military affairs. Though his method of constitutional interpretation anticipated this result, he never concluded that Congress enjoyed the general economic power that the commerce power and allied powers constitute today, a general power over the nation's economy comparable to Congress's power "over all the external relations." He believed that one set of specific powers licensed power over all the nation's external affairs, while another set of specific powers fell short of power over all the nation's economic affairs. And he believed this even though the expressed economic powers indicated powers beyond themselves, like the implied power to incorporate a bank. Marshall did find an implied power to construct canals and roads (a power of "internal improvements"), but only "for military purposes or for the transportation of the mail," not to promote Congress's view of the nation's economic well-being. His two reasons for pulling back from a general power over internal improvements were that (1) the founding generation "would not have granted" a general power of internal improvements, while it would have granted specific powers to build roads and canals for the military and the postal service, and (2) "farther than this, I know not why the government of the United States should wish it, nor do I believe it is desired."[15]

The first of these reasons (what the framers "would have granted") clashes with Marshall's own approach to constitutional interpretation; there is simply no way to reconcile his interpretations of the foreign affairs powers and the domestic economic powers. The second reason for pulling back from plenary power over the economy (what "I believe . . . is desired" in internal improvements) offends his stated view of the line between judicial and legislative power. Related problems afflict Marshall's opinion for the Court in *Gibbons v. Ogden* (1824), a case whose resolution turned on the scope of Congress's power "to regulate Commerce among the several States." A famous passage from *Gibbons* reads: "Commerce, undoubtedly, is traffic, but it is something more: it is intercourse. It describes the commercial intercourse between nations, and parts of nations, in all its branches, and is regulated by prescribing rules for carrying on that intercourse." Despite this sweeping conception of "commerce" ("commercial intercourse . . . in all its branches"), Marshall goes on to say that commerce "among" the states "may very properly be restricted to that commerce which concerns more states than one,"—and this because "[t]he enumeration [of powers] presupposes something not enumerated; and that something . . . must be the exclusively internal commerce of a state."[16] Marshall thus invokes what I am calling the federalism axiom and puts himself on the states' rights side of the federalism debate. Dual federalists have made the most of this passage in *Gibbons*. They have read the case as implying distinctions between inter- and intrastate commerce, manufacturing (an intrastate activity) and commerce that crosses state lines, and direct and indirect effects on interstate commerce. These distinctions are dual federalist distinctions; they serve the dual federalist strategy of defining Congress's power down as needed to avoid encroaching on the powers of the states. Add Marshall's opinion in *McCulloch* to the picture, and Marshall speaks on both sides of the states' rights debate.

Though Marshall deserves no authority beyond the quality of his arguments, we might still want to reconcile his contradictions in behalf of his dominant thrust, which, by all accounts, was nationalist. His reference in *Gibbons* to a state's reserved power over commercial activity of no concern to the nation's policy makers was pure dictum, unnecessary to resolve a conflict between a state-licensed monopoly and a federal licensee in interstate waters. Moreover, the power that *Gibbons* would deny Congress would hardly be much of a power. Intrastate activities of *no* concern to outsiders describes a class with no constitutional consequence, for no federalism issue could arise unless an intrastate matter were of some concern to an agent of the nation or a private party claiming a right under the nation's laws. Had Marshall said the Court would stop Congress from interfering with intrastate activity beyond Congress's *proper* concern, two tests of a "proper national concern" would have occurred, one distinguishing economic from noneconomic purposes, and the other distinguishing classes of economic activity in terms of impact on the nation. The first test (involving economic purposes) would say, for example, that it is improper for Congress to act under the Commerce Clause when motivated by concerns other than economic concerns. This test of what is proper would be a version of Marshall's no-pretext rule. It would apply to cases in which Congress used the Commerce Clause for noneconomic purposes, like curbing violence against women and banning partial-birth abortions. This test would serve as a rule against unauthorized pursuits; it would not imply states' rights against authorized national pursuits. Nor would it imply a narrow conception of any national end. Under this test, the commerce power and allied powers could result in a general power over the nation's economy, including broad powers to tax and spend for internal improvements.

The second test of when Congress is acting properly would ask whether Congress was interfering with an intrastate practice (economic or otherwise) that had a sufficient impact on the nation's economy to warrant national action. A court applying this test could ask whether farmers' raising grain not to sell but to feed their own livestock undermined Congress's attempt to benefit farmers who would go out of business without governmentally manipulated grain prices.[17] Since this second test of what Congress can properly do would apply in cases raising no issue of pretext (Congress would have an economic purpose), it would apply to cases where the Court wanted to review the wisdom of Congress's decision to regulate an intrastate activity. The propriety of a measure would be determined by the wisdom of the measure. Such a test would conflict with Marshall's understanding of the limits of judicial power vis-à-vis Congress, as stated in another oft-quoted passage of *McCulloch:* "where a law is not prohibited, and is really calculated to effect any of the objects entrusted to the government, to undertake here to inquire into the degree of its necessity, would be to pass the line which circumscribes the judicial department, and to tread on legislative ground."[18] The same would hold for the judicial assessment of the wisdom, and thus the propriety, of a law. Judicial assessment of impact would therefore raise a separation-of-powers issue, not a federalism issue, for it would simply give another national agency, the Court, a say in the formation of national policy. This would remain consistent with a nationalist view of congressional power, for a federal agency (the Court) would weigh the benefits to the nation of centralizing or decentralizing governmental response from case to case.

True, application of this test of propriety over the years could create a body of judicial precedents that might function as a list of categorical states' rights, like the states' right over child labor declared in *Hammer* and abandoned in *Darby,* and the states' right over state employees declared in *Usery* and abandoned in *Garcia.* But since all such decisions would turn on a contingent matter—national impact of local practices in changing circumstances—they would be policy judgments vested in national agencies (Congress and the Court) as conditions changed. One can therefore question whether any right flowing from an admitted policy judgment could be a constitutionally grounded right. It would hardly be a categorical right—one could not say categorically that a state could decide for itself questions like child labor and the hours and wages of state employees. The rule would be that a state could determine such matters for itself unless or until they affected the nation's economy to a degree determined by the nation's legislature and/or courts. What the states claim as rights would thus be reduced to matters of national policy. Aware of this fact, dual federalists like Jefferson and Calhoun insisted that the states, not the federal judiciary, have the final say in state-federal conflicts.

If two tests of a "proper" national concern are consistent with Marshallian federalism, a third is not. Justice Scalia employed this third test for the Court in *Printz v. United States* (1997). Here he reiterated the states' rights view of the founding as an act of separate sovereign states delegating narrow powers to a central government while retaining "residual sovereignty" in their reserved spheres. This "incontestable . . . 'dual sovereignty'" is manifest throughout the Constitution, he said, including the Tenth Amendment, the amending process, and even the Necessary and Proper

Clause, the usual "last, best hope[] of those who defend ultra vires congressional action." Dashing this "last, best hope," Scalia then claimed that an independent test of whether a congressional act was proper was Congress's restraint in behalf of the states' reserved powers.[19] Apparently, then, even without the Tenth Amendment, the very structure of the Constitution as a union of states would preclude Congress's pursuit of its ends in a manner that trenched on the states' reserved powers (in *Printz* the power of local sheriffs to decide for themselves whether to cooperate with a national gun control law). To this a modern Marshallian could say that even if "dual sovereignty" were "incontestable," Scalia's view of what is "proper" under the Necessary and Proper Clause is contestable by his own admission. For he himself notes that the clause is the "last, best hope" of those who reject his restricted view of national power. Gary Lawson, a scholar who shares Scalia's view and whom Scalia cites in *Printz*, has admitted that his rendition of "proper" is "highly controversial."[20] This means Scalia and Lawson will need to show what good for the nation as a whole is served by reading the word *proper* their way. They need a substantive argument for their reading of "proper" because, as a logical matter, the mere description of the United States as a federal system implies neither a specific view of the founding nor a rule for settling state-federal conflicts. I have indicated in a general way why no substantive argument can support states' rights in Scalia's sense, and I'll develop that position further in Chapters 4. If my argument proves right, no substantive argument can support the states' rights reading of any term in the Necessary and Proper Clause, including the term *proper*.

The states' remaining power to influence the outcome of a state-federal conflict would be exercised in one of two ways: by petitioning Congress to do something (repeal a statute or call a constitutional convention) or by unilaterally nullifying a national law. In the former case, as in a lawsuit, the state would implicitly abandon its claim to sovereignty by accepting its part in a national process of either constitutional amendment or congressional legislation, and states' rights federalism would graduate to process federalism. This leaves unilateral nullification as the only genuine states' rights method of deciding state-federal conflicts. Yet unilateral nullification is constitutionally inadmissible. A state's power to nullify a national law would ultimately depend on the state's right to use its armed forces against national authorities seeking to enforce the law. Jefferson recognized the connection between states' rights, nullification, and armed force in a letter to Madison of October 1, 1792. Here Jefferson proposed that because power to incorporate a bank in Richmond remained solely with Virginia, doing anything that recognized Congress's authority, like "signing notes, issuing or passing them [!], acting as director, cashier or in any other office relating to it [the branch national bank] shall be adjudged guilty of high treason [against Virginia] & suffer death accordingly."[21] By Jefferson's reasoning national authorities seeking to enforce the bank law would be foreign enemies of Virginia, against whom Virginia could legitimately use lethal force. Jefferson's premises thus lead to a conclusion that the Constitution excludes, for Article I, Section 10 prohibits the states from "keep[ing] Troops, or Ships of War in time of Peace" without Congress's consent, and Article I, Section 8 places the state militias under national control.

Whatever Marshall's motivation (on which, more in Chapter 4), his failure to be explicit about a general power over the economy and his position on internal improvements were inconsistent with his premises in *McCulloch*: that the Constitution was the voice of the American people as one political community; that the Constitution's ends were the most important to the people's happiness; and that Congress could disregard state policies and practices when pursuing constitutional ends.

Checks and Balances and the States

Comprehensive terms like "all the external affairs" and the nation's "commercial intercourse . . . in all its parts" are considerably more than the sum of Congress's enumerated powers. They signify unifying goods like national security and prosperity. Power construed in Marshall's "ample" terms effectively meant that when a policy-making majority of Congress wanted to pursue what a national agency like the Supreme Court could agree was a commercial purpose, it could do so as a matter of constitutional prerogative without regard for policies enacted under the reserved powers of the states. This view of the states' "reserved powers" implicitly denied that the states were coequals with the national government; they had to respect Congress's prerogatives when exercising their powers, while Congress had no such duty in return. Marshall's view also implied that when the states acted as individuals or in any manner outside their roles in the Constitution's representative, electoral, and amending processes—all processes of *national* decision—they were not part of the constitutional system of checks and balances. Marshall made this clear in the second half of his opinion in *McCulloch*. Deploying a doctrine of national supremacy under the Supremacy Clause of Article VI, he declared that Maryland could not tax transactions of the Maryland branch of the national bank. Maryland, in other words, could not use its taxing power in any way that obstructed (or checked) Congress's pursuit of authorized nation ends.[22]

Marshall's critics, including Jefferson and Madison, charged that Marshall's argument for unlimited means and no state check on national power amounted to unlimited national power in relation to the states, contrary to the Constitution's enumeration of national powers, which implied powers reserved to the states.[23] This criticism accurately captured the logic of Marshall's position. The charge that Marshall sought unlimited national power was a serious one because all sides of the states' rights debate seemed to accept a proposition that remained axiomatic in constitutional discourse at least until the time of Woodrow Wilson: that (independently of the bill of rights and internal structural restraints) the national government was one of "limited powers." Marshall anticipated the charge and tried to meet it by declaring that the Supreme Court would (1) continue to scrutinize Congress's actions and (2) void uses of power that were "pretextual." Marshall meant by this that the Court would void exercise of power for purposes other than their ostensible ones. Marshall's promise failed to silence his critics because it was no more than a promise to limit congressional purposes or ends. It still left unlimited means, and unlimited means reserved no area of social practice to the states. No categorical exclusion from national power in behalf of the states meant unlimited national power for authorized reasons.

A further reason Marshall failed to satisfy his critics involved another implication of his position. The Antifederalists and their Jeffersonian heirs had long seen the specter of a wealthy aristocracy or, more precisely, an oligarchy (an aristocracy of wealth) occupying a consolidated government whose legislature was too small relative to the size of its constituencies and geographically too remote from them for a meaningful measure of accountability to them.[24] The fear of consolidated government was thus linked to the fear of oligarchy. Oligarchy was also suggested by Marshall's view of substantive national ends and their relationship to other ends. Marshall saw that relationship as one of supremacy, not equality; state policies had either to yield or be shaped to avoid conflict with authorized national policies. For example, the nation could, under appropriate circumstances and through a variety of governmental instruments, shape educational policies in the states to serve national ends like security and economic prosperity. And the superior powers enumerated in Article I amounted, in Marshall's view, to two or three broad ends that comported with Lockean or bourgeois liberalism: national security, personal economic growth, and national unity in security and economic growth. Missing from the national list were powers linked to ends that included public morality, cultural integrity, and religious salvation. By Marshall's theory, exercising these reserved powers and pursuing their associated ends had to avoid conflict with Congress's pursuit of its authorized ends. And since "ends" entail "purposes" they also presuppose patterns of preference or "dispositions." By construing authorized power as plenary and in terms of certain ends, purposes, and therewith dispositions, Marshall at least suggested relatively unlimited power for persons with the right values and dispositions. Under Marshall's theory a Congress of businessmen and their professional allies could pretty much do what they wanted to do relative to forces representing conflicting religious, moral, racial, and environmental values—as long as the businessmen remained true to their typical interest, maximizing profits.

Marshall's saw the Constitution's substantive ends as the ends of Lockean liberalism: liberty conceived in terms of physical safety, the security of property, economic growth, commodious living, and a secular public reasonableness whose manifestations would have included toleration and accommodation of religions that supported Lockean values. Marshall was fully aware of regimes dedicated to ends like religious purity, military empire, and the aesthetic and/or moral value that attaches to republican citizenship in self-governing communities. But Marshall joined leading political figures of his era (Washington, Hamilton, James Wilson, the early Madison) in agreement with the bourgeois philosophers from Locke to Hume against not only the pagan and Christian traditions in political philosophy but also the civic republicanism of the Constitution's Antifederalist opponents.[25] For Marshall, the Constitution was dedicated to a bourgeois way of life, not to whatever ends might attract elites in the states or even popular national majorities. The merits of Marshallian federalism turn ultimately on whether reason favors the bourgeois way of life under foreseeable conditions or an essential element of that life under any and all conditions.

3

THE IMPLICATIONS OF MARSHALLIAN FEDERALISM

States rights' federalists construe national power narrowly. They deny that the national government has a general regulatory responsibility for the nation's economic health. They also exempt from national power social practices (like child labor and the working conditions of state employees) that they say are reserved to the states as rights. States' rights federalism represents a general theory of the Constitution's founding. This theory describes the original thirteen states as separate sovereigns contracting with each other to create a central government. In this founding act, the separate sovereigns delegate to the central authority the right to govern specific areas of social practice that the separate sovereigns feel they cannot govern successfully or efficiently on their own. These areas include foreign affairs, relations with Native American tribes, interstate trade, bankruptcy, weights and measures, immigration and naturalization (originally including importation of enslaved persons), and domestic insurrections.

The direct beneficiaries of these delegations of power are said to be the several state sovereigns—the separate communities as self-governing entities. Their delegations to the center are supposed to enable and facilitate their self-governance, the beneficiaries of which are their several peoples. The delegations of power to the central government do not directly benefit the people of all of the states considered as one whole community, for states' rights federalists deny the existence of one national community. This states' rights interpretation of the founding takes its bearings from the Tenth Amendment and the way Article I, Section 8 lists specific national powers. States' rights federalism construes the Preamble, the Supremacy Clause, and the ratification provisions of Article VII to fit a broader picture of separate contracting sovereigns. It construes the ratification debate in the same way, placing greater emphasis on the state ratifying conventions than on the Philadelphia Convention and emphasizing the occasional disclaimers of nationalist intent in *The Federalist* at the expense of that work's dominant thrust, which is clearly nationalist.

While states' rights federalism's account of the founding is controversial, there is no denying the importance in constitutional debate of theories of the Constitution's beginning and the Constitution's normative character (a contract? a charter?) as a whole. National federalists have their own account of both the whole and the beginning. They see the founding act as Marshall did: a revolution of one united people against their several governments and the old confederation of their governments. This one people went over the heads of their several establishments to establish a new government better to serve their paramount needs—like security, prosperity, and the freedoms to travel, to relocate, and to trade in national markets. Precisely because nationalists see these needs as paramount, they see community in these needs (the national community) as the paramount community, and they refuse to allow governments representing lesser needs to burden or veto the nation's pursuit of paramount needs. Accordingly, they deny states' rights exemptions from the pursuit of authorized national ends, which ends they construe broadly. In particular, they construe the Commerce Clause and related economic powers as vesting the national government with a general power over the nation's economy—power both to promote a general material prosperity and to regulate in pursuit of a general material prosperity.

Two broad theoretical problems confront national federalists. They must show (1) why their view of the beginning and the whole is superior to the states' rights view and (2) that their view is compatible with the axiom of "limited national powers." Before discussing the relative merits of the states' rights and nationalist theories we must examine the full implications of each, and that must await the conclusion of Chapter 4 on states' rights federalism. There I shall assume the obligatory force of constitutional text and/or history and argue that where these authorities are ambiguous, responsible choice can rest only on a moral argument. I'll then show why a successful moral argument for states' rights federalism is impossible and that, in fact, the "argument" for states' rights federalism is less an argument than an act of willful assertion. The present chapter asks whether the Marshallian variety can preserve some sense of the idea that the national government is one of limited powers and concerns. Answering this question involves working through problems with Marshall's rule against pretextual uses of national power, for aside from rights to participate in national decisions, the only states' right that a nationalist will allow is a right against pretextual uses of national power.

The Rule against Pretexts

We saw in the preceding chapter that Marshall tried to accommodate the federalism axiom by promising that the federal courts would strike down congressional pretexts. A rule against pretexts was necessary to limit Congress to authorized ends, and by so limiting Congress the courts would preserve a meaningful sense of limited national powers vis-à-vis the states. Yet the federalism axiom is widely thought to imply that some areas of social practice (education, domestic relations, sexual morality, land use, and so on) are left exclusively to state regulation, and a rule against pretexts simply fails to guarantee any such result. In fact, standing alone, a rule against pretexts is compatible with total, even totalitarian, national rule. In Plato's *Republic*, for example, the state regulates the population's sex life, including who beds with whom, for what purpose, where and when, and to some extent even how. These regulations result from a chain of reasons that begins in a concern for (what else!) national security. Thus we see how wide-ranging controls of social life—hyper "big government"—can result from a single authorized end. Add to national security responsibility for the nation's prosperity and the egalitarian aims of the Civil War Amendments (liberally construed, in nationalist fashion), and under the right circumstances Congress could regulate virtually any area of life. Congress could act under the Commerce Clause to stop farmers from growing food for their own families and livestock.[1] Under the most generous version of the Commerce Clause, Congress could stop terminally ill patients from growing medicinal marijuana for their personal use, as permitted under state law.[2] Congress could outlaw religious practices that conflicted with reasonable versions of authorized national ends, like national defense or equal opportunity for women.[3] Congress could use its taxing, spending, and regulatory powers to induce the states to protect people from "private" violence and discrimination and from undeserved hunger, homelessness, and ignorance.[4] A rule against pretexts would thus guarantee government that is "limited" in the sense of properly motivated—moved, as my examples indicate, by the values of today's progressive liberals. This would be anything but the kind of "limited" government that most states' righters have historically had in mind.

Another problem with Marshall's rule against pretexts concerns its judicial applications to congressional acts. A pretextual act is one whose actual motivating purpose is different from its stated purpose. The end that motivates a pretextual congressional act, typically the purpose by which the act is known to the public, would be different from the constitutional provision presented to a court as authorization for the act. A court that applies the no-pretext rule to Congress is prepared to suggest that Congress is misrepresenting its purposes. Reluctance to impute dishonesty to a coequal branch has occasionally moved the Supreme Court to disclaim a concern for Congress's motives. By this disclaimer the Court avoids offending a maxim of the separation of powers, namely, that the separate branches are coequal. We shall see, however, that a judicial rule against calling pretexts is itself a pretext. We shall see that courts cannot avoid imputing purposes to legislatures; they can only choose whether to permit legislatures to claim what everyone knows to be false purposes.

The judicial pretext of indifference to legislative motives might serve a purpose, however. Pretending to ignore motives that lie behind the "facial content or effect" of legislation avoids other difficulties, according to what is perhaps the best-known judicial opinion on this subject, that by Justice Hugo Black in *Palmer v. Thompson* (1971).[5] In this case Jackson, Mississippi, closed its municipal swimming pools rather than operate them on a racially integrated basis as ordered by a federal district court, which had also ordered the integration of other municipal facilities, including several parks, golf courses, and a zoo. The city council desegregated the other facilities but closed the pools, claiming that it could not operate integrated pools profitably and safely. Plaintiffs claimed that the city council closed the pools because the council members opposed integrating them, that the action was therefore racially motivated, and that the Equal Protection Clause of the Fourteenth Amendment barred racially motivated state and local action. But the district court accepted the city's claim, as did the Fifth Circuit Court of Appeals and, ultimately, the Supreme Court. Apparently these federal judges appreciated the city council's aversion to blacks and whites swimming together. But, of course, no one said so in public.

Justice Black reasoned for the 5-to-4 majority that closing the pools did not deny equal protection because the action affected both races equally and the Constitution guaranteed no affirmative right to state-provided recreational facilities. To reach this result, Black chose between competing descriptions of what the council had done. Everyone knew that the council had closed the pool at least partly for a racial motive and that this action stigmatized blacks. Black chose to describe the act as no more than an act of closing the pool, a facility to which no one had a constitutional right. To the plaintiffs' claim that a racist motive invalidated the act regardless of its effect, Black cited an opinion by none other than John Marshall for the proposition that bad motivation alone was insufficient to void an act that was legitimate on its face (here, officially concerned only with economy and safety) and that resulted in no unconstitutional effect (there being no constitutional right to municipal recreational facilities).[6] Black offered three reasons for avoiding the question of motive: (1) "[I]t is extremely difficult for a court to ascertain the motivation, or collection of different motivations, that lie behind a legislative enactment." (2) "It is difficult or impossible for any court to determine the 'sole' or 'dominant' motivation behind the choices of a group of legislators." And (3) "[T]here is an element of futility in a judicial attempt to invalidate a law because of the bad motives of its supporters. If the law is struck down for this reason, rather than because of its facial content or effect, it would presumably be valid as soon as the legislature or relevant governing body repassed it for different reasons."[7]

So Marshall's rule against pretexts is no more than a promise of well-intentioned power. And if Black is right, good-faith attempts to apply the rule are "extremely difficult," maybe "impossible," and eventually futile—in which case the rule cannot guarantee even well-intentioned power. We must now see whether and how a nationalist like Marshall might view Justice Black's reasoning in *Palmer*.

The (Pretextual) Rule against Examining Legislative Motives

The judicial policy against judging a legislature's motives has a complicated history in the constitutional cases of the federal courts. Justice Day invoked the rule in *Hammer v. Dagenhart* (1918), the child labor case, even as he compromised it by noticing Congress's intent to remedy unfair competition among the states.[8] In the previous decade, Justice Peckham, for the Court in *Lochner v. New York* (1905), recognized no general rule against examining legislative motives when he found that the reasons New York gave for setting the maximum hours for bakers were pretexts for what was actually a "mere labor law," an attempt to gain by law what labor had failed to gain at the bargaining table, an unconstitutional act under the laissez faire doctrines of the era.[9] In an influential analysis of judicial scru-

tiny of legislative motives, John Hart Ely noted that in the decades immediately preceding *Palmer v. Thompson,* the Court found numerous state
legislative enactments unconstitutional for their illicit motives.[10] Ely
noted that after *Palmer* the Court ignored Justice Black's opinion by requiring Fourteenth Amendment plaintiffs to prove discriminatory intent
on the part of state officials, including legislative bodies like the Jackson
city council.[11] Ely showed further that the Court's familiar approach in
civil rights cases—"strict scrutiny" of "suspect classifications" like race and
religion—enables judges to sniff out illicit motives even as they pretend to
be concerned solely with a law's facial aims and concrete effects.[12]

The Court has adhered more closely to a policy of indifference to legislative motives when the case involves Congress acting under the Commerce
Clause. But since there is no consistent policy of indifference to legislative motives, the question is how to explain the Court's policy under the
Commerce Clause. A plausible answer is the Court's approval of the commerce power as a national "police power," the residual power of a government to regulate private conduct for the sake of the public health, safety,
welfare, and morals—more generally, the power "to preserve the public order and to prevent offenses against the State, but also to establish . . . those
rules of good manners and good neighborhood which are calculated to
prevent a conflict of rights, and to insure to each the uninterrupted enjoyment of his own so far as is reasonably consistent with a like enjoyment of
rights by others."[13] As an official matter, Congress enjoys no such power.
Congress's powers are specified and enumerated, not residual.[14]

Yet in *Champion v. Ames* (1903) the Court upheld Congress's act of
March 1895, entitled "An Act for the Suppression of Lottery Traffic through
National and Interstate Commerce and the Postal Service, Subject to the
Jurisdiction and Laws of the United States."[15] For the 5-to-4 majority, Justice Harlan openly acknowledged that the act's restrictions on the interstate carriage of lottery tickets aimed to supplement the efforts of those
states "which, for the protection of the public morals, prohibit the drawing
of lotteries, as well as the sale or circulation of lottery tickets."[16] Here,
then, was an open use of the Commerce Clause not for an economic purpose but for a moral purpose. Under the narrow conception of activities "in
commerce" that prevailed until the mid-1930s, other "police power" purposes reached by Congress under the commerce power included outlawing
the interstate shipment of impure foods and drugs.[17] In *Hoke v. United
States* (1913)[18] the Court upheld the Mann Act (also known as the White

Slave Act of 1910), which used the Commerce Clause to prohibit transporting women across state lines for what the act itself described as "immoral purposes." And when the Court reaffirmed *Hoke* in 1917, it said "the authority of Congress to keep the channels of interstate commerce free from immoral and injurious uses has been frequently sustained, and is no longer open to question."[19]

Regulating the "channels of interstate commerce" had become a species of "regulating commerce," regardless of whether Congress sought economic ends of any kind. By the time the Court decided *Hammer v. Dagenhart* in 1918, Justice Day could say (disingenuously, in this case) that the Court had "neither authority nor disposition to question the motives of Congress in enacting this legislation."[20] However, Day did not say, as Black later said, that the Court was *unable* to describe Congress's motive or that doing so would be futile. In fact, Day had no trouble describing Congress's motive. He recognized that the child labor act "aim[ed] to standardize the ages at which children may be employed in mining and manufacturing within the States," which practice Congress regarded as "the evil" of "unfair competition" between the states.[21] Day's apparent point was that whatever Congress's motive, Congress could not enact a law that had the effect of reversing a state's decision to permit child labor, for labor conditions and practices were not aspects of commerce. Labor conditions and practices were incidents of manufacturing, which preceded commerce; goods were made before they were shipped, and Congress could govern the shipping, not the making.[22] Day had to separate the purpose of a law from its effect, even if, as is always the case where action is successful, the salient effect and the purpose were logically related— just as a window opener (the agent of a concrete act of window-opening) realizes her purpose when she does something that causes the window to go from closed to open. Day had to separate purpose from effect because he approved earlier decisions prohibiting interstate transportation of women for immoral purposes, lottery tickets, and impure food and drugs. These decisions were constitutional, he claimed, because they closed the channels of commerce to things that harmed the public, whereas children could produce goods that were not harmful to the public.[23] Here Day assumed that child labor and unfair competition were not harmful to the public. Justice Holmes aptly ridiculed this assumption in his famous dissent in the case,[24] and the Court and the country have long abandoned Day's narrow conception of commerce and the commerce power.

But Day's opinion is not inexplicable. It indicates a strategy for letting a legislature do what the justices regard as the right thing on those occasions when describing an act in terms of its real purpose or most salient effect would, under prevailing doctrine, invalidate the act. When a legislature (like Congress) seeks a result (like combating the manufacturing of impure drugs) that the justices approve but consider beyond the legislature's authorized or permissible ends, the justices can declare the legislature's motives irrelevant (or, in Justice Black's version, unknowable) and describe the act in ways that validate it. This strategy proved useful in many cases after *Hammer v. Dagenhart*, including those involving closure of swimming pools to avoid integrating them and other acts, like the Civil Rights Act of 1964 and, most conspicuously, the Partial-Birth Abortion Ban Act of 2003.

A veteran New Dealer like Hugo Black may have preferred not to cite a case as infamously reactionary as *Hammer v. Dagenhart*. But John Marshall's nationalism made him a hero to the New Deal, and Black could cite Marshall's opinion in *Fletcher v. Peck*. If Black was right about *Fletcher*—if it announced a rule against judging an act by its motivating purpose— then Marshall himself would have testified that a rule against pretexts is unworkable. Marshall, of course, is no constitutional authority beyond the quality of his reasoning, and even if Black were right about *Fletcher*, one could still say that *Fletcher* contradicts *McCulloch*, and that controlling principles make *McCulloch* sounder doctrine. But a closer look at *Fletcher* will show that Black did not have to read Marshall's opinion as he did and that Fletcher need not vitiate a rule against pretexts. I warn the reader that this "close look" at *Fletcher* is tedious, and readers may want to skip it. It is surely unnecessary, for regardless of what Marshall said, we human beings in fact do describe acts in terms of what we see as the purposes of the actors. Indeed, purpose, end, or motive is what distinguishes a mere change in the world from the kind of change we call action. I review Black's construction of Marshall not to prove what readers can confirm by reflecting on what they themselves do when they say that some individual or group does something. I review Black's construction of Marshall to show that Black erred in pitting Marshall against common sense. Readers who need no such proof can skip the next two sections and their unavoidably tedious fare.

Marshall's Opinion in Fletcher v. Peck

In 1795 four development companies bribed most of the Georgia legislature to sell around 35,000,000 acres of the state's western lands in the "Yazoo" area (most of what is now Alabama and Mississippi). The state "sold" the land for about 1.43 cents an acre. An outraged electorate booted out most of the legislature the following year, and the new legislature promptly passed a law rescinding the sale. Before the rescinding law, however, John Peck, one of the original speculators, sold 15,000 acres of the land for five dollars an acre to Robert Fletcher, an innocent third party. The price to Fletcher represented an increase in the original sale price of over 33,000 percent! After Georgia's new General Assembly tried to rescind the original sale, Fletcher sued Peck ostensibly for return of the purchase price but actually in hopes that a federal court would void the rescinding law and clear his title to the 15,000 acres. The question of the case was whether Georgia could revoke the original sale, and the Court said no. Marshall reasoned that rescinding the sale would violate both the state's implied promise to the developers (upon signing the sales contract) not to reassert its right to the land and Fletcher's right as an innocent purchaser to rely on a legally flawless title.[25]

Marshall acknowledged that the apparent bribery of the state legislature made the question a close one,[26] and his response to this complication contains the passage that Black cited in *Palmer*. I quote Marshall's language at length in fairness to Black, whose reading was not unreasonable, and so that the reader can see that a different reading is also reasonable.

> That corruption should find its way into the governments of our infant republics and contaminate the very source of legislation, or that impure motives should contribute to the passage of a law or the formation of a legislative contract are circumstances most deeply to be deplored. How far a court of justice would, in any case, be competent, on proceedings instituted by the State itself to vacate a contract thus formed, and to annul rights required under that contract by third persons having no notice of the improper means by which it was obtained is a question which the court would approach with much circumspection. It may well be doubted how far the validity of a law depends upon the motives of its framers, and how far the particular inducements oper-

ating on members of the supreme sovereign power of a State to the formation of a contract by that power are examinable in a court of justice. If the principle be conceded that an act of the supreme sovereign power might be declared null by a court in consequence of the means which procured it, still would there be much difficulty in saying to what extent those means must be applied to produce this effect. Must it be direct corruption, or would interest or undue influence of any kind be sufficient? Must the vitiating cause operate on a majority, or on what number of the members? Would the act be null whatever might be the wish of the nation, or would its obligation or nullity depend upon the public sentiment?

If the majority of the Legislature be corrupted, it may well be doubted whether it be within the Province of the judiciary to control their conduct, and if less than a majority act from impure motives, the principle by which judicial interference would be regulated is not clearly discerned.[27]

Yet later the opinion reads:

If a suit be brought to set aside a conveyance obtained by fraud, and the fraud be clearly proved, the conveyance will be set aside as between the parties, but the rights of third persons who are purchasers without notice, for a valuable consideration, cannot be disregarded. Titles, which, according to every legal test, are perfect are acquired with that confidence which is inspired by the opinion that the purchaser is safe. If there be any concealed defect, arising from the conduct of those who had held the property long before he acquired it, of which he had no notice, that concealed defect cannot be set up against him. He has paid his money for a title good at law; he is innocent, whatever may be the guilt of others, and equity will not subject him to the penalties attached to that guilt. All titles would be insecure, and the intercourse between man and man would be very seriously obstructed if this principle be overturned.[28]

Analysis of Marshall's position should begin with some reminders regarding the nature of legislative acts. These observations apply to the acts of Georgia's General Assembly, operating under the constitution of that state (established in 1789 and amended in 1795) in force when the Yazoo land grant was executed and later when the Court decided *Fletcher.* They apply also to Congress and to all legislatures under American-style constitutions. By the manner in which these constitutions refer to their legislatures, the legislatures are man-made, rule-constituted institutions designed to perform specified acts (legislate, investigate, and so on) in pursuit of public purposes. These institutions are operated by human beings sworn to act as officials whose responsibilities are defined by the rules constituting the institutions. These institutions have identities over and above the separate identities of the individuals who occupy their offices, and this institutional identity enables us to personify these bodies, as all of us (citizens, academic observers, officials) regularly do.

We regularly attribute agency to Congress, just as we attribute agency to natural persons. We say that Congress inquires, deliberates, declares, and acts by conducting hearings, passing bills, appropriating money, and so forth. We say that people trust or distrust Congress, implying that Congress can bear moral qualities. We approve or disapprove Congress's conduct in particular cases and its record as a whole over stretches of time and during the two-year periods (the 1st Congress, the 100th Congress) designated by law to elect the entire membership of the House of Representatives. Even though Congress does few things with the involvement of each and every member, we still refer to Congress as the responsible agent for every decision ("act") made by a vote of the membership. We even hold Congress responsible for what it declines to do when some of us feel that it should do something; hence the references to "do-nothing" Congresses. Luckily for me and the reader, I need not defend the metaphysics of these references, for they are stable and unchallenged features of the nation's civic discourse, to which this book would contribute, and any analysis that would disable these references (by claiming, for example, that Congress is a legal fiction with no real existence and that calling Congress trustworthy is meaningless) would disable the entire discourse.

The language of the American Constitution, specifically the Preamble, indicates that Congress is supposed to act only in good-faith and reasonably competent pursuit of public purposes like the national defense, justice, and the general welfare. Article I, Section 15 of the Georgia Constitution of 1789 indicates the same by requiring each member of the General Assembly to "solemnly swear (or affirm, as the case may be) that I have not obtained my election by bribery, or other unlawful means; and that I will give my vote on all questions that may come before me, as a senator, (or represen-tative,) in such manner as, in my judgment, will best promote the good of this State; and that I will bear true faith and allegiance to the same, and to the utmost of my power observe, support, and defend the constitution thereof."

Language of this kind yields a two-part test of legislation: (1) Does the constitution authorize the act—is it the *kind* of act that the constitution authorizes? Is it, for example, a regulation of commerce as distinguished from a morals law? And (2), is the particular act (a) reasonably calculated to advance the public toward (b) a reasonable version of its true interest? In the Yazoo land grant, the General Assembly passed the first test: the legis-lature was authorized to sell this tract because it was authorized to sell public land generally, and this tract was public land. What the General Assembly failed was the second test. By all accounts, even Marshall's, the General Assembly betrayed the people of Georgia. Evidence of this fact was the enormous gap between the penny and a half that the people of Georgia received per acre and the five dollars per acre that Fletcher paid less than a year later. Here was a surpassing outrage, and the question was what to do about it.

Permitting Georgia to revoke the sale would reaffirm that government has no legitimate power to act in a manner that is demonstrably contrary to the public interest. Notwithstanding his decision in the case, Marshall did not deny this principle. In the second passage quoted above he indi-cated that in a lawsuit between the state and one of the original develop-ers, the Court would permit the state to rescind a fraudulent sale. But the state was not the plaintiff here. Fletcher, an innocent investor, had brought this suit in hopes of clearing the title to what he had purchased, and ap-proving the state's attempt to revoke the sale might itself have been con-trary to the public interest. In Marshall's view, a commercial life was the Constitution's conception of the good life, and maintaining the confidence of bona fide investors was crucial to the health of a commercial society.[29] Moreover, Article I, Section 10, par. 1 expressly prohibited the states from passing laws "impairing the Obligation of Contracts," and since the sover-eign people of Georgia had signed the Constitution, they had agreed that a scrupulous adherence to contractual obligations was best for them too. Marshall thus let the title stand for reasons that reflected his view of what the Constitution was chiefly about. These reasons were substantive in na-ture. They enjoyed no special connection to a rule against judicial review of legislative purposes. And judicial inquiry into legislative motives would have been necessary in a decision whose possibility Marshall left open: voiding the original sale in a different suit between different parties. Thus, Marshall's opinion in *Fletcher* does not foreclose inquiry into legislative motives, inquiry that would be necessary to redeem the promise against pretexts that Marshall made in *McCulloch*. Black's reading of *Fletcher* was therefore not the only reasonable one.

Black's Opinion in Palmer v. Thompson

But aside from his reading of *Fletcher*, Black had arguments of his own for declining to review legislative motives. As we have seen, he contended that (1) ascertaining the motive or the different motives "behind a legislative enactment" is difficult; (2) "[i]t is difficult or impossible for to determine the "sole" or "dominant" motivation of a group of legislators; and (3) voiding a law for the motives of its supporters rather than its facial content or effect is futile because the legislature could repass the same law "for different reasons."[30] The first two of these arguments misrepresent what happens when a plaintiff asks a court to judge a legislature's motivating purpose.

Consider the facts in *Palmer*. Here the city said it was closing the pools due to reasons of economy and safety. The plaintiffs in the case disputed this rationale; they said the city's real reason was not economy and safety but avoiding the court's desegregation order. The trial court thus had to decide a factual question: whether the city closed the pools wholly or partly to avoid the desegregation order. Though Ely believed that the plaintiffs made "a strong showing of racial motivation,"[31] a different assessment of the evidence was possible, as was the possibility of an evidentiary toss-up. In any event, the question was the city's truthfulness in disclaiming a racist motive. Though Black failed to confront this question forthrightly, doubtlessly because he knew the answer, he pretended to decide it. He did this when he said "there was substantial evidence supporting the [city] council's stated reason for closing the pools." Justice Byron White gave a different answer when he said in dissent that "the only evidence in this record is the conclusions of the officials themselves, unsupported by even a scintilla of added proof."[32] White placed the burden on the city and asked for more than the city's stated reason. Though Black effectively placed the burden on the plaintiff, he at least pretended that the city had evidence to support its stated reasons.[33] White looked "behind" the surface of the legislative enactment and its effect on the pool, and Black either did the same or pretended to.

Palmer displays the structure of any case in which a legislative body is charged with misrepresenting its purpose. The legislature claims to be motivated by one purpose; an opposing party says the legislature has a different purpose or a mixed purpose, one element of which, as a matter of law, is enough to sink the enactment. These cases ask judges to weigh the evidence and decide between conflicting accounts of the legislature's purpose—specific accounts like economic purpose *versus* racial purpose. One or both of these accounts are part of the public's understanding of the legislation in any system where laws are made in public view and in response to what the public expects. The people of Jackson surely knew that the pools were losing money and that a racial sentiment called for closing them. These accounts don't always conflict; they can coexist without opposition in many contexts. A journalist or a historian as well as the typical citizen would find no internal contradiction in the proposition that the city closed the pools both to avoid integration and to save money. The accounts did compete in court, however, because there they had different legal consequences.

What motivates a legislature in these cases is therefore controversial, and deciding who is right requires evidentiary and interpretive judgments that judges make routinely. Resolving these issues is never a matter of searching for private motives beyond competing descriptions of an act's salient effects. These questions can be easier in some cases than in others. Some might wonder, for example, whether the motivating purpose behind the Federal Child Labor Act of 1916 was economic or moral or one more than the other. Some might debate who bears the burden of proof in cases of different kinds along with the rules for handling evidentiary toss-ups and acts that serve mixed public purposes. But a mature legal system has ways of dealing with these difficulties other than refusing to question the legislature's description of its acts. Applying settled Fourteenth Amendment doctrine, for example, the Court in *Palmer* would have ordered Jackson's pools reopened had it declared Jackson's motive to be mixed. A firm finding of motive would have been the better course in *Palmer*, for to the extent that a legislature or any other agent controls how others describe its conduct, it is beyond the law. Where courts refuse to examine legislatures' accounts of their own conduct, laws cannot effectively apply to them. Justice Black did not want to say that the Fourteenth Amendment was inapplicable to the Jackson city council. That is why he pretended to find "substantial evidence supporting the [city] council's stated reason for closing the pools." In saying this, however, Black contradicted the putative rule against looking behind an enactment's stated purpose or effect.

Black argued finally that it was futile to examine a legislature's stated purpose because doing so would allow the legislature to reenact the same act for a different purpose. The short answer to this objection is that reenacting the same act for a different purpose is passing a different act. When Jack says that Jill opened the window he imputes to her (1) a desire to open the window; (2) a belief that some movement on her part would open the window; and (3) the movement that opened the window. These three claims are about Jill, the agent of the act. Jack implies a further claim, this time about the window, namely, (4) that the window was closed and is now open. Though (4) is not about Jill, its membership in this one set of claims [claims (1)–(4)] is due to its connections to Jill's intentions, beliefs, and movements: (4) is what she wanted, schemed, and worked to realize. Jill's act thus displays three components: an intentional component (her desire for a specific change in the world); a procedural component (comprising her causal beliefs and her causal movements); and a teleological component (the end that she both wanted and worked for).[34] If observers want to describe Jill's act as both an act and Jill's act, they will make the same imputations and claims that Jack makes, and their description will incorporate reference to the three components of Jill's act. When they say, as Jack does, that "Jill opened the window," they will implicitly refer to a causal movement (the motion of *opening* the window) and the effect of this movement (the window *opened*); the two temporal states of the same window (closed then, open now); and the desire, intent, and causal beliefs of Jill, to whom the act belongs in some sense of "belongs" (it is *her* act). If we could think about Jill's act in a manner altogether separated from her desire to open the window, her intent actually to do it, and her bodily exertions to have it done, we would be thinking not about an act but (at most) about an event or events.[35] It is far from clear, however, what events we'd be thinking about. Take Jill's agency out of the picture and the individual events formerly unified as parts of one phenomenal whole ("Jill's act") evaporate to leave a chaos of disconnected states to be described in innumerable ways (a burst of fresh air, jet overhead, cat sleeping, dog barking, knock on the door, and so on).

As it turns out, Black was like Jack—that is, Black's references to the act of the city council exhibit the same logical structure as Jack's references to Jill's act. Though in one part of Black's opinion he advises judges to ignore questions of "motivation" and judge only the "facial content or effect" of legislative acts, a subsequent part accepts the city council's "stated reason for closing the pools." It could not have been otherwise, for a law's "facial content or effect" would be entirely indeterminate (in a sense they wouldn't exist) if really separated from some notion of legislative purpose. Why not describe the Partial-Birth Abortion Ban Act as an event that added to the workload of the Government Printing Office? Why not notice that the act's initials (part of its "facial content") are almost the same as those of the Patrolmen's Benevolent Association? Though these observations would be true, they would have no bearing on the act's constitutionality. Relevant observations would have to link the act to some agent and to some purpose with constitutional consequences. The act would be known and named by its purpose, which would typically be the same as its most salient expected effect. Different purpose, therefore, different act. Should the city council have enacted the same act under a different stated purpose, and should the Court have described it as the same act under a different stated purpose, the newly stated purpose would be a pretext.

Can Pretexts Be Fairly Called?

Though Marshall's rule against pretexts is not unworkable, it might be objectionable on other grounds, like democracy and the separation of powers. After all, when a court declares a legislative act a pretext, the court is accusing a legislature of dishonesty, and this might offend some notions of democracy and the separation of powers, for democracy favors elected legislators over unelected judges and the separation of powers assumes the equality of the several branches of government. These considerations would make calling pretexts a special case of the familiar problem of judicial review in a democracy. I note here, for what it's worth, that elsewhere I have joined other writers who see an assertive judiciary as crucial to democratic aspirations.[36] I therefore see no good argument from either democracy or the separation of powers against a no-pretext rule. But this question belongs to a debate different from the present one, which is whether the no-pretext rule can be fairly applied—by anyone. This question arises because we can doubt that judges can choose between competing descriptions of an act in an objective, nonpartisan way.

An observer who asks whether Congress is "regulating commerce" as constitutionally authorized does so in a context marked by controversy between two act descriptions, one falling under an authorized type of action, the other falling outside authorized types of action. We might ask, for example, whether the Partial-Birth Abortion Ban Act was a commercial regulation or something else, like a morals law or a civil rights law. The context is more than one of controversy; it is also one of constitutional controversy— that is, a controversy in which the observer describing Congress's action speaks not for himself but for the Constitution. Though our political practice has progressed (or declined?) to the point where the Supreme Court's account of congressional action is final, members of the Court are not supposed to represent their personal preferences. They at least pretend to speak for the constituent people ("We the people"). The Court therefore presupposes an ability to describe a congressional act as a truthful and public-spirited citizen would describe it. Everyone has reason to doubt this possibility, of course; yet the possibility of a fair and public-spirited observer is impossible to deny. What makes it impossible to deny is that one who would deny it assumes that, in denying it, she herself is truthful and public spirited *and* that a "candid world" (her readership) can recognize her as such.[37] So if our best theory of the Commerce Clause should conclude that a "commercial purpose" is requisite for action under the Commerce Clause, we must be able to say that the disinterested public sees the act as aiming for either a commercial result or for a mixed result that includes a commercial result.

In addition, and analogous to what we saw in the Yazoo case, Congress has no authority to regulate commerce per se, but only to regulate commerce in the public interest, for the Constitution makes the provisions that follow the Preamble instrumental to the ends therein, which ends, as a whole, amount to the public interest or equivalent comprehensive good. The observer who would speak in the Constitution's name, therefore, would speak not only truthfully but also patriotically. This complex possibility— the possibility of speaking truthfully and patriotically—is an ineluctable presupposition of constitutional discourse. No participant in this discourse can coherently declare that judges as a type are incapable of being fair, whatever might be said of individual judges or courts.

Now the question is what constitutional principles might suggest about a congressional act itself—that is, the intentional, procedural, and teleological components of an authorized congressional act. Consider the procedural component of an act authorized by the Commerce Clause. As a rule-constituted act, a congressional act is realized by motions that conform to a set of rules. Unlike Jill opening a window, Congress regulating commerce follows steps made fairly determinate by law, the law-making procedures set forth in Article I. Not that Article I provides law-making procedures only or only one law-making procedure or that Congress can influence the public's behavior only through acts of one kind. Congress can regulate through taxation, for example, as it sought unsuccessfully to do in 1919 by imposing a 10 percent tax on the profits of companies employing children.[38] Congress can also influence social behavior through spending policies and the power to investigate. Though these law-making and other processes are subject to formal and informal internal changes and constitutional problems of their own, as we shall see in the case of the spending power, these processes are limited in number and stand with the regulatory power as a set of complementary (carrot and stick) strategies for governing society. The fixed number and rule-structured nature of these options remove most doubts about what physical steps count as actions of Congress.[39] This leaves the intentional and teleological components of congressional acts as the principal areas of difficulty in describing the acts. Since, as a logical matter, the intentional component and the teleological component imply each other (intending to open a window is intending that the window be open, and, in an action context, an open window is an opened window), our remaining questions relate to Congress's reasons for action. How do we know when Congress is doing what it is authorized to do and not something else?

Recall the kind of situation in which this question arises. Here an observer faces a choice between two public purposes offered as descriptions of the act, each of which is present in either the public's understanding of the act or in the government's presentation of the act (in court, in the title or preamble of the act, in the recorded statements of politicians, in press reports, and elsewhere). For example, the title of the act may label it as a regulation of commerce, and denying that the act is a commercial regulation, an opposing party may call it a morals law, or a "mere labor law," or a civil rights law. Accepting the government's account saves the act; accepting the other account sinks it. Which account best describes the act?

Consider the 1964 Civil Rights Act, upheld in *Heart of Atlanta v. United States* (1965).[40] Congress claimed authority for the public accommodation section of this act (Title II) under both the Commerce Clause and the enforcement provision of the Fourteenth Amendment. For reasons connected with precedents and principles of privacy that I need not elaborate here, upholding the act under the Commerce Clause was easier for the Court than upholding it under the Fourteenth Amendment. The Court chose the easy way; it approved Title II as a commercial regulation and declared that it need not decide the Fourteenth Amendment question. This may have been the best course in view of considerations that can always compromise or even trump a law when following it would defeat purposes that include domestic tranquility. But "commercial" was hardly a faithful account of Congress's motivating purpose. We can see this by applying a simple test: what was the general public's understanding of the act? One need not conduct a content analysis of media coverage of the 88th Congress to confirm what no one will deny: that in the months before July 1964, the public knew the act to be the kind of act described in the act's official title: "The Civil Rights Act of 1964." One can rightly say, of course, that the act was both a civil rights law and a commercial regulation since it proscribed discrimination in businesses whose "operations affect commerce" (Sec. 201(b)). After all, a law can be both a commercial regulation and a civil rights law without contradicting itself. But if the Constitution forces a choice between these two descriptions, "civil rights law" is the only honest answer to the narrow question of the act's purpose. And if the federalism axiom is a genuine constitutional principal, the Constitution did demand a choice between the two descriptions. For permitting Congress to treat the Commerce Clause or any other constitutional power not as implicating a public purpose like national defense and prosperity but as a strategy for pursuing any ends for which it may be fitted—ends beyond national defense and prosperity—is to abandon any sense of the national government as one of limited responsibilities.

This brings us to a point where we must ask whether any version of the federalism axiom can be a genuine constitutional principle. Because no one could value anything and everything that some entrenched authority might call national security and prosperity, and because everyone acknowledges that some conceptions of these ends can be wrong and of no value, all will eventually conclude that, at bottom, people value only what they believe to be the true or probably true understanding of national security and prosperity. People differ about the true understanding, however. A fundamentalist Muslim will see true security and prosperity as inseparable from his religious beliefs and observances, and he is not unique.

Define national security and prosperity as you will and it will be inseparable from some belief about how best to live, which will in turn implicate some moral or religious belief. The idea of separating security and economic concerns from moral and religious beliefs is therefore illusory, and clearly, the pursuit of any given conception of security and prosperity necessitates the suppression, in one way or another, of at least some religious and moral beliefs. Extending First Amendment freedoms to schools that program children to act on jihadist beliefs is out of the question in this country because jihadist acts would defeat ends like security and prosperity, as liberals conceive these ends.

But what if the jihadist or some other antiliberal conception proved to be better? Though any such conclusion would make the Constitution a mistake, constitutionalists should at least consider this possibility because they should be committed to real security and prosperity, not to a bourgeois version of these ends—especially where the latter seems on a collision course with the earth's carrying capacity. What rational actor would raise his children committed to what he concedes merely seems a good while having reasons to doubt its real goodness and acknowledging that experience may prove it a false good? Marshall's no-pretext rule implicitly separates economic from spiritual and aesthetic concerns in a way that shapes the latter to the demands of the former; hence the value that many Americans place on moderate religiosity and the relaxation of aesthetic and moral restraints in ways that are good for business. But can we be certain that what is good for business will approximate ends like real justice and the kinds of security and liberty that constitute real well-being? If not, we cannot apply the no-pretext rule in good faith, for in historical context, this rule would keep Congress focused on bourgeois ends, which, again, can constitute no more than a conception of comprehensive ends like the public interest. To put the point differently: When a present-day Marshallian speaks for the Constitution and says no pretexts, he must mean (1) pursue only bourgeois ends because, in view of what is foreseeable and affordable, (2) bourgeois ends best approximate true security and prosperity. If, in keeping with his own fallibility and in light of modernity's problems, he doubts (2), then (1) becomes arbitrary, and the Constitution excludes an admittedly arbitrary rule (including one that secures admittedly false ends). Our question now is whether Marshallian federalism can meet these difficulties: can it connect itself to a good that is both comprehensive and rationally undeniable? I shall submit my answer to this question in conjunction with a defense of Marshallian federalism against process federalism, which occurs in the concluding chapter of this book. I can preview that answer here, however.

The Constitution's Deepest Commitment?

Marshall was a Hamiltonian, and the leading Hamiltonian interpreter of the Constitution of the last two generations was Martin Diamond. As Diamond read *The Federalist* and its philosophic precursors, the Constitution is committed to the practices and attitudes of "the Large Commercial Republic," an urban-industrial order committed to property, growth, and liberal values like toleration and equal opportunity.[41] Yet no preambular end or comprehensive good (like justice or the general welfare) is reducible to "Large Commercial Republic." And if existing institutions embody the attitudes and practices of the Large Commercial Republic, that does not make this state of affairs an essential constitutional commitment, for the Constitution itself provides lawful ways to change existing institutions. The Constitution's amendability and the nonreductive nature of comprehensive ends combine to make the Large Commercial Republic no more than a conception of constitutional ends—a controversial conception from the days of Hamilton and Jefferson to the present era of greenhouse, income gap, oligarchy, and distrust of public institutions. The Large Commercial Republic is thus a mere conception of constitutional ends; it is not the Constitution's ultimate commitment.

If there were an "ultimate constitutional commitment" it would have to be some value, institution, or practice that lies beyond the power to amend. A candidate for this honor would be what justifies amendability itself—the value placed on a people's power "to alter or to abolish" an inadequate government and "institute new Government" as seems "most likely to effect their Safety and Happiness." *The Federalist* supposes the same power ("power" in the combined sense of moral right and material competence) when it calls on Americans to prove mankind's capacity to rise above "accident and force" and "establish[] good government from reflection and choice" (1:3).

The Federalist has much to say about the capacity to form and reform institutions. *The Federalist* indicates that at its best this capacity involves a public debate in which "reasons" are "freely" submitted at one and the same time to the "philanthropy," "patriotism," and self-interest of individuals who are concerned with "the existence of the Union, the safety and welfare of the parts of which it is composed, [and] the fate of an empire, in many respects, the most interesting in the world" (1:3–6). By promising the reader "the safest course for your dignity, your liberty, and your happiness" (1:6), by invoking a modern "science of politics (9:51), by describing the "distribution of property" as a more "common and durable" source of factions than religious "zeal" (10:58–59), and by appealing to no religious authority of any kind, *The Federalist* indicates (rightly, as we shall see) that this will be a secular debate.

The Federalist indicates further that the right to form and reform political institutions cannot be structured or rightfully contained by any political establishment, including the amending provisions of a written constitution. Because, as a matter of political feasibility, the constitutional proposal of the Philadelphia Convention could not have attracted the unanimous support of the states required by the Articles of Confederation, the Convention had proposed adoption by and among as few as nine of the thirteen states. Congress accepted this course when it sent the constitutional proposal to the states, and *The Federalist* defends this decision simply by pointing to the "absurdity" of the alternative: leaving the fate of the union to "*a majority* of 1–60th of the people of America" (40:263, referring to the population of Rhode Island; original emphasis). Madison thus treated the obligation of a law as contingent on its continuing reasonableness. He recognized also that under some conditions the principle of amendability can clash with and legitimately bypass the positive law designed to give that principle practical effect. Invoking the Declaration of Independence, Madison said the Convention realized that "in all great changes" of governments, "forms . . . ought to give way to substance" lest the people's "precious right" to revolution be negated. He added that since spontaneous and leaderless popular movements are "impossible," changes in government must "be instituted by some informal and unauthorized propositions, made by some patriotic and respectable citizen or number of citizens" (40:265, original emphasis).

The Declaration of Independence and the founding thus indicate that a disposition to exchange reasons in justification of questionable beliefs and policies is morally prior to formal governmental institutions and specific conceptions of constitutional ends, like the Large Commercial Republic and its ends of security, prosperity, and equal opportunity. I call this disposition a "secular public reasonableness," and, following *The Federalist*, I conceive it as a virtue—a good and praiseworthy disposition for both an individual and a community. I argue in the concluding chapter of this book that the value of this disposition is an inference from the Constitution as written; that this disposition comprehends the economic and noneconomic dimensions of lived experience; and that while chance may account for both the possession of this disposition and its loss, neither an individual nor a community can actively elect to abandon it. If I am right about these matters, a secular public reasonableness will prove to be the ultimate constitutional end and the key to the answers that Marshallians submit to their critics.

4

WHY STATES' RIGHTS FEDERALISM IS
IMPOSSIBLE TO DEFEND

The federalism axiom says the powers of the national government are enumerated and therefore limited in number. A nationalist theory compatible with this axiom would have to include a theory of nationally authorized ends and a rule against pretextual uses of power, acts seeking unauthorized ends under cover of authorized ends. A no-pretext rule and a list of national ends would not suffice for states' righters, however. To see why, consider some examples.

The Gun-Free School Zones Act was a pretextual act. Gun possession in school zones could very well be a national problem, and one with serious economic consequences. Yet the end sought by this particular act was safe schools, not the production of goods or the distribution of wealth or any other economic end. The *Lopez* Court correctly reasoned that a different conclusion would permit any act with economic consequences to pass under the Commerce Clause, thus defeating any and all versions of the federalism axiom. Though guns in schools could diminish the nation's wealth, and, as the Court observed, safe schools (along with low divorce rates) could be part of a comprehensive plan to improve the nation's material well-being, meeting an economic threat happened not to be the purpose of this particular act. By contrast, in 1908 child labor was seen as both a humanitarian problem and an economic problem. Lower labor costs gave states that permitted child labor a competitive advantage over states that prohibited it, and the *Hammer* Court cited that fact as an actual reason for the act. Under a welfarist reading of the Constitution, the Child Labor Act was an honest exercise of the Commerce Clause, and the Court erred in voiding the act.

Pretextual acts of recent years include the Controlled Substances Act as applied to medical marijuana and the Partial-Birth Abortion Ban Act.

Though enacted under the commerce power, these acts were not concerned with the production and distribution of the nation's wealth; they were motivated by health and moral considerations, not creating jobs, reducing the income gap, or reducing the trade deficit. Yet each of the acts could have been constitutional under different circumstances or different constitutional provisions. Medical marijuana could get out of hand and threaten to produce a nation of potheads unfit for productive citizenship.[1] A welfarist theory of the Fourteenth Amendment—a command to protect people and to do so equally—and a secular demonstration of the fetus's personhood could justify national laws protecting the fetus. Pursuant to the amendment's command to protect people (presupposed by the command to protect people equally), Congress could use its power to enforce the amendment to require local officials and taxpayers to protect children from gun violence in schools.

While some will deny that Congress has authority to educate the youth to an ideal of intellectual excellence formed independently of the nation's military and economic needs, none will deny that circumstances could justify Congress's promoting the training needed for fighting wars and meeting foreign economic competition. We could not say, therefore, that the states enjoyed unqualified sovereignty over education or any sovereignty over education in all circumstances. The same holds for all other categories of social practice. Consider public morality. A society whose political constitution promises equal opportunity and entrusts economic and political power to private hands cannot be indifferent to the racist and sexist attitudes that move these "private" hands.[2] The promise of equal opportunity might thus necessitate governmental efforts to change people's attitudes on race and sex, and because such measures might be necessary to fulfill a constitutional promise of equal opportunity, the Constitution should be read to authorize such measures as circumstances required.

These examples show that a states' rights federalist would need more than a no-pretext rule. A measure that is pretextual on one occasion need not be pretextual on all occasions, and a no-pretext rule would leave the national government free to do as it wished vis-à-vis the states as long as it did so for nationally authorized purposes. Under an ends-oriented constitution, virtually the only states' right other than process rights like representation in Congress and a role in constitutional amendments and the electoral college would be the general right against pretexts itself. The focus in federalism cases would remain the broad responsibilities of the national government: national security, national prosperity, and the equal economic and political opportunities of the nation's people. Given the content of these ends, a right against pretexts would amount to a right against the uses of national power for racial, sectarian, and other antiliberal ends. An example would be deploying the Commerce Clause against practices that offend a sectarian view of when human personhood begins. Reducing states' rights to a right against pretexts might therefore argue for process federalism over national federalism, for the aims of national federalism might be served simply by guaranteeing the states' process rights and enforcing the constitutional rights of individuals against the states, which the federal courts already do. Thus, a court would not have to say that the Partial-Birth Abortion Ban Act pursued an unauthorized end; it could say that the act offended a woman's right to choose. I discuss this prospect further, especially in Chapter 7, where I show that a constitution of negative liberties (like a woman's right to choose) is no substitute for a constitution of positive ends (like a society whose members are accountable to each other in a manner free of sectarian imposition). But the present point is that a no-pretext rule will not satisfy a dual federalist conception of "limited national power." A no-pretext rule is merely the negative side of a focus on positive constitutional ends, and a positive focus defeats any notion of substantive states' rights. Our question now is whether there is any case for states' rights beyond process rights and a general right against pretexts, and we shall see that there is not and cannot be.

Defending States' Rights

States' righters have two ways of restraining national power. They can read national power narrowly or they can carve exemptions from national power broadly conceived. We begin with the first strategy. Because no one defines *all* national power narrowly, states' righters must justify reading some powers narrowly and others broadly. Though the several enumerated powers over foreign commerce, war, and the military in Articles I and II fall far short of all that would be required to defend the nation and conduct its foreign affairs, national power over defense and foreign affairs has always been regarded as plenary; in C. Herman Pritchett's words: "dual federalism never got a foothold in the field of foreign relations."[3] The justification for this fact is (1) the unquestioned need for a united front abroad, and (2) the incompetence of the several states to speak and act for the nation as a whole. Yet a united face abroad implies a union at home that dual federalists deny. And the incompetence of the states abroad is the foreign affairs counterpart of the principle of generality and locality which dual federalists also deny. How, then, can dual federalism explain one face abroad and many at home? And if incompetence of the several states in foreign affairs demands plenary national power in that area, how could the incompetence of the several states over domestic matters of national concern not demand plenary power to address the nation's domestic problems?

A dual federalist answer to these questions can be found in an opinion for a unanimous Court by Justice George Sutherland in *United States v. Curtiss-Wright Export Corp.* (1936).[4] Justice Sutherland contended that with the Declaration of Independence sovereignty passed from the British Crown to the colonies in a divided fashion: domestic sovereignty passed from Crown to each of the original states, and sovereignty over foreign affairs passed to the union as a whole and its agent, the Continental Congress. The states then elected to divide their domestic powers, delegating some to the national government and reserving the rest. The states passed no foreign powers to the nation because no such powers had initially passed from the Crown to them.[5] From this, said Sutherland: "It results that the investment of the federal government with the powers of external sovereignty did not depend upon the affirmative grants of the Constitution. The powers to declare and wage war, to conclude peace, to make treaties, to maintain diplomatic relations with other sovereignties, if they had never been mentioned in the Constitution, would have vested in the federal government as necessary concomitants of nationality."[6]

What Sutherland neglected to do is offer a reason why anyone should read constitutional history his way. Sutherland's account is an interpretation of events, not an uncontroversial description of them. Why not a different interpretation? Why not say, with Lincoln, that the union came before the states, and that through a successful revolution the union turned colonies into states? Why not add, with Marshall, that in 1787 the people of the whole resumed their sovereignty and upon ratification redistributed power between the national and state governments? (Marshall's account would explain the appearance of foreign affairs powers in Article I, Section 8, powers whose enumeration Sutherland held superfluous.) Why not adopt a principle of generality and locality and say with Lincoln that the people of the whole established the national government to do what it alone can do: address the nation's problems, at home and abroad? Because Sutherland faced an interpretive choice, he needed an argument from goodness or rightness to justify his choice. Yet he offered no such argument.

So we have yet to answer our question. If the domestic powers of Article I, Section 8 were construed as the foreign affairs powers have been construed, the national government would have plenary responsibility for the nation's economy—a duty to take all reasonable and feasible measures to promote the material well-being of the nation's population. As we assume power to tax and spend for military research and development, for example, we would assume power to tax and spend for dams, canals, roads, railroads, and other "internal improvements." As we assume power to regulate for the sake of national security, we would assume power to regulate for national prosperity. As we grant that the nation does not have to rely on a voluntary army, we would grant that the nation does not have to rely on voluntary purchases of health insurance. Why, then, should we read the Constitution one way regarding national defense and foreign affairs and another way regarding the nation's economic life?

Beyond Justice Sutherland's answer, another way for states' righters to deal with this question would be to deny that there exists one conception of prosperity that ought to apply to the entire nation. Or, equivalently, states' righters could deny that the American population constitutes one nation whose prosperity government can promote. Thus, it can be said that while military research and development helps achieve a security from foreign powers that all Americans can share, a canal in New York not only fails to benefit Pennsylvanians but harms them by enabling New York City to beat out Philadelphia in the race for distribution centers for goods to and from the interior. This brings us to the compact theory of union associated chiefly with John C. Calhoun: the United States is not a nation in the fullest sense; it is not a collection of individuals who typically see themselves as belonging to one sociopolitical entity. The United States is rather a contractual union of separate communities, the ever-sovereign states. I analyze Calhoun's theory at some length in Chapter 5, but I should make a preliminary observation here.

As an account of how the nation's residents saw themselves at the founding, the compact theory was never demonstrable. Aside from problems of whose self-understanding should count, the compact theory assumes what is implausible and cannot be proved: that the typical franchised male of the 1780s valued membership in an altogether separate political community (a fictional entity in view of the Articles of Confederation) more than membership in a union of political entities whose contiguous and porous parts permitted him to travel and relocate at will from one part of the country to the next. No evidence whatever supports this assumption, and Calhoun himself held different beliefs at different stages of his career, as we shall see.

Nevertheless, the compact theory of the union traces back to Antifederalist thought and the Kentucky and Virginia Resolutions of 1798, authored, respectively, by Thomas Jefferson and James Madison. At odds with at least some parts of the constitutional text together with the constitutional theory of Hamilton and the early Madison, versions of the compact theory may have fit the nation's mood for some of its history after the Revolution and the founding and before the nationalizing effects of internal improvements, industrial development, innovations in transportation and communications, and the mobilization to fight two world wars. Versions of the compact theory resurfaced in the aftermath of the school desegregation case and again in the 1980s as theorists sought to formulate the constitutionalism of the Reagan Revolution.[7] Vestiges of the compact theory survive to the present in the constitutional doctrines of rightist jurists like Justice Clarence Thomas and twenty-eight state attorneys general who are presently challenging the constitutionality of the ACA ("Obamacare"). The compact theory remains influential, therefore, and I shall examine it in Chapter 5. But first we must see if the states' righter can make a case for states' rights in a manner that assumes Americans are members of one national community.

Why States' Rights? An Overview and Some Preliminaries

Our question is why we should read the domestic powers of the national government narrowly while reading the foreign affairs powers broadly. What good will come to the nation by denying Congress power to do all that it reasonably can to secure the nation's prosperity? Answers to this question derive from what are now five standard claims for states' rights federalism. In an oft-cited statement of these claims in *Gregory v. Ashcroft* (1991), Justice Sandra Day O'Connor conceived American federalism as a "structure of joint sovereigns" that "preserves to the people numerous advantages." These advantages are, she said:

1. "a decentralized government that will be more sensitive to the diverse needs of a heterogeneous society";

2. "increase[d] opportunity for citizen involvement in democratic processes";
3. "more innovation and experimentation in government";
4. government that is made "more responsive by putting States in competition for a mobile citizenry"; and
5. "[p]erhaps the principal benefit . . . a check on abuses of government power" for the sake of liberty.[8]

Elaborating this last benefit, O'Connor treated the state governments as parts of the national system of checks and balances. She claimed that "[j]ust as the separation and independence of the coordinate Branches of the Federal Government serves to prevent the accumulation of excessive power in any one branch, a healthy balance of power between the States and the Federal Government will reduce the risk of tyranny and abuse from either front."

To support this proposition she quoted two passages from *The Federalist*, one by Hamilton, the other by Madison. Hamilton said that "[p]ower being almost always the rival of power," both levels of government "will at all times stand ready to check usurpations" of each other, and [t]he people, by throwing themselves into either scale, "will decide."[9] Madison said that as the people "[i]n a single republic" guard against "usurpations" by dividing the government "into distinct and separate departments," the people in a federal system divide power "between two distinct governments," thus creating "a double security" for their rights.[10] Though one "can dispute whether our federalist system has been quite as successful in checking government abuse as Hamilton promised," said O'Connor, "there is no doubt about the design. If this 'double security' is to be effective, there must be a proper balance between the States and the Federal Government. These twin powers will act as mutual restraints only if both are credible. In the tension between federal and state power lies the promise of liberty."

O'Connor of course exaggerated when she said there was "no doubt about the design." Dissenters in *Gregory* had doubts that traced back to *McCulloch*, where Marshall denied that Maryland could check Congress's decision to charter a bank with branches in the states. The initial difficulties in any suggestion that the states can check the national government are the Supremacy Clause and the absence of any explicit check in the constitutional text. Notwithstanding O'Connor's quotes from *The Federalist*, a specific and unequivocal state check is mentioned in no part of that work.

In the passages O'Connor cited, Hamilton and Madison contradicted the clear nationalism of their collaboration in the Philadelphia Convention and the nationalism that characterizes most of what they say in *The Federalist*. Despite the dominant theme of *The Federalist*, O'Connor could have cited other passages that favor states' rights (for example, 10:63, 52:358–359, 83:560), and the resulting discrepancy between the larger theme and these passages calls for an explanation.

Edward Purcell suggests the most plausible explanation: a disingenuous campaign motive. He simply doubts that Hamilton and Madison "held much faith in their claim that the states would commonly unite against intrusive actions by the national government."[11] Such unity would seem "to fit awkwardly" with Madison's general view of the nation's "numerous and varied internal factions," says Purcell. Congress, after all, is a reasonably representative body, and the interests there represented overlap sufficiently with the combined interests represented in the state legislatures to make it rare that a majority of the state legislatures would oppose an act of Congress. Despite several challenges in the nineteenth century to national authority by states acting alone or in groups, at few points in the nation's history have most of the states united against an act of Congress.[12] The states did act with sufficient unity against the Supreme Court when they adopted the Eleventh Amendment in 1795. In the passages that O'Connor cited, Hamilton and Madison could have been referring either to the states' role in constitutional amendments or to the military potential inherent in the state militias.

As reiterated here several times, amendments result from a national process in which the states play a part, and though an erstwhile sovereignty may explain why a state has a part to play, a part remains but a part. Moreover, as we saw in Chapter 1, if the constitutional text supports military action by one domestic government against another, it supports national force against the states, not vice versa. In the states' rights phases of their careers, Madison, Jefferson, and Calhoun did deduce states' rights checks from their understanding of constitutional fundamentals; these checks were known variously as "interposition" and "nullification," with the latter culminating in a states' right to secede from the union. A right to secede followed upon a refusal to recognize both judicial review and the amending process as substitutes for the ultimate right of an individual state to answer constitutional questions for itself. Secession was the true implication of the compact theory because, within the premises of that theory, the alternative to secession was living under a rule to which one had not consented, and that was tantamount to loss of the "power[s] of self government . . . [and] self protection," the antithesis of independence and sovereignty.[13] Unlike Madison and maybe Jefferson, Calhoun recognized the secessionist implication of the compact theory and was prepared to act on it.

O'Connor's view of the fundamentals was close to Calhoun's. Intentionally or not, she implicitly denied the existence of one conception of what prosperity is or one assessment of its value relative to other goods, like state control of school zones and the pay of state employees. But unlike Calhoun, O'Connor had to view states' sovereignty in a postwar light. The Civil War left her no choice but to assume that a state's act of checking national power would proceed only through a federal lawsuit or a constitutional amendment. The protesting state cannot act alone in these national processes. It can act only as a part of a larger whole to whose authority it must submit—to whose authority it is in fact submitting in the very act of protesting through channels prescribed by the whole. If there are postwar state's rights against national authority, they are the rights to sue on grounds of pretext and to amend the Constitution. These rights are derivative of, and defined by, the Constitution. These rights could not have preexisted the Constitution, and the Constitution could not have resulted from their exercise. Because the states enjoy only these subordinate and derivative rights, one can dispute O'Connor's claim that the Constitution is "a structure of joint sovereigns."

An account of constitutional structure more faithful to the constitutional text, at least in its postwar light, would follow Marshall in *McCulloch* and describe one sovereign, the "People of the United States," establishing agent-governments that occupy two levels, one state, one national, with the latter supreme when pursuing authorized ends. That the constituent authority granted supremacy to the national government in cases of conflict indicates that "the People" is one cultural entity—one entity, that is, with a more-or-less specific cultural identity.

The later Calhoun held a different view of the nation. For him cultural differences between North and South were both manifest and stable, with no prospect for convergence, and this meant separate peoples' contracting as equals and reserving rights of nullification and secession. Because nullification was no part of O'Connor's understanding of federalism, she should have seen the founding as one sovereign people establishing two governments, with one government representing the sovereign's overriding values. Rejecting nullification, she had no warrant for describing the Constitution as "a structure of joint sovereigns" and reasoning from that premise to a states' rights exemption from Congress's pursuit of authorized national ends. We'll return to this issue in Chapter 5.

O'Connor's five arguments for states' rights look better in the abstract than they do in light of the nation's experience. Consider her fifth argument. As an abstract proposition, mutual governmental checks may seem to result in more liberty for the individual. But the nation's experience exposes this claim as most contentious. From the nation's beginning a principal impetus for the advance of national power at the states' expense has been the vindication of personal rights against the abuses of the state governments. The American founding vindicated the rights of lenders from state laws that altered the obligations of borrowers; the Civil War and its constitutional amendments ended slavery; federal courts applied most of the Bill of Rights to the states; federal judicial and legislative power sought to end racial discrimination by state agencies and private businesses and employers; and federal courts have tried to secure reproductive choice for women and liberty for homosexuals at the expense of the states' power to define the health and morals of their people.

Of course, the states had their versions of the rights involved in these contests, including the rights of slaveholders, the rights of individuals to live in communities of their own racial and religious kind, and the rights of unborn persons. One can deny that the national answers to these disputes have been uniformly correct, and Justice O'Connor might have shown that sometimes the states sought to protect liberties that right-thinking persons (that is, right-thinking persons nationwide) would have vindicated against national authorities. After all, Calhoun once convinced himself and tried to persuade others that slaveholding was a moral right and ought to remain a legal right (because slavery "in the present state of civilization" was "a positive good").[14] And many academics profess to believe that rights are merely conventional, never simply "real," in which case "rights" no longer recognized may yet be revived, for conventions change. So I don't contend that history refutes O'Connor's fifth claim. I contend only that the claim is debatable, and that it therefore needs the help of further analysis and evidence before it can serve as a decisive argument for denying Congress power to do what it reasonably can for the nation's prosperity. (I shall contend ultimately that no such argument is possible.)

O'Connor's second claim may also look good in the abstract. It too needs help, however. That honoring states' rights "increases opportunity for citizen involvement in democratic processes" implies a conception of constitutional democracy that breezes past the framers' aversion to populist democracy in the states, their disgust with the states' conduct during the Revolution and after, their view of constitutionalism as reconciling democracy to objective standards of political morality, and their belief that the value of democracy depends on that reconciliation.[15] The framers' reservations about participatory democracy are hardly out of date.[16] Even if devolving power to local levels fostered increased citizen participation and a self-critical public-spiritedness, well-meaning and moderate government would not guarantee competent government at any level.

Nor would devolving power in democracy's name imply either a free hand in defining democracy or separate local standards for measuring state performance. Justice O'Connor herself assumed one true conception of democracy (participatory democracy) in arguing for states' rights. And no one can successfully argue that we should conceive power over a given territory as power to describe reality as one might wish. No one could say, for example, that in the early fifties the Southern states were even trying to prepare black children for productive roles in an industrial economy, not to mention providing an educational opportunity that equaled that provided to white children. The only question would be whether Congress could respond to such neglect under its constitutional duty to promote national prosperity. If the answer to this question were no, then Congress would have no general duty to promote national prosperity, which would return us to the problem we started with: How or why could Congress have a general duty to defend all of the nation and not have a general duty to pursue the prosperity of all of its people? In any case, O'Connor did not and could not have freed the states to define democracy as they wished. By implying a national standard of "democracy" in her very argument for the states' "independence" and "sovereignty," she leaves us wondering what meaning these words might have.

O'Connor's first and fourth arguments need help because they contradict each other. She first assumes that the states are culturally too diverse to be governed peacefully by one central authority. She then assumes that residents of each state are free to live in whichever state they please. Yet Jones can't move from a transitional neighborhood to a legally secure WASP neighborhood anywhere in the country because the Civil War Amendments and related statutes guarantee Sister Xiao-Lin's right to buy an available house in Jones's block no matter where he might move.

As for O'Connor's third argument, while it may be her best one, it is not really a states' rights argument. Malcolm Feeley and Edward Rubin point out that the kind of experimentation O'Connor assumed is useful only when the states "share a single goal," not when the states' goals "are different from each other." What experiment would one design, they ask, to determine whether the Southern states should have retained slavery?[17] Who will stand up and declare the good served by letting Texas experiment with the white primary or Alabama experiment with capital trials without lawyers for poor defendants? If the nation had a more-or-less uniform understanding of what it wanted by way of public purposes like the public's literacy and health, letting the states experiment with different means would hardly entail suspending national standards for evaluating the results or surrendering national power to rule out some experiments.

States' Rights and Competitive Federalism

Justice O'Connor's fifth claim deserves a closer examination, which I shall conduct together with a closer look at her fourth argument. Her fifth claim is that liberty is "perhaps the principal advantage" of mutually checking national and state governments. To separate this claim from Calhoun's checks on national power, we must reformulate it. Today, the only way for a single state to check national power constitutionally is to ask the federal judiciary to declare federal action a violation of some national law, including the Constitution. A court can check national power in one of two ways. It can either find that Congress or another national agent has acted without affirmative constitutional authorization, as Congress did when it passed the Gun-Free School Zones Act under the Commerce Clause. Or a court can declare a constitutional or a statutory exemption to an otherwise authorized act. The First Amendment, for example, exempts freedom of speech from congressional regulations of commerce; Judge Vinson held that mandating insurance coverage was exempted from the national commerce power, and the Court in *Gregory v. Ashcroft* held that Congress itself had exempted the retirement of state judges from the federal Age Discrimination in Employment Act.

Updating O'Connor's fifth argument, it reads: Courts can enhance the liberty of Americans generally by narrowing Congress's power over the economy and/or exempting some state practices from admitted national power. Thus construed, O'Connor's fifth claim (that states' rights enhance liberty) is practically equivalent to her fourth claim (that liberty is enhanced by states' competing for mobile citizens). The combined argument would be that restraints on Congress's responsibility for the nation's economy (a narrow commerce power with some exemptions thrown in) would enable the states to offer different packages of regulations, taxes, and services, and these different packages would provide a greater array of choices for citizens who can move from state to state. More options for mobile citizens assumes meaningful differences among the states, and this assumption connects the now-combined fourth and fifth claims with O'Connor's first claim: that more power for the states enhances the nation's ability to serve the diverse needs of a heterogeneous national community. I shall therefore discuss arguments (5), (4), and (1) together, and I shall do so by examining a general thesis that relies on all three. Constitutional theorists now call this thesis "competitive federalism."[18]

The leading competitive federalists are Randy Barnett, Richard Epstein, and Michael Greve. These economic libertarians read the domestic commerce power and other economic powers (over bankruptcy, coinage, patents, the powers to tax and spend, and the like) as falling far short of a general power over the nation's economy. They seek the erosion and eventual reversal of New Deal judicial landmarks that recognize Congress's authority to set price supports and production quotas, tax and spend for social welfare purposes, and regulate the labor relations and working conditions of the nation's workforce. They claim that restoring Congress's power and the states' responsibilities to pre–New Deal levels will force state governments "to compete for business, investment, and productive citizens." Different "regulatory regimes and packages of governmental services" will then yield more choices for citizens who are generally free "to vote with their feet." And "citizen choice" will then "discipline" state governments "the same way in which consumer choice, in competitive markets, disciplines producers."[19]

Different writers defend "competitive federalism" with arguments that range from historical and lexicographical to social-scientific (psychological and economic) and even moral, and no aspect of the position, substantive or methodological, is uncontroversial.[20] We need not examine all of the issues here, however, for even if the tenets of competitive federalism are true in all contexts (historical, social-scientific, legal-moral), competitive federalism turns out to be a species of national federalism, not states' rights federalism.[21] Though competitive federalism may redirect national power, it does not diminish it relative to its conception of national ends. It simply reduces "national prosperity" to one of its contingent means, minimally regulated markets.

The logic of competitive federalism is a nationalist logic. It begins in a vision of the nation's economic health and resolves constitutional issues in ways that serve that vision—and it does so without regard for states' rights. Competitive federalists would entrust the national government with power that they think adequate to the nation's economic health, which they conceive in terms of low taxes, minimal regulation, free trade, and maximum citizen choice. Michael Greve, who currently directs the American Enterprise Institute's Federalism Project, is clear about the nationalist logic of his position. He says that competitive federalism "does not seek to restore some elusive balance between the states and the federal government or to reinvest sovereign states with the glory they may have possessed in Andrew Jackson's days."[22]

Greve's federalism, unlike that of Calhoun, Jackson's first vice president, is made for people who leave home. Greve reports that 40 percent of respondents to a survey conducted in 1990 had relocated from their native states. The survey also shows Americans "who stay put do so for reasons other than a sentimental attachment to their home state and its government." Competitive federalism wants the states to compete for these unsentimental people. "Federalism is about *competition* among the states," Greve says. "It serves not so much to empower the states as to discipline them."[23] The agents of that discipline are the businesses and "productive citizens" who will move out (leaving the unproductive behind) if they dislike the mix of burdens and benefits offered by the states in which they temporarily reside.

Greve assumes, of course, as must other competitive federalists, that the "productive citizens" have a *right* to move out—a right to move with their personal property, including their capital. This right is actually a collection of several rights enforceable against states that would try to hold people back or, on the terminal end of the move, keep them out.[24] These rights of exit and relocation are hardly cost-free or uncontroversial; they either preclude or severely abridge claimed rights of individuals who want to associate with people of their own racial, ethnic, or religious kind in enclaves protected by civil and criminal laws governing things like trespass, inheritance, housing, marriage, education, and, especially, citizenship (rights to vote, sue, petition government). Basic rights of exit and relocation presently fall under the Privileges and Immunities Clause of Article IV and the Civil War Amendments, especially Section 1 of the Fourteenth Amendment, which grants U.S. citizenship to native-born and naturalized persons, a right to citizenship in the states where they reside, and therewith rights of exit, entry, and choice of residence. The Constitution did not recognize all of these rights at first, of course; some achieved legal status following the bloodiest exercise of domestic power in American history, and the full power of the national government continues to guarantee their enjoyment.

"Competitive federalism" thus seems an odd kind of federalism, for its central promise—"citizen choice"—is a right achieved through and maintained by national power, historically at the expense of state power. Though citizen choice is the selling point of competitive federalism, the strong national character of competitive federalism seriously limits the range of citizen choice. As an abstract idea, federalism is associated with difference; its special concern is preserving difference in unity. Federalism is also distinguished from nationalism, which is associated with union (sameness) and emphasizes the unity that envelopes (smothers?) a subordinate diversity. Because Greve would maximize choice by multiplying options, he emphasizes diversity: hence competitive *federalism*. And, in federalism's fashion, Greve promises that the advantages of competitive federalism will "extend not only to economic matters, but also, and with equal force, to social or lifestyle issues."[25] Here he mentions communities that do and do not permit public smoking and gay marriage. The citizens of his federal republic will be able to choose among this array of communities.

But Greve is whistling "Dixie" here. His promise of diversity cannot be serious. The communities of his system will not differ significantly from each other in terms of the issues that have historically divided Americans. We can see this by the way Greve pulls some options off the table. "Some matters are so fundamental that we do not permit any jurisdiction to provide a choice," he says, in a nationalist voice. Among these forbidden choices he lists slavery, racial segregation, and polygamy—and, he adds, "one can have a long, difficult debate about whether abortion should fall into that category."[26] The problems for Greve at this point are obvious: If abortion depends on the outcome of a debate, so do other matters, including gay rights, polygamy, and smoking. And Greve cannot guarantee diverse communities because the debate he assumes must be a national debate. The very existence and character of diverse communities will depend on the outcome of a national debate. Even if Congress decides to leave some matters to the several states, regarding marijuana for example, the decision to decentralize—a national policy decision—will precede and enable diversity in the states.

As the nation's law presently stands, state and local communities are free to debate smoking tobacco and act immediately on the outcome of the debate. The same does not hold for smoking pot or cocaine or reinstituting official segregation. Although people in the several states can still debate such matters, they cannot act on conclusions that offend national policy. To produce and distribute cannabis for public consumption would require repealing, amending, or declining to enforce the Controlled Substances Act. To reestablish segregation would mean repealing the Fourteenth Amendment. No state or any number of states can constitutionally achieve any of these results on their own. The states or their certified representatives can work only as parts of national majorities acting through national processes. Greve therefore can promise the mobile citizen little beyond a range of options that a long, difficult, and continuing debate has revealed as approximately the right thing for the country as a whole.

If Greve is unhappy with the present level of diversity in the country, he is out of luck, for the very rights of exit and relocation on which his "competitive federalism" depends have helped to restrict the range of permissible styles of life in America. The nation cannot have legally protected racial, ethnic, and religious enclaves partly because of the individual's rights to travel and relocate her residence. She may be able to find a neighborhood here and there of her racial, ethnic, or religious kind, but the law stops her kind from doing everything necessary to perpetuate the neighborhood's character. And since the law is written in the name of a national community of which she is supposed to be a part, the law has its own view of what she essentially is. It holds, in effect, that her true and relevant kind is not really a racial, ethnic, or religious kind. Nor is it a kind defined by sex or sexual preference. And since she can move about and raise her children elsewhere, she is not essentially a Hoosier or a Yankee.

You could say the law makes her an American, but that leaves the question of what being an American is. Being an American cannot be defined in terms of fidelity to the Constitution because the Constitution is amendable and because its background principles and the precedents set by the framers themselves give Americans the right to revolution or the right to bypass unworkable amending procedures.[27] As the options are eliminated one remains: our citizen belongs to a Rational Kind, distinguished from other kinds by the capacity of its members to give and exchange reasons in community with each other.[28]

Greve suggests something like this when he says abortion in the states will be decided by a long debate, which must mean debate at the national level. No such debate could occur among persons whose identity was inseparable from their birthplace (a point Greve would acknowledge) or religious beliefs. This debate could not occur if people failed to connect their authentic selves to a desire for truth that all in the debate could come to see—a shareable truth not dependent on some special revelation, or special inheritance, or specific cultural commitment. So when Greve says the right to abortion depends on a debate, he would disfranchise Americans who believe there is nothing to debate, either because they believe God condemns abortion or because they believe moral questions are matters of arbitrary personal choice. Thus, Greve cannot promise people on either extreme of the abortion debate much that is important to them.

People like Greve (people willing to debate and live with the outcome) can have a state of their own; not so with the millions of people who think there is nothing to debate. Full-blooded true believers of either extreme (people who won't debate either their beliefs or anyone's beliefs) cannot vote with their feet because there is no place for them to go. The Constitution precludes their kind of place. The serious moral skeptic can find no political community that admits that its laws are fundamentally arbitrary, especially not in the United States, for the Constitution is supposed to void fundamentally arbitrary laws. The Constitution also voids laws through which the true believer would perpetuate his faith, laws that would control the education of the community's youth, the religion of its population, the sex lives of its people, the products they consume, the messages they hear, and the people they marry, live next to, work with, and fight beside.[29]

Competitive federalists recognize that rights to travel, relocate, and sue are rights of individuals who have additional rights as producers and consumers. The rights to relocate would have little meaning or value without these additional rights. Among them are property rights that are especially dear to competitive federalists, including the old liberty to contract, which they would revive, and the recently fortified freedom from uncompensated regulatory takings.[30] In addition, competitive federalists make a point of their opposition to racially discriminatory state action.[31] Competitive federalism's support for this array of rights, economic as well as civil, highlights a feature of competitive federalism that provides further evidence that federalism is far from what competitive federalism is about. This feature is a broad reliance on national judicial power, including national judicial power over the states.

Richard Epstein shows his support for a strong judiciary by his intemperate words for those who call for judicial deference to the elected branches of the national and state governments. Though pointedly denying that he accuses the Progressive movement of racism (and raising the question in the process), Epstein does suggest a connection. The Progressives' narrow view of individual liberty and broad view of the police power "supported a strong conception of judicial quiescence" that abetted decisions like *Plessy v. Ferguson*[32] and Woodrow Wilson's 1913 order segregating the civil service.[33] Waxing bolder, Epstein informs the reader about Justice Holmes's "sympathy for the great Progressive cause of eugenics." He says Holmes's denial of the liberty to contract in *Lochner v. New York*[34] parallels Holmes's notorious denial of a right to procreate in *Buck v. Bell*.[35] He observes that a narrow view of liberty combined with a broad view of the police power moved Felix Frankfurter to approve a state policy of forcing school children to salute the American flag, contrary to their religious beliefs.[36] This policy, says Epstein, testing decency's limits, was a demand "of public fealty that typified the Nazi regimes with which we were soon to come into mortal conflict."[37] Such, apparently, are the devastating associations in store for all who disagree with Epstein's "judicial oversight of the political process."[38]

As Greve notes, in the five decades prior to the Rehnquist Court, a broad view of Congress's powers and a broad view of judicial power under the Fourteenth Amendment developed together and "spelled the death knell of federalism as a principal constitutional concern."[39] Epstein, it appears, would break up the old nationalist team of strong-Court-strong-Congress and substitute strong-Court-weak-Congress. But appearances can mislead, and showing how they mislead in Epstein's case will underscore my claim that defending states' rights is self-defeating.

Epstein and the Commerce Power

Epstein favors a commerce power that is much narrower than that which presently gives Congress power over any significant activity that is generally recognized as "commercial" or "economic." Today, for example, the Court and most academic observers agree that Congress has constitutional authority to regulate agricultural production, protect domestic industries from foreign competition, set the maximum hours and minimum wages of the nation's workers, mandate safe working conditions, force employers to help fund workers' retirement, impose price controls on the nation's businesses, punish monopolistic practices, ensure product safety, ensure the safety of goods and persons in transit, punish fraud, require sound banking practices, grant monopolies, rescue insolvent banks, insure bank deposits, regulate gas mileage, and so on down an endless list of economic activities or other activities that affect the nation's economy. Today it is generally acknowledged that Congress's power over the economy is limited by a small list of exemptions, not by an indefinite store of "reserved powers." Today the national government has wide authority to do what it reasonably can to promote the economic growth of the nation and the personal economic security and advancement of its people—all this mostly under the Commerce Clause. Epstein dissents from this near consensus, however, and his grounds are scientific and moral. He admits that the historical record is insufficient for him to know all that the framers intended to accomplish through the commerce power, and he acknowledges the textual and historical evidence that the framers intended mercantilist policies that he and other free marketeers strongly oppose.[40]

Text and history thus force Epstein to think for himself, and individual choice in a competitive market becomes his test of both good policy and good institutions. Applying this test, he finds that Congress has used a broad power over the economy for good purposes and for bad. He thinks the bad outweigh the good, however, and to prevent the bad he will sacrifice the good. So he defines the commerce power narrowly, as not much more than power to regulate the carriage of goods and the conduct of business across state borders (for example, power over who may carry interstate passengers), the instruments of that carriage (responsibility for things like airport security, the length of freight trains, and the size and weight of interstate trucks), and the channels of that carriage (power to set rules of the road on waterways and air routes). What Epstein opposes most is government specifying hours, wages, and other terms of employment, for, he holds, such measures guarantee inefficiencies that inflate the cost of goods and diminish consumer choice. Epstein thus imports into the Constitution a conception of the commerce power that reflects his view of what is best for the well-being of the nation as a whole. And his justification for proceeding in this manner is precisely his conception of the national interest and his forthright acknowledgment that constitutional text and history force him to consult his view of the national interest.[41]

By shaping the commerce power to fit his view of good policy, Epstein conflates a constitutional question and a policy question. Normally this would be a category mistake, but here it reflects Epstein's well-considered commitment to two propositions. Criticizing the Rehnquist Court for not moving beyond a few exemptions from national power to a full-throated return to the narrow Commerce Clause of the 1920s, Epstein says flatly: "The greater the scope of permissible government action, the higher the level of abuse."[42] This proposition supposes (1) that a constitutional right to regulate always results in a net increase in the number and/or scope of regulations over specified activities within a specified period, and (2) that regulation does more harm than good. Here, then, is essentially a scientific judgment that acknowledging that government has broad constitutional authority guarantees abusive policies, and this judgment becomes the factual premise of a legal-moral argument for reading the Constitution (the Commerce Clause and the Due Process Clause) to limit the authority of both the national and the state governments. But Epstein's scientific premise does injustice to the facts, even as he describes the facts, and he eventually compromises his case for a narrow commerce power.

Consider first the historical facts. The broad commerce power of the New Deal remained entrenched in Supreme Court doctrine throughout the Burger and Rehnquist years, a fact Epstein assumes by decrying it.[43] Yet this broad commerce power was not enough to stop deregulatory waves from 1976 to 2008, in transportation, banking, finance, telecommunications, broadcasting, and utilities. The nation's experience over these years confirms a logical point: the right to do x does not entail the actual doing of x. A constitutional power to regulate is a right to choose to regulate; this right is a normative entity that entails no event in the physical world, including the act of choosing to regulate. In fact, one way to promote minimal regulation of the economy overall might be for Congress to preempt all constitutional power over the economy and then choose to exercise that power minimally. It is at least plausible that the greater the number of regulating authorities, the more actual regulation. But Epstein takes a different course. Instead of preempting state power and regulating minimally as a matter of national policy, Epstein would meet a threat of over regulation by urging the courts to (1) truncate the commerce power and (2) restrain state economic policies, mostly under the Fourteenth Amendment. He would use the courts to keep both Congress and the states down, in other words. But consistently followed, this strategy ill serves Epstein's free-market ends. If the past is any indication, Epstein will eventually need a commerce power broader and a Congress more powerful than he would presently allow—and in spite of himself, he concedes the point.

Epstein forgets his rule that power guarantees abuse when he comments on what he calls "the one sensible but measured expansion of the affirmative Commerce Clause." This is the "expansion" that occurred "in connection with the antitrust laws," which combated mergers that "intended to monopolize or cartelize particular products [like steel pipes and meat] or labor markets."[44] A narrow view of the commerce power would reach only those few monopolies and cartels that affected the "cross-border shipments of goods" (collusive stockyard fees and state-mandated freight rates, for example), leaving "immense difficulties" for other industries, such as subjecting "individual mergers . . . to attack under the law of each state in which the firms did business." It was "not surprising," therefore, that the Old Court eventually put aside the strict dichotomy between commerce and manufacturing announced in *United States v. E. C. Knight Co.*[45] and "took the position that the Sherman Act and, later, other antitrust laws, were within the scope of the commerce power on the ground that these private cooperative arrangements had a 'substantial effect on nationwide economic activity.'" Thus, says Epstein approvingly, "the justices on the Old Court . . . took into account problems of social organization that were not envisioned at the founding."[46]

Unsettled by the clear implication of this last observation, Epstein moves quickly to contain the damage. He insists that the Old Court's departure from *E. C. Knight* was a "measured expansion," not a new view of Congress's relationship to the economy or the states. He claims that "no one before 1937 thought that the difficult matters pertaining to interstate mergers or price-fixing arrangements that involved transactions in two or more states undercut the basic logic of *E.C. Knight.* Manufacturing was still regarded as an exclusively local subject."[47] His evidence for this last proposition seems so weak that I fear I've misunderstood it. He seems to rely on the unstated assumption of the Twenty-First Amendment (repealing Prohibition) that individual states could decide whether to permit the manufacture of intoxicating beverages within their borders. The amendment, it seems, did not have to spell out this assumption because of the general understanding that "manufacture was already under the exclusive control of the states."[48]

If this indeed is Epstein's argument, readers need no help judging it. They can easily see that (1) the states' power to regulate x does not imply even a superior power to regulate x, much less an exclusive power to do so; (2) an exclusive states' right to determine the manufacture of intoxicants within a state's borders would not preclude national power over the wages and working conditions of that industry's workers; (3) exclusive control over the manufacturing of strong drink would not imply exclusive control over the manufacturing of other products, for there could be something special (culturally and medically) about strong drink; and (4) leaving a state with power to decide whether x may be manufactured within its borders would not cancel the supremacy of national power pursuing national ends or the possibility that national ends might require overriding state policies—the possibility that any and all matters left to the states could have "substantial effects" on matters admittedly within national control. In addition, readers can surely question Epstein's statement that "no one before 1937" thought Congress had power to regulate manufacturing. One wonders how this statement squares with Epstein's earlier report that the Progressive movement had been pushing for an "expansion" of the commerce power since the late nineteenth century.[49] How could cases like *Hammer* and *E. C. Knight* have arisen if "no one before 1937" believed Congress could reach practices incident to manufacturing?[50]

But put these problems aside. For argument's sake, let us accept Epstein's contention regarding what people thought before 1937. The next question would be: so what? If everyone before 1937 believed Congress had no power over manufacturing, it hardly follows that we should agree. It might follow if either the constitutional text or the framers were clear on the matter, but Epstein holds otherwise, as we have seen. It might also follow if one accepted the premise that one should believe what all or most others believe. But if Epstein's position depended on which side had proved conventionally most persuasive about the Commerce Clause, he would be a Progressive. Of the Progressives he says: "Although they ultimately prevailed . . . they and their ideas come out second best as an intellectual matter."[51]

So by his own example he entitles his critics to ask, "as an intellectual matter," and regardless of what others believe or believed, why anyone should deny Congress the authority to do what it reasonably can to advance the nation's economic well-being. Instead of answering this question, Epstein draws a line between commerce and manufacturing, crosses the line when it serves his view of the nation's economic health, and insists that the line he just crossed remains a good line. Would it not be better to acknowledge the principle of the crossing: that the Constitution empowers Congress to do what it reasonable can to promote reasonable versions of the nation's material well-being? Why suggest that defenders of this principle have things in common with racists and Nazis? The principle is not all that bad; it is open to a free-market understanding of what Congress can reasonably do. It flatters that understanding by assuming it can compete successfully with other ideas, a possibility the Constitution leaves open *as a question of public policy* that Congress is free to answer as the evidence indicates.[52]

Epstein has no substantive reason for a narrow view of the commerce power—no reason in terms of the public interest. We have seen, in fact, that his substantive argument favors a broad view of the commerce power: the public interest demands a free market; to promote a free market Congress may sometimes have to regulate incidents of manufacturing, and Congress cannot decide when to regulate manufacturing unless it has the power to do so. Epstein thus shows by example that substantive arguments for states' rights end up being arguments for nationalism. But Epstein does have another argument for a narrow commerce power. This further argument is not an argument from some public purpose; it is an argument from judicial authority. It is a lawyer's argument, a kind that often works in court, where people don't always seek what is sound "as an intellectual matter." Epstein's further contention is that a narrow commerce power conforms to something John Marshall said in *Gibbons v. Ogden*, the dictum about commerce whose effect is entirely intrastate.[53]

In fora where what counts is sound "as an intellectual matter," an obvious point makes Epstein's further argument a weak argument: neither John Marshall nor anyone else speaks definitively for the Constitution. Critics of Marshall's performance in *Gibbons* have included some of the most renowned constitutional scholars (Thayer, Crosskey, Frankfurter, Powell),[54] and in Marshall's case as in all others, the question is who is right "as an intellectual matter." Appeal to Marshall's opinion in *Gibbons* is a weak move even if one acknowledges Marshall's preeminence among constitutional authorities, as I do, owing to the quality of Marshall's arguments generally and especially in *McCulloch*. The problem with Marshall's opinion in *Gibbons* is its notorious ambiguity; it can bear both a states' rights and a nationalist reading. Epstein himself acknowledges Marshall's overriding commitment to a strong national government; he also acknowledges the nationalist reading of *Gibbons*.[55] But this doesn't stop Epstein from giving *Gibbons* a states' rights reading. Our question now is whether Epstein's reading of *Gibbons* is more Epstein than Marshall. I think it is an easy question, but it is not an uncomplicated one, and I ask the reader to bear with me a bit longer. My aim is not to deconstruct Epstein but to show through a criticism of Epstein that libertarians cannot justify interpreting the Constitution to deny Congress authority to do what it reasonably can for the nation's economic well-being.

Gibbons involved a conflict between competing steamboat companies operating ferry services between New York and New Jersey. One operator held a federal license to work in coastal waters, the other held an exclusive franchise from the State of New York—a monopoly—to operate in New York waters between New York City and Elizabethtown and up the New York side of the Hudson to Albany. Declaring a conflict between the federal license and the New York franchise, Marshall invoked the Supremacy Clause and held against the monopoly. The monopoly had argued that the word *commerce* included only the buying and selling of goods, not their carriage, and therefore Congress had no power to license anyone engaged in navigation. Marshall rejected this vacuous claim. Citing broad usage and legislative precedent involving foreign commerce, he held that power over "commerce" certainly embraced power over "navigation." This plus an application of the Supremacy Clause was all Marshall needed to decide the case. But he added two sets of dicta, one set pointing north, the other south (Epstein would say east and west). These dicta concerned the scope of the Commerce Clause.

As counsel for the federal licensee, Daniel Webster had urged the Court to extend the commerce power to the "commercial intercourse between nations, and parts of nations, in all its branches."[56] Most of Marshall's opinion reflects Webster's nationalist view. Marshall begins by rejecting a theory of "narrow construction, which would cripple the government and render it unequal to the objects for which it is declared to be instituted, and to which the powers given, as fairly understood, render it competent." The opinion then proceeds to describe the commerce power as broader than necessary to decide the case. Adopting Webster's language, Marshall declares that commerce covers more than buying and selling; "[i]t describes the commercial intercourse between nations, and parts of nations in all its branches." He declares that commerce "among the several states" means "intermingled with them," and that "[c]ommerce among the states cannot stop at the external boundary line of each state, but may be introduced into the interior."[57] Then Marshall hedges. In a second set of dicta, he says:

> It is not intended to say that these words comprehend that commerce which is completely internal, which is carried on between man and man in a state, and which does not extend to or affect other states. Such a power would be inconvenient, and is certainly unnecessary. Comprehensive as the word "among" is, it may very properly be restricted to that commerce which concerns more states than one. The phrase is not one which would probably have been selected to indicate the completely interior traffic of a state. . . . The genius and character of the whole government seem to be, that its action is to be applied to all the external concerns of the nation, and to those internal concerns which affect the states generally, but not to those which are completely within a particular state, which do not affect other states, and with which it is not necessary to interfere, for the purpose of executing some of the general powers of the government.[58]

Ignoring the nationalist parts of *Gibbons,* states' righters have invoked the above passages to draft the great chief justice to their cause. Epstein does the same. He says Marshall "had no intention whatsoever of claiming that any manufacturing or agriculture was covered by the [commerce] power" and that Marshall's "entire point was that some *commerce* was exclusively intrastate and thus beyond the power of Congress to regulate."[59] Yet Pritchett observed that Marshall's "conception of commerce 'which concerns more states than one' was considerably more sophisticated" than the "hard and fast dichotomies" of the states' righters.[60] To say, for example, that Congress cannot regulate commerce that does not "extend to or affect other states" is far from drawing a rigid line between categories like "commerce" and "manufacturing," for there is no telling what species of commercial activity might affect future states of the national economy. Despite Epstein's own willingness to cross or deny the line when doing so serves his libertarian ends, as in the antitrust cases, Epstein holds the line when commenting on the New Deal's restricting the sale of dairy products and the production of wheat to support farm prices. The Constitution authorizes no such legislation, Epstein says, citing *Gibbons*, because "[t]here is no need to regulate production or consumption to have plenary power over transportation."[61]

Epstein's last statement is hard to defend. Here Epstein reduces *commerce* to *transportation*, despite ordinary usage that makes "commercial" overlap substantially in meaning with "economic," as reflected in Epstein's own reference to manufacturing (an economic activity) as intrastate "commerce."[62] We have seen that Marshall joined Webster in holding that the word *commerce* in the Commerce Clause refers to "commercial intercourse between nations, and parts of nations in all its branches." This phrase could be used to mean the intercourse called "transportation" and all branches of transportation, but usage hardly limits commerce to transportation, and the question is: what does?[63] We will turn to this question momentarily.

A second difficulty with Epstein's statement appears when one realizes that he is talking not just about the Commerce Clause but also the Necessary and Proper Clause. He is not just saying that manufacturing and transportation are two different things and that facilitating one differs from facilitating the other. He implies that under no possible circumstances can manufacturing and incident practices have a substantial effect on transporting goods from place to place. He is implying that regulating manufacturing could *never* be a good-faith means to regulating transportation or facilitating an adequate transportation system. If this were true, Epstein would have an important category of economic activity—production in such forms as manufacturing, farming, and mining—that is reserved to the states. Our immediate question is whether Epstein can fairly attribute this position to Marshall, and here is where things get tricky.

Why might Marshall have wanted to say that manufacturing, agriculture, mining, and production fall into a different category of social practice than the transportation of goods to market? Epstein truncates the commerce power because he believes, falsely, that more authority to regulate means more actual regulation, and because he believes that the more Congress regulates, the worse off the nation is. But why would Marshall think like Epstein? In view of Epstein's testimony that Marshall was more interested in legitimating Congress's power vis-à-vis the states than in facilitating free trade, why would Marshall want the truncated commerce power that Epstein wants? This question has an answer, and Epstein cites it. But it is the kind of answer that Epstein cannot deploy as his own. The answer is slavery. Epstein has pointed out that Marshall said what he did in *Gibbons* from a concern "not to tread on Southern sensibilities regarding Congress's power to regulate slavery."[64] This hypothesis makes sense, and other writers have proposed it.[65] To protect slavery from Congress, Marshall did not have to mention slavery; he had only to say that Congress could not regulate "commerce . . . between man and man in a State."

Slavery might explain Marshall's dictum in *Gibbons*, but slavery is no answer to why today's Americans should interpret the Commerce Clause as Epstein does. The broader legal-moral context of the present-day federalism debate defeats any suggestion that we should follow a doctrine that Marshall fashioned to protect slavery—that is, *solely* to protect slavery, for Epstein attributes no other end to Marshall. Epstein still needs an argument, therefore, and he eventually lapses into a familiar one. A broad reading of the Commerce Clause (or a reading of the Necessary and Proper Clause that would permit Congress to reach manufacturing) "makes pointless the entire system of enumerated powers."[66]

Epstein thus works his way around to begging the question. He assumes what has to be shown: that the public interest demands a states' rights view of the enumeration of powers. He assumes that the point of enumerating powers is not to maintain a hierarchy of ends that define a specific way of life but to maintain the reserved powers of the states as rights against national powers. He assumes this after acknowledging that neither history nor text compels the states' rights view. He assumes this despite his own free-market theory of the national interest—an understanding that has no substantive connection to states' rights and whose administration (by the federal judiciary, according to Epstein) rejects the states' righter's essential claim: that some good or other is always best served by state and local rather than national institutions. Epstein thus begs the question, and it is Epstein who does it, not Marshall.

Whatever Marshall's motivation, the Supremacy Clause speaks against a truncated commerce power. In *McCulloch*, Marshall focused on constitutional ends. He showed no concern for the subordinate ends left to the states because the Supremacy Clause favors Congress over the states when Congress is pursuing its ends. Had Congress's ends been defined to avoid encroachments on areas left to the states, the Constitution would preclude legitimate clashes between state and national power, and the mere occurrence of a clash between state and national power would void the national act. This would upend the Supremacy Clause, whose natural and traditional reading assumes that pursuit of national ends can conflict with state prerogatives *and* that on such occasions, national power prevails.[67]

Marshall does recognize that congressional majorities might pursue unauthorized ends, hence the rule against pretexts, whose function differs from that of the Supremacy Clause. Marshall's focus throughout is the Constitution's ends, chiefly national security and national prosperity. Epstein sees government in a negative light and the Constitution as designed not chiefly to enable government but to restrain it. Libertarian that he is, and convinced that government generally does more harm than good, Epstein reads the Commerce Clause narrowly from a greater concern that government not exceed its limits. Marshall sees the Constitution and its government in a positive light: an instrument of the goods listed in the Preamble.

The rule against pretexts, the Supremacy Clause, the enumeration of powers—all assume that something is "reserved to the States." The question is how to describe what is left to the states and the relationship between powers granted and powers reserved. Epstein takes a categorical approach: manufacturing is reserved to the states; transportation is entrusted to Congress; and Congress can never have a legitimate reason for encroaching on the states—except when Congress does have a reason for encroaching on the states. Marshall recognizes the possibility of congressional encroachment as well as pretext, and he holds that the Supremacy Clause legitimates good-faith encroachments. This possibility of legitimate encroachments (Congress displacing the states in matters traditionally theirs when doing so is an effective way to advance reasonable conceptions of national ends) precludes a categorical line between state and national powers. While Epstein talks of the line between manufacturing and transportation, Marshall describes "[t]he genius and character of the whole government" as a division between "concerns which affect the states generally" and those local concerns "with which it is not necessary to interfere, for the purpose of executing some of the general powers of the government."[68] Lincoln was later to call this "the principle of *generality* and *locality*."[69]

Applying this principle is different from applying some action-type like manufacturing something or transporting something. The intentions and intended results of these actions are fixed in advance of their occurrence by the logic of the action-types that they instantiate. We know in advance that an act of window opening must (1) flow from an agent's intention to move the window from a closed to an open state and (2) proceed through some movement of the agent's body to end in a window opened. All unequivocal acts of window opening—past, present, and future—display these features. All acts of window opening are named for their intended results, not their consequences, most of which are unpredictable. An act of window opening that causes a cold that results in a death that brings about a succession crisis, a civil war, and an empire's collapse, remains an act of window opening, not to be confused with acts of killing people and destroying empires. "General" and "local" are attributes here of conditions or concerns; they are not action-types. A condition or state of affairs that bears the property "local" today can bear the property "general" tomorrow. Examples abound. Poverty in America might have been a local problem until the poor started migrating en masse throughout the county. Slavery in America might have been a matter of mere local significance until, for reasons both racist and humanitarian, the nation's whites started worrying about its spread. Substandard public education might have been a local problem before the age of integrated regional economies, mobile workers, high-tech war making and high-tech domestic production, distribution, and finance.

What is general is also what is general relative to something and to some population. Given the nature of Congress as a widely representative body that is normally hard to move, a problem is at least presumptively of general interest simply by virtue of Congress's taking an interest in it. Though I argue in Chapter 3 that the Constitution is at least provisionally committed to what Diamond called the Large Commercial Republic, and that this state of economy and society is reasonably well defined and distinguishable from other states of affairs (like the Christian Commonwealth or the Aryan Nation), no one can say in advance what the general and local problems of the future might be. Some might say (though I would not) that problems like the death of Terri Schiavo will never be economic problems, but no one can say that these problems will never be problems of general interest.[70] A principle of generality and locality embraces much more than the Constitution's enumerated powers, and Marshall believed, as Lincoln was to believe, that the former is the principle of the latter. Presupposing a principle of generality and locality, Larry Kramer has said "federalism . . . [is] not just preserving state authority where appropriate, but also enabling the federal government to act where national action is desirable."[71] Marshall made the point in connection with the Necessary and Proper Clause: "This provision is made in a constitution intended to endure for ages to come, and consequently to be adapted to the various crises in human affairs."[72]

Thus, Marshall's language in *Gibbons* does not have to bear the interpretation Epstein gives it. Why, then, should we interpret Marshall as Epstein does? Epstein can hardly answer this question by saying Marshall said we should interpret Marshall Epstein's way. Given Marshall's ambiguity— "that grand Marshallian ambivalence," Epstein calls it[73]—a defense of Epstein's interpretation would have to appeal to some substantive good, like a free and open national market. Yet we have seen that such an argument might work as a policy argument, depending ultimately on whether a society that follows free-market principles will, in Epstein's words, "find itself better able to obtain prosperity for all its members than one which deviates" from those principles.[74] We have seen also that Epstein's attempt to convert this policy argument to a constitutional argument depends on premises that clash both with undeniable facts or with facts as Epstein sees them. We have seen, in sum, that Epstein fails to show why Congress should be denied power to do all that it reasonably can to promote the nation's prosperity.

No further effort on Epstein's part will work. No one can defend a narrow view of Congress's power because constitutional text and framers' intent admit conflicting interpretations and because a narrow view of Congress's power serves no substantive good. A weak Congress would serve liberty and citizen choice only if Congress could do nothing to enhance liberty and if Congress were liberty's only threat, suggestions that would make liberty meaningless as an end of government. A weak Congress might serve cultural diversity (abolishing Congress might serve it better). But a weak Congress would not serve cultural diversity as a thing of value to the nation as a whole, which cultural diversity would have to be to serve as a reason in a national forum. To competitive federalists like Epstein and Greve, cultural diversity is a value only if diverse communities can be seen as optional residences for individual Americans—in principle, all socially responsible Americans

Cultural diversity as a value *to* Americans generally would depend on both a right of individual Americans to relocate and the acceptability of the resulting options to socially responsible Americans. The right to relocate is guaranteed by national power, including congressional power. Congressional power also shapes the quality of the options. As Greve notes, the nation has chosen to forbid segregationist and polygamist options. Each of these policy choices involved exercises of congressional power over what local populations declared to be local matters. The nation decided that a less diverse nation (one that excluded segregated and polygamous communities) was more attractive than a more diverse nation (one that included segregated and polygamous communities). The practical requirement that options be acceptable to some population would place qualitative limits on the options, and legislative power would be needed to maintain those limits.

No Argument for States' Rights Federalism

I shall summarize the main points of this chapter by commenting further about the second and third items on Justice O'Connor's list. Among the benefits that Americans will realize if courts restrain national power in behalf of states' rights, O'Connor lists (2) an increased opportunity for citizen involvement in democratic processes and (3) scope for more innovation and experimentation in government. Earlier I challenged (2) as assuming too much about the meaning and value of democracy. For argument's sake at this point, however, let us accept (2) and (3) at face value, for by doing so we can see again why no substantive argument can justify a narrow view of Congress's power.

Begin by noticing the context of any concrete claim that democratic participation justifies a narrow view of Congress's power. Today, thanks to the Civil War, such a claim would be made in a national forum. It would be addressed to a national court, and its content would have to make sense to that court as an agent of the sovereign people for which the Constitution speaks. This claim would arise when someone claiming to speak for a state disagreed with Congress about the scope of congressional power. Congress would want to address a problem that was within its jurisdiction, broadly conceived, and the state would say that by narrowing the scope of Congress's jurisdiction and letting the states handle the problem their separate ways, a court would enhance democratic participation.

This complicated claim would assume (1) a correct or currently best conception of democracy, and (2) the value of democratic government, as conceived, relative to other values, like competent government. This ranking of values would in turn presuppose (3) a correct or currently best view of the ends of government. One could hold, for example, that the Constitution's most important end, if not always its most urgent end, must be either a self-critical and public-spirited electorate or a competent leadership community that enjoys the public's trust.[75] These claims would require moral arguments. Upon concluding these arguments one would proceed to a social-scientific claim: (4) that a population's participation in legislative give-and-take over important public questions tends to make its members less self-serving and more public-spirited. All such claims appeal beyond local standards, moral and scientific. No one would contend today that *for democracy's sake*, the federal courts should have let the old white-primary state of Texas practice its version of democracy. Few today would say that democracy demands that states that disfranchise women (say, on a "men's club" theory of party primaries) should be free to determine the wages and working conditions of women. Only a national standard can justify letting the states govern what Congress wants to govern and could otherwise govern, and the national standard that justifies state power also limits it.[76]

A narrow view of Congress's power would thus depend on whether the states invariably behaved themselves, and that means the nation would need good luck. Actually, the nation would need much more than good luck. For the states invariably to behave themselves, they would have to display a pattern of behavior so stable that it surpassed luck to achieve the status of a behavioral regularity, the equivalent of a scientific law. This situation would be incomprehensible within constitutional discourse because the standard of good behavior would have to be a national standard, and if the states invariably conformed to that standard there could be no state-federal conflict that would impart meaning to claims of states' rights.

The only admissible position, therefore, is what common sense could have confirmed at the start: that sometimes local control can foster public deliberation and public-spritedness and sometimes it can't. Sometimes and on some issues more public deliberation might take place at the local level than at the national level, but sometimes the reverse will be true. It all depends. Had there been a pattern of events so stable as to guarantee that local government is always the best feasible government, the founding itself would be a mystery. And because it all depends, the best practice is to devolve or centralize policy as contingencies require. Yet this practice presupposes (1) national standards of what is best, (2) centralized constitutional authority to devolve or centralize policy as contingencies require, and (3) a central authority to assess the results.

The ambiguities of constitutional text and history, the discursive requirements of the national forum in which the states' rights debate takes place, and the requirements of practical reasonableness in an unpredictable world—all conspire to defeat a substantive defense of states' rights federalism. The adequacy of the national government to the nation's needs is not a question of constitutional authority; it is a question of political science. As a matter of formal constitutional principle, the nation may have the power it needs to address its problems—I mean real problems, not some restricted class of "legally cognizable" problems. But formal constitutional principle cannot guarantee a system that enables the nation actually to approximate its true needs, as distinguished from and even opposed to the immediate preferences of its "likely voters." The Constitution's adequacy as an instrument of real goods is a family of questions whose members include the moral, the social-scientific, and the natural-scientific. The answers to none of these questions will be "local," even if some of these answers involve carefully measured and scrutinized devolution of discretion to state and local institutions—institutions whose responsibility to national standards justify describing them as national institutions operating at subnational levels.

5

JOHN C. CALHOUN'S FALSE THEORY OF THE UNION

Why should we read Congress's power in a manner that avoids conflicts with the states' practices and policies? What is so valuable about the states that the nation should restrain its government from doing what it reasonably can to promote the security, well-being, and liberties of its people? I have examined the standard states' rights answers to this question and the standard responses, and I join writers who find that restraining national power makes sense as an occasional matter of policy, not as an unqualified constitutional principle. Put differently and more broadly, restraining the nation's power to pursue national ends makes sense only when the national government decides that the best course is to leave a matter to the states—in which case there would be no state-federal conflict.

Occasionally a state like Georgia may have legitimate reason to experiment with something like tougher voter ID requirements; Georgia could be suffering widespread and persistent vote fraud that state-issued voter IDs might ameliorate. But the abstract value of experimentation cannot be a reason for stopping Congress or its delegate, like the Justice Department, from assessing the motive behind the experiment, reviewing the experiment's results, and judging their consistency with constitutional ends. Nor can liberty justify restraining Congress or the Justice Department, for all would agree that Georgia's voter ID law could be a pretext for discouraging some Georgians from voting, and no one claims (in public) that a liberty to suppress the vote is a liberty that the nation stands for. The same holds for "democracy." Democracy can hardly be a reason for deferring to Georgia when it comes to voter qualifications, for the Fourteenth and Fifteenth Amendments make Georgia answerable to national standards of democracy, and those standards condemn bad-faith voter requirements or any voter requirements that fall unequally on identifiable classes of the state's law-abiding adults.

When states' righters argue for narrowing national power, they presuppose national conceptions of the values they invoke (liberty, democracy, good-faith experimentation), and national conceptions of these values call for oversight and ultimate enforcement by national agencies. Sometimes a state policy or practice might happen to serve or be compatible with a national end. But the right to determine this—the right to interpret and apply this national standard—would be that of a national agent, like Congress or the Supreme Court. States' righters cannot successfully challenge this conclusion. We have seen why they cannot show that states' rights are good for the country. Let's now see whether they can defend their position in some other way.

They might begin by claiming that they have no obligation to show that their position is good for the country. States' righters might assume a radical skepticism about values and contend that words like *liberty* and *democracy* have no true meaning that could justify preferring one national conception over many local conceptions. Thus, they would say, there can be no real reason for denying Georgia's right to define democracy in any manner that the representatives of its people might wish. This argument would be met by doubts about who represents the state's people. For who can know who really represents a state whose officials repress the vote? But this complication aside, "Georgia" would face an unanswerable objection. Without a true or truly better understanding of democracy, there can be no real reason for leaving Georgia alone—no reason for letting its government define democracy as it might wish. Skepticism about values thus proves unavailable to the states' righter as a ground for opposing a broad view of national power. States' rights federalism is itself a normative position, part of a theory of the right way to conduct the nation's affairs. As a normative position, states' rights federalism presupposes both the possibility and the attractiveness of true propositions about notions like liberty, democracy, rightness, and goodness. If there were no true propositions about ideas or concepts like these, it could not be true that states' rights federalism is either morally right or reasonably instrumental to some good.

Nor can states' righters successfully retreat from a radical skepticism about values to conventionalism about values, which is a more moderate skepticism. They cannot contend that ideas like liberty and democracy mean different things to different communities and that, *therefore*, the meaning of all such ideas should be left to each state or region of the nation.

Arguments like this cannot work even if the meaning and relative importance of values have no more than conventional status or if views about them vary from place to place. Assume, for example, that "prosperity" had no more than conventional meaning. The question then would be: so what? That prosperity meant different things to different communities would be a proposition that, standing alone, could justify no conclusion about what anyone ought to do. It could not be a reason for Congress to alter its view of prosperity to accommodate the conflicting view of some of the states. Nothing of a normative nature follows from the proposition that prosperity means different things to different people. Except for arguments in hypothetical form (if you want x, do y), only an argument with a moral premise can justify a practical conclusion. One could say that if Congress would avoid South Carolina's secession, it would repeal the Tariff of Abominations. But no such conclusion would flow from the mere fact that different parts of the country have different views of prosperity or how to pursue it. ——

Moral premises that occur in actual political arguments involve what the parties assume to be real goods (like liberty) or true standards of right conduct (like fairness).[1] To deploy a moral premise that could justify a narrow commerce power, states' righters might argue that where different communities define prosperity differently, a principle of self-determination (a kind of liberty) demands that each community permit each of the others to define and pursue prosperity for itself. Yet the very deployment of any moral premise assumes that both parties agree or can agree about the meaning of the good (like "self-determination") that the premise invokes. Both parties would also have to agree that the value invoked is important enough to settle the debate about what to do. To have sufficient weight, the common moral ground must be considered nonconventional or real by participants in the debate. So we would have to see "self-determination," the subject of the moral premise in our example, as a real good for us to conclude that we ought to let each community define prosperity for itself. By a real good I mean a good whose meaning is independent of what different persons or communities believe its meaning to be. A real good, in other words, is a good about whose meaning and means people can be wrong. If "self-determination" meant what each party wanted it to mean, it could not be a reason for any party to act against its wants. In this case, the so-called value of self-determination could not be a reason for a more powerful state (like the United States) to deny Georgia self-determination. The more powerful state could say that as it sees the world, self-determination for some depends on slavery for others, predation is no better or worse than coexistence as equals, and that predatory states have a right to self-determination too. Self-determination about the meaning of prosperity could not function as a reason for letting Georgians govern themselves if doing so conflicted with what a more powerful state saw as its prosperity.

Yet if there were objectively better and worse meanings of self-determination, and if self-determination were seen as a value of great weight, then it could be a reason for letting Georgians govern themselves, as long as they did so consistently with self-determination itself. In that case, Georgians could find it hard to claim, as they once tried to do, that the value of self-determination justified their right to choose to be a slave state, for slavery seems the antithesis of self-determination, and if some people in Georgia could justify enslaving others, other states could use the same argument to deny Georgia self-determination. Nor could some people in Georgia easily invoke self-determination as their basis for suppressing the vote of other Georgians, for self-determination is rooted in an idea of political equality that vote suppression seems to deny. This example shows yet again that defending states' rights discursively—that is, offering a reason for states' rights—is a self-defeating act. You can assert states' rights constitutionalism without giving reasons, of course. You can defend it with bullets or ballots. You can "defend" it in a sense by putting a wall around it—that is, simply by refusing to debate its nationalist opponents.[2] But you can't enter the field and defend it with reasons. Defend it with reasons and you defeat yourself.

Calhoun's Nationalism

John C. Calhoun argued that each state of the union should be free to determine its own economic institutions without national interference of any kind, from outlawing slavery where it existed to stopping its spread to the territories. This seemed to be a straightforward states' rights argument. But James Read's important new analysis of Calhoun's thought should revise the conventional view of Calhoun. Calhoun was always difficult to classify as either a states' righter or a nationalist because he offered his theory of the union and its resulting rights of nullification and secession as means for holding the union together. In an era that had lost the good feeling between the sections that had marked the founding period, Calhoun reasoned, the threats of nullification and ultimately secession would force the union's parts into saving compromises.[3] Nevertheless, an advocate of nullification and secession is an unlikely nationalist, and Calhoun surely considered himself a states' righter, at least in the second half of his political career. But whatever Calhoun's self-understanding, his argument for slavery was a nationalist argument, and his final theory of the Constitution was a nationalist theory. Calhoun's career thus illustrates the futility of defending states' rights in a national forum. The requirements of the forum in which Calhoun chose to participate—that is, the expectations regarding what counts as reasons for action in a national debate—gave his conclusions a nationalist character, regardless of his intentions.

Calhoun's argument for slavery occurred at a time when slavery needed defending. Free labor needed no defense because the nation's public philosophy held that each person was born with a property right to his own body and that none could legitimately govern another or take his property without his consent. This was the philosophy of John Locke and the Declaration of Independence, and increasingly after the Revolution its hold on the country put slavery on the defensive. Arguing for slavery meant arguing either against Lockean principles or their application to particular situations. Arguing not against Locke but against applying Lockean principles to slavery in the South had been the strategy of Jefferson and other Southern leaders at least through the 1820s. This strategy conceded that slavery was unjust. It claimed, however, that abolition would bring economic and political ruin. Calhoun realized that this "necessary evil" argument had failed slavery's cause, for antislavery sentiment had grown steadily since the founding period. In fact, Calhoun attributed the march of antislavery to the necessary-evil argument. The view that slavery was a necessary evil conceded that it was an evil. So Calhoun sought to displace the prevailing public philosophy with one in which slavery would be not evil, but a permanent blessing for the nation and all its people, black and white (36–39, 121). To this end he rejected the individualistic assumptions of the Declaration of Independence and its claim that men are born equally endowed with liberty (36–38). Liberty was not a birthright, Calhoun contended, but a "reward to be earned" (36). Because liberty for some was impossible without slavery for others, he argued, defenders of slavery were liberty's true friends (124, 126–130, 136).

African slavery in America, according to Calhoun, was a condition not only of freedom for white but also of progress for blacks, as evinced by improving birthrates of blacks in the South and the rates of "vice and pauperism . . . bodily and mental afflictions . . . deafness, blindness, insanity and idiocy" of free blacks in the North (136). African slavery in the South, said Calhoun, was also a key element of national prosperity. It ensured a harmony of the nation's economic interests by providing raw materials for northern manufacturers and customers for their products (140–141). Calhoun reasoned that because a slave was the property of his master, the master's interest included the interest of the slave, and the presence of this fused perspective in the nation's deliberative councils would be a model for labor-management relations in the industrializing North (122–124). Calhoun contended further that the founding had committed the nation to slavery and that the national government had an affirmative duty to protect the institution (101). In view of this affirmative duty Calhoun urged the national government to avoid actions (like receiving ambassadors) that might imply recognition of nations governed by blacks (135). He urged that Congress decline to consider abolitionist petitions and proposals, from both state and private sources, for excluding slavery from the territories and the District of Columbia (100–102).

Calhoun would also have imposed duties on the states. Each state, he argued, had a constitutional obligation to protect slavery because each state had signed a proslavery constitution. As Calhoun saw it, Vermont violated its constitutional pledge when its legislature sent Congress an antislavery memorial (98, 101–102). States that honored their commitment would suppress abolitionist activities within their borders and cooperate in returning fugitive slaves (103). And in view of what he saw as slavery's benefits and the degraded conditions of free blacks, Calhoun even suggested that abolition in the North after the Revolution had been a mistake (136). To protect slavery and honor background principles of liberty and the rights of contracting states, Calhoun proposed amending the Constitution to remove all doubt about a states' right to nullify federal law. He also proposed a dual national executive, one elected from the North, one from the South, each with a veto over the decisions of the other (85–86).

Read shows that this is hardly the leave-us-alone Calhoun described by other historians (87–89). This is a Calhoun who saw his state as part of a national system and who fully appreciated the dependence of his aims, including slavery, on national power. To make slavery and its alleged benefits secure, Calhoun proposed a new public philosophy for the nation as a whole, complete with a new understanding of liberty, its nature, and its social prerequisites. He urged the nation's people to adopt a favorable attitude toward black slavery and to make corresponding adjustments in their views regarding their economic self-interest and fairness to others. In the name of liberty and union, he would have obligated both the national government and all of the states to adopt policies favoring slavery in both their domestic and foreign affairs. In the name of these principles, he would have changed the Constitution to give the slave interest multiple vetoes over national action. Here then was a fairly comprehensive position on the ends of government, their institutional means, and their economic and attitudinal prerequisites. Our question is what room states' rights had in this picture, and the answer is little to none. This conclusion emerges most clearly in Calhoun's opposition to abolitionist activities.

Read points out that the abolitionist threat to slavery extended beyond formal proposals to abolish slavery or limit its spread. Abolitionist literature and activities could incite slave revolts, encourage runaways, and discourage the return of fugitives. Abolitionists could also diminish the moral status of slavery in the eyes of the nation and eventually the South itself—a disastrous consequence for a thinker convinced of slavery's benefits, including its crucial role in maintaining a free society as Calhoun saw it (96). To meet the abolitionist threat, Calhoun advanced a legal-moral argument and a prudential argument. We have seen that the latter described slavery as an instrument of all good things (freedom, security, prosperity, civilization) and the former described the founding as a pledge among contracting states to respect and protect each others' domestic institutions, including slavery.

By this last argument, the legislature of Vermont violated that state's founding pledge when, in December 1837, the legislature sent Congress a memorial opposing the admission of Texas as a slave state and defending Congress's power to outlaw the interstate slave trade and ban slavery in the territories and the District of Columbia (98). Calhoun thought that Maine and other states also violated the pledge by letting the likes of the Maine Abolition Society operate within their borders (103). These actions and omissions by free states posed a problem for Calhoun: how, in the Constitution's name, to demand affirmative congressional action in slavery's behalf without treading on the sovereign prerogative of the free states.

National agents could not just march into the headquarters of the Maine Abolition Society and close it down. "State sovereignty" precluded that. What, then, could Congress do?

Calhoun answered that Congress and the national government generally could and should use its several powers in ways that would secure slavery's future. Calhoun referred rather vaguely to actions beyond fugitive slave laws, refusing antislavery petitions, permitting slavery in the territories, and refusing to host foreign dignitaries who were black. He suggested Congress could close all of the nation's mail to abolitionist literature (not just abolitionist mail to the South, banned by the Jackson administration) and deploy its powers over foreign and domestic commerce as might be suitable to support policies of the slave states (105).[4] Though Calhoun was less than generous with examples, one comfortably within the scope of his words would be a federal ban on interstate travel by abolitionist speakers.[5] Such a ban would offend the First Amendment no more than Congress's closing the mails to abolitionist literature and certainly no more than Congress's refusal to receive abolitionist petitions, actions Calhoun supported against First Amendment claims.[6]

Calhoun was also less than clear on Congress's receipt of antislavery petitions from the state governments, as distinguished from petitions from private abolitionist groups. He was clear that these state petitions were unconstitutional—violations of what he saw as the states' original pledge to support each other's domestic institutions. But he declined to vote either for or against the Senate's receipt of the Vermont memorial of December 1837 (100). His strategy was to substitute a set of six resolutions designed to persuade the Senate that while Vermont, "a sovereign State, a party to the constitutional compact, . . . had a right to enter our doors," it had no right to propose a violation of the Constitution, and the Senate had no power to consider violating the Constitution.[7]

Combining all that Calhoun said on the Vermont memorial, Read finds that Calhoun effectively denied "that even a sovereign state could bring antislavery resolutions to Congress." Despite Calhoun's commitment to states' rights, says Read, he placed "restrictions on how they could be legitimately deployed." So, Read concludes, "In the end, for Calhoun protecting slavery was a higher principle than states' rights."[8] Calhoun thought he had a citizen's duty to defend and promote slavery pursuant to his oath to preserve and defend a constitution committed to slavery. Vermont had neither a First Amendment nor a structural right as a "sovereign state" to oppose slavery in any way because slavery's preservation was both a constitutional end and a necessary condition of other constitutional ends, like union, the blessings of liberty, and the general welfare. Vermont, it seems, had no right to oppose a correct view of constitutional ends or to propose an incorrect view of constitutional ends—no right, therefore, to determine constitutional meaning for itself. Starting from an effort to defend a state's right to choose slavery, Calhoun ended by denying a state's right to oppose slavery. He left the states only with rights whose exercise either advanced or did not impede a view of the national interest in which slavery was essential. This was a corrupt nationalism in several ways. It betrayed foundational moral principles and contradicted itself. But a corrupt nationalism remains a kind of nationalism, and Read's analysis shows that Calhoun was more a proslavery nationalist than a states' righter.

Calhoun and the Compact Theory

But what can Calhoun's position on slavery illustrate about states' rights arguments generally? Calhoun had arguments that bore on the nature of the Constitution other than his argument for slavery, and even if these other arguments conflict with his argument for slavery, they may show that some states' rights arguments can reach adequate levels of coherence and plausibility. Let us test this possibility by examining Calhoun's compact theory of the Constitution. Calhoun's point of departure was the theory (or theories) embodied in the Virginia and Kentucky Resolutions of 1798, authored, respectively, by James Madison and Thomas Jefferson and defended at length by Madison's Report of 1800 on the Virginia Resolutions. According to Calhoun and the Virginia and Kentucky Resolutions, "the People" that ratified the Constitution was neither an aggregate of individual persons nor the one cultural entity spread throughout thirteen geopolitical entities to which The Federalist had occasionally referred (e.g., 2:9–10; 14:88) and that Marshall had described in McCulloch. The constituent "People" was rather an aggregate of thirteen sovereign, independent, and separate political communities, the "states." The United States, so the argument went, was a union (construed as an aggregate) of states, not individuals, and the national government was a creature of these states.

This is the compact theory of Calhoun and the Virginia and Kentucky Resolutions. The question is what this theory imports for state-federal conflicts. Grant that separate communities ratified as separate communities, not as parts of one nation. Would this fact bear in any way on whether OSHA, a congressional delegate, could require ventilation systems and methane alarms in the mines of West Virginia? Could some mining company rightfully contend that power over commerce falls short of working conditions in the mines because mine safety is a matter for the states?

Jefferson and Madison might well have thought so, since at one time or another each favored narrow constructions of national power, with heralded exceptions like the Louisiana Purchase and the Second National Bank. Calhoun would have thought so too, if we consider the matter in light of the second half of his career, when he opposed federal regulation of slavery in the territories, and when he came to oppose things he had favored in the early part of his career, like protective tariffs, internal improvements, and a national bank. Calhoun's elaboration of the compact theory was richer than that of the earlier compact theorists. Calhoun reached farther back than Jefferson had done to reexamine and reject the individualist premises of Locke and the Declaration of Independence,[9] and he reached beyond Madison to a right to secede from the union, constitutionally and in peace.[10] When Calhoun defended nullification and secession in 1831 as extrapolations from the Jeffersonian Revolution of 1800, the aged Madison rejected both nullification and secession for himself and the then deceased Jefferson (42–44). Madison's opposition to Calhoun saved his reputation as a patriot, but it did little for his reputation as a states' righter. As between Madison, Jefferson, and Calhoun, the leading states' rights theorist must be Calhoun. He more than they (as far as we know, in Jefferson's case; see Read, 33–34, 45) was more willing to embrace the implications of his position, whether reasoning backward to heterodox first principles or forward to disunion—but not really to states' rights *within* the union, as we have seen and shall further see.

Treating Calhoun as the preeminent compact theorist may seem unfair to that position, for an association with Calhoun has its liabilities. Of course, these liabilities stem from what the Civil War did for the cause of nullification and secession. Nullification and secession now serve the role that mathematical absurdities serve in the classical reductio ad absurdum. Euclid proposes that if two triangles coincide in all other respects, their bases will be equal, for otherwise straight lines of different length could occupy the same space, which is absurd (due to what is meant by "same space"). But this kind of argument works better in mathematics than in religion and politics. Abraham's anguish at the prospect of killing his beloved Isaac did not cause him to deny God's goodness. And jurists still cite "dual sovereignty" even after Calhoun proved that there is no middle ground between national supremacy and secession. To be fair to the compact theory, therefore, we must bracket its inadmissible implications. Let us see if Calhoun's compact theory, sans nullification and secession, can justify states' rights as constitutional restraints on national power. We shall see that it cannot.

Calhoun's account of the Constitution's beginning involves political entities of three kinds: (1) thirteen separate political communities, the "states"; (2) the several governments of these separate communities, the "state governments"; and (3) the joint government of these separate communities, the "federal government." Calhoun apparently felt that each of the states had been and remained composed of persons who saw themselves as members of but one political community. This political community was the "state," properly so called—the state in its "sovereign" aspect, not to be confounded with the government of a state, which was a mere agent of the state. Each of these sovereign peoples or states created two governments. Each people created its state government by itself and for its own interests. And each people jointly with the other peoples created the federal government. Each state acted for itself in agreeing to create the federal government. That is, each state understood the purpose of the federal government to be the promotion of its own separate interests.[11] South Carolina thus ratified the Constitution not for the joint security and prosperity of South Carolina and New York or any other state, but to secure its own shores from foreign invasion; to secure its foreign exports from piracy; to shield its foreign customers from tariffs and thereby maintain their power to purchase its exports; to maintain an unobstructed national market for its goods; to ensure the return of its fugitives; to secure its frontiers from the Indian tribes; to suppress its slave rebellions; and so forth.

These state and federal governments, the theory continued, were mere agents of each of the several sovereign peoples or states, each of which retained its full independence and complete sovereignty over both its governments. The state and federal governments were equal and coordinate agents of each of the several peoples. The Constitution was a compact *between* the ever separate and sovereign peoples or states and *over* both their governments and individuals in the states—individuals as distinguished from the sovereigns of each state, which sovereigns were organic communities, not mere aggregates of autonomous individuals.[12] The theory then implied propositions that we are bracketing momentarily: (1) that, retaining its separate sovereignty, each state had the right to judge infractions of the Constitution for itself and to respond as it might—by acquiescing, nullifying, or seceding; and (2) that a state's residents owed allegiance to it alone—not to the union of states.[13]

Missing from Calhoun's picture were entities that were central to John Marshall's account of the founding: the one people of the United States as a whole, and the individual citizen, whose right to move from place to place would have justified some interest in and loyalty to the nation as a whole. From the early 1830s to his death in 1850, Calhoun denied the existence of one national community. Near the end of his life he repudiated his early views and denied that one American people ever had existed or ever would exist.[14] He acknowledged, however, that the existence of one national people had been disputed since the founding, and that "an argument of some plausibility" favored the nationalist view that one people did exist and that the Constitution was the voice of this one sovereign people.[15] The question of one people or many was pivotal for Calhoun. Answered one way and the allegiance and obedience of citizens would be "due to their respective states," the state and national governments "would stand as equals and coordinates in their respective spheres," and the union between citizens of different states would be political "through their respective states," not social. Answered differently and "sovereignty would reside in the whole—or what is called the American people," allegiance and obedience would be due the whole, the states would be "inferior and subordinate" to the national government, and "the individuals of the several states" would be "fused . . . into one general mass . . . united *socially*, and not [only] *politically*."[16]

Calhoun's theory of still separate and sovereign states is not as anachronistic as it may appear. It connects in several ways to recent and current concerns. Segregationists resurrected it in the aftermath of the *Brown* decision.[17] It formed the core of Justice Thomas's dissent in *U.S. Term Limits, Inc. v. Thornton* (1995), which was joined by three other members of the states' rights block of the Rehnquist Court, including the Chief Justice.[18] Without mentioning Calhoun by name, a leading conservative theorist once offered a Calhounian denial of nationhood as the theoretical ground of the Reagan Revolution.[19] And, of course, from the time that *Lopez* was decided in 1995, Supreme Court majorities have cited "state sovereignty" as a basis for restraining national power. For these reasons, Calhoun's argument for a nation of states would seem to warrant close examination, and I would expect it to founder on its disagreement with the egalitarian individualism of the Declaration of Independence and its depreciation of the autonomous individual whose moral rights preclude unqualified allegiance to any political community and include freedom to criticize the community of the individual's formative years and live accordingly by moving to a different place. Yet, as a logical matter and despite its historical associations with states' rights, nothing in Calhoun's theory of the union entails a narrow view of national power.

Grant that the union is one of ever-sovereign states; that these states established the federal government to serve their separate interests; that no national community exists for any government to serve the interests of; that citizens owe exclusive allegiance to their states—grant all this, and you still have no argument for denying Congress broad powers to regulate and to tax and spend, including power to tax and spend for internal improvements, power to regulate labor relations, and power to protect domestic industries. Under the right circumstances any such measure could serve the interests of the separate states, as Calhoun himself assumed when supporting the Tariff of 1816 and urging Congress to refuse consideration of Vermont's antislavery memorial in 1825. True, a narrow view of Congress's power would follow from a state compact theory that assumed narrow power for Congress meant more power for the states, and more power for the states guaranteed better results for the states. But these assumptions are clearly false, and Calhoun's theory excludes them. Narrow power for the national government guarantees more usable power (that is, more institutionalized power) for the states only if you confound the states with their governments. But, as we have seen, Calhoun pointedly distinguished the states as sovereign communities from their creatures, the state governments. And narrowing Congress's power might mean more power not for the state governments but for the states themselves. This separation of the states from their governments is not an invention of Calhoun. As interpreted by *The Federalist*, Article VII of the Constitution also distinguishes the states' peoples from their state governments.[20] Madison drew this distinction with care in his Report to the Virginia General Assembly of January 1800 on the Virginia Resolutions of December 1798.[21]

Marshall makes the same distinction in *McCulloch*.[22] These authorities aside, the distinction between a state's people and its government is essential if we are to justify the founding, or even to make sense of it. If the electorates of the states believed that, as a general rule, more power for their state governments guaranteed better lives for themselves, the Constitution's ratification would be a mystery and the failure of the Articles of Confederation would be an illusion, perhaps a deliberate fraud.[23]

At any rate, Calhoun conceived the federal government as no less the agent of a given state than its state government. Each state either created or helped create and adopted *both* its state government *and* its national government; and, Calhoun held, each state did so for its own interests. Each state can claim that the government in its state capital and the government in the District of Columbia are both its governments—framed and ratified by it and for its interests. From this it would follow that a conflict between the government in Columbia and the government in the District of Columbia need not be a conflict between the state of South Carolina (that is, the sovereign people of South Carolina) and some other political entity. Thus Calhoun argued, in effect, that the legislature of Vermont had betrayed Vermont—that is, the authentic will and the best interests of the people of Vermont—when the state's legislature submitted the antislavery memorial to Congress in December 1827. Calhoun also argued, in effect, that congressmen sworn to uphold the interests of Maine and Vermont could legitimately tax and spend and deploy Congress's postal and commerce powers to discourage abolitionist activities in those states. If Calhoun's criticism of Maine and Vermont reflected his constitutional principles, he implicitly recognized that sometimes the interests of the states demand congressional action in areas traditionally left to the state governments. Of course, Calhoun also believed that sometimes the states' interests demand that Congress restrain itself. Calhoun therefore believed the states' interest demanded that their agents act or not, as contingencies might require. Ordinary practical reason confirms the need for such flexibility. The pursuit of any substantive goal—slavery, freedom, or whatever—calls for action or forbearance as contingencies require.

But power to act or not is power to act. Power-not-to-act is thus the antithesis of no-power-to-act. A constitutional government cannot decide between action and restraint unless it has constitutional authority to act. Broad *constitutional* authority is therefore logically prerequisite to choice between action and restraint, which choice in concrete cases is a question of contingent *policy*. Calhoun's substantive understanding of the public interest and his distinction between a state and its government implies that a state's interest is poorly served by prior constitutional restraints on what he conceives as *its* federal government. The optimal situation indicated by Calhoun's premises and illustrated by his criticism of abolitionist states would be a national government with broad constitutional power and wise officials dedicated to constitutional ends. By contrast, broad power for the states and narrow power for the nation would mean multiple versions of the public interest, a multiplicity whose validity Calhoun denied in his stances on the nature of prosperity and the nature and distribution of liberty. To Calhoun, the New England abolitionists were an anticonstitutional force; they were not participants of a process seeking a true version of the common good.

This is not to say that Calhoun offered nothing to the states' rights cause. Calhoun's theory of union supports three states' rights when exercised by, or under the authority of, state conventions: a right ultimately to nullify national laws, a right to secede from the union, and a right to the exclusive allegiance of a state's citizens. Though these rights would be logically compatible with broad delegations of power to the general government, they would have constituted no small gain for states' rights in antebellum America, despite continuing doubts about their meaning and the conditions for their exercise. Calhoun himself created these doubts when he criticized, on constitutional grounds, states that permitted blacks to vote; fought enforcement of (sometimes effectively nullifying) the Fugitive Slave Act; petitioned Congress to stop the spread of slavery; and permitted abolitionist activities within their borders. But however Calhoun might have conditioned rights to nullify and secede, if these rights were all that states' righters could gain from Calhoun, they would amount to nothing today. What states' righters need today are reasons why the nation's courts should restrain national power over the nation's economy, race relations, civil liberties, public health, public morality, criminal justice, civil justice, and environmental protection. Calhoun's theory of union offers no such reason.

Calhoun's Theory Amended

At this point we might conclude that the only states' rights that Calhoun's theory served would be rights that the Civil War erased. This would make

Calhoun useless to present-day states' righters. But Calhoun, and therewith the compact theory, may not be entirely useless to modern dual federalism. With one not unreasonable modification, the theory could justify reading national power narrowly. The modification would be that, at least presumptively, a state's government serves the interest of the state's people better than the national government does. I emphasize that this would not be Calhoun's theory. He saw the Constitution committed to substantive ends, like slavery and free trade, as objectively good for the whole country, notwithstanding the disagreement of some state governments. Calhoun's separation of a government—any government—from its people reflected his assumption of an objective public interest and his recognition that any administration could fail to perceive that interest. In this respect Calhoun joined the Declaration of Independence and *The Federalist*; they also assumed an objective public interest and, as a consequence, a distinction between a people and its government. Thus Calhoun indicated that when Congress declined to consider Vermont's antislavery petition, Congress represented the interests of Vermont better than Vermont's legislature did, for, he claimed, union with slavery (if not universal slavery) was both a constitutional mandate and in Vermont's true interest, despite the ill-thought abolitionist convictions of her nineteenth-century population.

But whatever Calhoun believed, the assumption that state governments speak for their people is hardly uncommon, and, except in anarchic or revolutionary contexts, claims for a people's rights are often conflated with claims for the power of some government. An obvious explanation of this fact lies in the norm-constituted nature of what is meant by a separately identifiable people. A population altogether lacking institutional glue is not a people, and reference to the people of Vermont is ordinarily a reference to an institution of some sort, if only a political culture to be described in terms of informal beliefs, dispositions, and expectations.

We see the conflation of popular rights and governmental power throughout the states' rights debate. Though Madison's Report on the Virginia Resolutions distinguishes a state's government from its people and defends the people's right "to interpose," and though the penultimate paragraph of the Resolutions speaks for "the good people of this Commonwealth," the first sentence of the Resolutions speaks for "the general Assembly of Virginia," which body adopted the Resolutions.[24] In his famous debate with Robert Y. Hayne, Daniel Webster said the nullification doctrine "leads us to inquire into the origin of this government and the source of its power. Whose agent is it? Is it the creature of the State legislatures, or the creature of the [nation's] people?"[25] The Constitution itself, in the text of Article V, treats "the legislatures of three-fourths of the several states" as equivalent to "Conventions in three-fourths thereof" for purposes of ratifying constitutional amendments, leaving to Congress the choice between these methods. Finally, as a matter of historical practice, state constitutional conventions are usually called by state legislatures, and state legislatures are unlikely to call conventions when their opinions differ markedly from the opinions of their constituents. Thus, nullificationists completely dominated the legislature that called the South Carolina convention of 1832, whose overwhelming majority (of more than 5 to 1) "nullified" two national tariffs and authorized legislation to implement the nullifications.[26]

These links between the people and the government of a state support a presumption that a state's government speaks for its people. This presumption enables states' righters to claim that less power for Congress means more power for the state governments. With this claim, the compact theory gives states' righters their reason for a narrow view of national power: restrained national power is a sworn contractual obligation. Whether this is a good reason or not returns us to the question about the existence of one American people at the founding. Did one set of dominant political values unite the original thirteen populations into one people?[27] Lincoln indicated the importance of this question when he opined that "much, perhaps the whole" of the states' rights position derived from a negative answer to it.[28] Herbert Storing did the same when he called an affirmative answer "the foundation of the nationalist position" in both the Constitutional Convention and the argument of *The Federalist*.[29] Calhoun eventually treated this question as pivotal even though he initially identified a different question as "by far the most important" of "all the questions which can arise under our system of government."[30] Let's look at Calhoun's initial question.

Near the beginning of his posthumously published "A Discourse on the Constitution and Government of the United States," Calhoun "reduced" the states' rights debate "to a single question: whether the act of ratification, of itself, or the constitution, by some one, or all of its provisions, did, or did not, divest the several states of their character of separate, independent, and sovereign communities, and merge them all in one great community or nation, called the American people?" Here Calhoun assumed what *The Federalist* and Marshall denied: many separate communities before ratification. He then proceeded to ask whether ratification transformed many peoples into one. But Calhoun's opening assumption (many peoples before ratification) virtually decided his "most important" question (whether ratification made one of many). Change from many communities to one community would be, he said, "a mighty change," and precisely because the change would be a mighty one, he put the burden on those who contended for it. And a mighty burden it was. Nationalists had to establish their case "by the most demonstrative proof," said Calhoun (89).

By "most demonstrative proof" Calhoun required more than the stronger argument. He required an apodictic argument, a knock-down argument, a nationalist argument powerful enough to stun states' righters to silence. This requirement was evident in the way Calhoun treated even weak, confusing, and embarrassingly question-begging replies from his side as good enough to win the debate. To nationalists who would cite the Preamble's reference to "a more perfect Union" and George Washington's approving reference to "the consolidation of our union," Calhoun replied that Washington and the framers "intended to make more perfect" (or 'consolidate') "the old union of the confederacy," a union of ever-sovereign states. They could not have intended to create a nation, said Calhoun, for that would have destroyed the old confederacy.[31] To nationalists who said that the states surrendered at least part of their sovereignty when shifting from the Articles' requirement of unanimity for constitutional amendments to the Constitution's three-fourths requirement, Calhoun replied that the states "still retain" their "high sovereign right . . . to change or abolish the present constitution and government at their pleasure," since "sovereigns may, by compact, modify or qualify the exercise of their power, without impairing their sovereignty."[32]

To nationalists who cited the Supremacy Clause of Article VI, Calhoun replied that the clause guarantees no victory for the general government in clashes with the states, even when the federal measure is safely within delegated authority. Reading the Necessary and Proper Clause as a restriction on national power, Calhoun said that laws of the national government must not only be strictly necessary, they must also be "proper" in the sense of consistency with "fundamental rules of universal application."

These rules guarantee state sovereignty in general and in particular the right of individual states ultimately to decide state-federal conflicts for themselves.[33] Under these rules, "these States, in ratifying the constitution, did not lose the confederated character which they possessed when they ratified it, as well as in all the preceding stages of their existence; but, on the contrary, still retained it to the full."[34]

Calhoun thus proceeded as if it were impossible for the nationalist view of the founding to overcome the heavy presumption against "mighty change"—the change from many peoples to one people. This returns us to the question whether the American people existed prior to ratification. What evidence did Calhoun have that there was no "American people" prior to ratification? Read points out that Calhoun's claim was not an empirical claim about the public's "subjective degree of attachment" to one government or the other. That one American nation cannot exist and never existed was simply "an axiomatic and normative claim" on Calhoun's part and "Calhoun conspicuously assumed what he claimed to demonstrate."[35] Defenders of Calhoun might reply that Calhoun did not just assert his no-nation conclusion, he argued for it, and that Read errs in accusing him of begging the question. But the evidence favors Read.

Calhoun's no-nation argument centered on the "style" or name: the "United States of America." He observed that this name was used in the Declaration of Independence, the Articles of Confederation, and the Constitution. The Declaration declares that the states are "free and independent"—free and independent from each other, not just Great Britain, according to Calhoun—"with full power to levy war, conclude peace, contract alliances, and do all other acts and things which independent States may of right do." The Articles declare that "Each State retains its sovereignty, freedom and independence; and every other power, jurisdiction, and right, which is not, by this confederation, expressly delegated to the United States in Congress assembled." Then Calhoun simply asserted that the same name at every stage was nearly "conclusive evidence" for the same "political relation" at every stage, from the revolution to the present. Otherwise, said Calhoun, the framers would have "practiced a deception, utterly unworthy of their character, as sincere and honest men and patriots." The change from confederation to more perfect union was therefore "not in the foundation" but merely "in the superstructure of the system."[36]

Read concludes that with this argument Calhoun begged the question. The question involves the existence, relative strength, and development of an American national consciousness. If you assume that Americans saw themselves as one people against the colonial power during the Revolution,[37] you will not read the Declaration of Independence as the states' declaring independence from each other, as Calhoun did. Assume even a relatively weak national consciousness and you will not emphasize the separatist parts of the Articles of Confederation (like the declaration in Article II that each state retains its sovereignty, independence, "and every Power . . . which is not . . . expressly delegated") to the total exclusion of its nationalist parts (like the preamble's reference to "perpetual Union" and Article IV's aim "to secure . . . mutual friendship . . . among the people of the different states"). Assume either a vestigial (from the Revolution) or an inchoate (postwar) national consciousness augmented by the reaction against the performance of the states during the Revolution and immediately thereafter, and it is understandable that a strong national government surfaced as an alternative to the Confederation.[38]

That the issue turns on the existence of a national consciousness is supported both by Calhoun's theory of sovereignty and by Calhoun's personal history. Regarding the former, Calhoun located sovereignty in an extragovernmental entity: the people of a state. The government and the people of a state were not the same; the former was rather the agent of the latter. Man was "created for the social state, and . . . accordingly so formed as to feel what affects others, as well as what affects himself."[39] Society thus seems to be essentially an empathic bond, and this suggests that, questions of law and residence in abeyance, whether an individual belongs to a given community with others depends on a psychological state of affairs: his feelings toward them and their feelings toward him. As for Calhoun's personal history, Read observes that in the early part of Calhoun's career, probably until the mid 1820s, Calhoun was a nationalist; he supported the Second National Bank, a program of internal improvements, and the tariff of 1816, a mildly protective measure whose support he was later to repudiate.[40]

From his analysis of Calhoun's speeches, Read finds "three key elements in his vision of an American nation": (1) the country's regionally distinct economic interests (southern agriculture and northern manufacturing) which together constituted a national economy of complementary parts; (2) "roads, canals, a reliable common currency" and other means for

"facilitating political, economic, and intellectual communication between . . . parts" of the country; and (3) "an ethic of political and economic reciprocity" that precluded one part of the country aggrandizing
itself at the expense of another (56). In an oft-quoted statement, Calhoun
said: "Neither agriculture, manufactures, nor commerce, taken separately,
is the cause of [national] wealth; it flows from the three combined, and
cannot exist without each,"[41] At some short-term sacrifice to his region, Calhoun supported the tariff of 1816 for the sake of "the security and permanent
prosperity of our country" (301). "[M]anufactures . . . grown to a certain
perfection, as they soon will under the fostering care of Government" will
provide "a ready [domestic] market" for southern agriculture and enable
the country to avoid "that languor of industry and individual distress now
incident to a state of war and suspended [foreign] commerce" (303–304).
The highly protective and seemingly permanent tariffs of 1828 and 1832
proved to Calhoun and other Southern leaders that what Read calls the
"ethic of reciprocity" was a thing of the past. Read concludes that this de-
moralizing loss of mutual good will among the sections explains Calhoun's
later denial that an American nation existed.[42]

The upshot of Read's analysis for our purposes is that "Calhoun believed there once existed a spirit of sectional reciprocity" (65). Read cites
passages from Calhoun's speeches and writings as late as 1833 to support
this conclusion (62–63). At both the early and middle parts of his career
Calhoun believed that Americans had what Feeley and Rubin call some
"sense of collective political identity."[43] This belief on Calhoun's part un-
dermines his claim in the Discourse that Americans "never . . . in any
stage of their existence" constituted "one people or nation" in a political
sense.[44] Read says that at career's end Calhoun despaired of restoring a
spirit of sectional reciprocity and hoped instead that a mechanism of nullification "would force a sectional accommodation that could no longer
occur through the ordinary democratic process" of majority rule.[45] This is a
fair judgment on Read's part. Calhoun did say near the end of the Discourse
that "[w]hat has been done cannot be undone" and that exclusion of slavery from the territories has "permanently destroyed" an original "equilib-
rium" on which the ethic of reciprocity depended.[46] Yet this statement,
like the Discourse generally, addressed a political proposal to a national
readership. Because any such proposal will assume common ground that
is conclusive with the reader, it implicitly affirms either the existence or
the possibility of a common identity. Calhoun thus said that the vetoes he

proposed for "the weaker section" (via nullification and a plural executive) "would make the union a union in truth—a bond of mutual affection and brotherhood—and not a mere . . . instrument of domination and aggrandizement . . . submitted to by the weaker only from the lingering remains of former attachment, and the fading hope of . . . restor[ing] the government to what it was originally intended to be, a blessing to all."[47] This thought alone—independent of his proslavery nationalist argument against the antislavery states' rights arguments of New England—complicates any attempt to describe Calhoun as a states' righter. The best one could say is that his position was mixed.

A Mixed History

"Everything has been mixed," said John Marshall when trying to describe the degree of national unity from the colonial period to ratification. In a letter of May 7, 1833, Marshall said, "we never have been perfectly distinct, independent societies, sovereign in the sense in which the Nullifiers use the term. . . . [W]e have always been united in some respects, separate in others. We have acted as one people for some purposes, as distinct societies for others." Marshall concluded that the mixed character of the nation's history "demonstrate[s] the fallacy of the principle on which either nullification or the right of peaceful constitutional secession is asserted," namely, "[t]he idea of complete sovereignty of the State[s]. . . . [an idea that] converts our government into a league, and, if carried into practice, dissolves the Union."[48] That the nation had a mixed history before ratification is easier to accept than Calhoun's separatist account of the nation's history if for no other reason than Calhoun's own inability to maintain consistency with that account. Calhoun needed a separatist account because a mixed account would have implied divided sovereignty, and divided sovereignty meant national supremacy in pursuit of authorized national ends—the very doctrine of *McCulloch* that precludes categorical state's rights and opens the possibility of eventual consolidation. Because, as a logical matter, divided sovereignty in the presence of the Supremacy Clause meant potential if not eventual consolidation, Calhoun was right to conclude that no real middle way existed between full state sovereignty and full national sovereignty. Eventual consolidation was anathema to him because it all but guaranteed the end of slavery and the destruction of what he considered a superior way of life.

A modern states' righter shares Calhoun's difficulty with a mixed account of the nation's history: mixed history implies divided sovereignty and the Supremacy Clause makes divided sovereignty untenable. "Divided sovereignty" eventually means a national answer to all policy questions of any salience. "Divided sovereignty" eventually means national sovereignty. So a modern states' righter has to construe what is most plausibly a mixed history as a separatist history. He has to claim, as Justice Thomas has claimed, that the union was originally not one of mobile individuals but of separate and independent sovereign communities intent on maintaining their separate sovereignty. Yet even if this separatist account of the founding generation were true as a matter of historical fact, nothing of present normative import would follow from that fact alone. States' righters would need a moral premise to bridge their version of the past and their prescription for the present. This normative premise would have to invoke a good recognized by the nation as a whole as applicable to its present situation. If a separatist past had any relevance to the present, it would lie in a separatist future.

On those occasions when Calhoun offered his separatist history of the nation, he had reasons for doing so. He believed that slavery and free trade served both his sectional interests and the national interest, and his separatist version of constitutional history served to rationalize slavery and free trade. That the nation's history itself, separated from moral premises, compelled no separatist reading is indicated by Calhoun's own occasional nationalist readings, as when he supported a national bank and claimed that Vermont had committed itself to support slavery. Calhoun's reasons for a states' rights reading of the founding reveal what he wanted the nation to be, not just what he wanted Carolina to be. This last point marks Read's contribution to our understanding of Calhoun: Calhoun was not content with restricting national power relative to slavery. He needed and demanded national power in the service of slavery. And he construed national power and states' rights to accommodate that end.[49] We know more about Calhoun's conception of the good society than about the conception or conceptions of the states' righters on the Rehnquist and Roberts Courts. What we do know is that the justices are moved by neither history nor states' rights, but by some vision of the nation as a whole.[50]

6

STATES' RIGHTS AS RIGHTS ONLY TO PARTICIPATE IN NATIONAL PROCESSES

Walter Berns once said that the debate in *McCulloch* was at bottom a debate over "the kind of country the United States was intended to be." Maryland favored a Jeffersonian ideal whose economic basis was agriculture and whose philosophic defense stemmed from Rousseau; Marshall and the government favored a Hamiltonian vision of industrial power whose principal philosopher was Locke. Though the country may originally have been open to Jefferson's vision, said Berns, Marshall favored the Hamiltonian option, partly because 1819 was too late for the nation to reverse course.[1] The authors of *The Federalist* and others might disagree with Berns about the nation's early options (see 6:31–32, 7:40, 8:47, 10:59). But none can quarrel with Berns about the kind of thing at stake in *McCulloch*.

McCulloch occurred in a national forum; it was part of a national debate. Participants in national debates must invoke principles that are broader than local. Debate about the meaning and application of these norms is debate about what the nation ought to be. To argue that America should be, say, a commercial society is implicitly to claim that given the world as it is likely to be, a commercial society best promotes the true well-being of the nation's people.[2] Calhoun's conduct illustrates the point. He insisted that the free states support Southern slavery as essential both to the national interest and a correct (that is, more than merely local) understanding of liberty, including their own interest and liberty. Calhoun's argument was thus a nationalist argument—an argument about "the kind of country the United States was intended to be." Moreover, as we have seen, Calhoun deployed this nationalist argument against the rights of the New England states—their states' rights to actions opposing slavery.

More than arguments about the future, federalism arguments are also arguments about the law. They occur when constitutional language and history lack sufficient clarity to avoid controversy over what the Constitution means. From the Constitution's Preamble and from what the Declaration of Independence says about why "Governments are instituted among Men," we know that constitutional questions are ultimately about means and ends.[3] The instrumental nature of constitutional debate explains what Purcell calls the instrumental nature of federalism arguments: the tendency of partisans to switch sides on states' rights depending on their underlying substantive aims.[4] Federalism is an institutional arrangement; as such, it is neither reducible to nor essential to any substantive good. An institutional arrangement that once shielded slavery and child labor can hardly be the embodiment of liberty and prosperity. Nor can an arrangement that enabled the states to violate treaty obligations and renege on war debts be essential to national defense.[5] Had the founding generation considered states' rights ends in themselves or the basis for burdening the pursuit of national ends, one could hardly explain the nation's decision to abandon the Articles of Confederation.[6]

Renowned dual federalists have attested through their conduct that the utility of federalism is contingent. Jefferson compromised his states' rights scruples when he changed his mind about the constitutionality of West Point and when he ignored the enumeration of national powers, invoked the interest of the nation as a whole, and purchased Louisiana.[7] Madison approved the Second National Bank in 1816 notwithstanding his opposition to the First National Bank in 1791. Calhoun mocked states' rights when he argued not only against Vermont's position on slavery but against its right to take that position. And pro-lifers who attacked *Roe v. Wade* for usurping states' rights were pro-lifers, not dual federalists, for they displayed few reservations about Congress's making partial-birth abortions a federal crime.[8]

To history's testimony against states' rights federalism—that is, that no national figure has consistently treated "state sovereignty" as a fundamental value—one can add the testimony of practical reason. The contingent value of institutional means makes states' rights federalism irrational, for states' rights restraints on central power preclude the policy flexibility that contingencies demand. The rational pursuit of liberty or any other substantive end requires a government to centralize or decentralize policy as opportunities and challenges materialize. Plenary constitutional authority at the center permits policy flexibility; narrow constitutional authority at the center restricts it. A central government can always decentralize as a matter of ordinary legislative policy. But provincial governments cannot hold a central government responsible for addressing a matter beyond its jurisdiction. Where constitutions are instituted to pursue substantive ends like liberty and security, and where threats to these ends are unpredictable, narrow national authority offends practical reason.

Narrow national power makes sense only where broad provincial power is seen as an end in itself, as might be the case among contracting communities who subordinate values they share to values that separate them from each other. Such was the occasional constitutional contract of Calhoun's later imagination—the one he ignored in his stance on the antislavery policies of the New England states. Narrow national power makes no sense where people believe, as Publius did, that the sole value of any institutional arrangement is as means to "the public happiness" and where fallible actors acknowledge the need for diverse views about the concrete meaning of that end and how to pursue it.[9] Narrow national power makes no sense where people understand their aspirations and therewith themselves as more than the sum of their immediate preferences and the products of their local conventions—as the authors of *The Federalist* did, as Calhoun also did, despite himself, and as every reflective person does by virtue of what it means to be a reflective person, namely, one who seeks to measure his immediate preferences and beliefs by standards that apply to people generally.[10]

Locating Process Federalism

A vague but widespread appreciation of the nationalist case prevailed in American law and public opinion from the late 1930s through the late 1960s, except among opponents of the civil rights movement.[11] The presidential campaigns of Barry Goldwater in 1964 and Richard Nixon in 1968 promised a revival of states' rights, and in 1971 President Nixon successfully nominated a dual federalist, William H. Rehnquist, to the Supreme Court. Less than five years later, Rehnquist led the Court to the first vindication of states' rights against national power in some forty years. The case was *National League of Cities v. Usery*.[12] Here a plurality of the Court held that although Congress had power to prescribe the hours and wages of the nation's workforce, the Tenth Amendment exempted the hours and wages of state employees from this power—just as the First Amendment exempted freedoms of speech and press from Congress's otherwise admitted powers. *Usery* inaugurated the federalism revival now associated with Rehnquist's name.

The Court overruled *Usery* nine years later in *Garcia v. San Antonio Metropolitan Transit Authority*,[13] a decision based on the process conception of federalism, to be discussed in this chapter. Yet the Court silently abandoned process federalism in *New York v. United States*,[14] decided only six years after *Garcia*. And subsequent states' rights victories under the Commerce Clause, the Eleventh Amendment, and the Fourteenth Amendment manifest the continuing influence of Rehnquist's opinion in *Usery*. At present, therefore, *Usery's* holding is officially dead though its principle lives in fact, and *Garcia's* holding remains good law though its principle is at least comatose.[15]

This chapter asks whether *Garcia* deserved its fate. Dual federalists say yes, heedless of the fact that *Garcia* offers them the only defensible version of states' rights beyond a right against pretexts. One would expect the nationalist answer to be an unqualified no; but the nationalist answer is equivocal. On the one hand, process federalism is a nationalist position, and we shall see later in this chapter that in important ways process federalism may perfect Marshallian federalism. Under modern conditions, the differences between process federalism and Marshallian federalism may be largely rhetorical—a matter less of any substantive import than how observers choose to rationalize nationalist results. Yet process is inconceivable apart from substance. Process never stands alone, and process federalist must eventually acknowledge that fact. Process federalists who would link process to substance can conceive process as means either to public purposes or to private purposes. Any version of the former abandons process federalism. Link constitutional processes to national public purposes, like economic growth and equal opportunity, and process federalism becomes Marshallian federalism or something formally like Marshallian federalism. If constitutional processes seek most to preserve spheres of autonomy for the states, over education, say, or sexual morality, process federalism lapses into dual federalism.

To avoid a free-floating process that is beyond human imagining and to distinguish itself from dual federalism on the one hand and Marshallian federalism on the other, process federalism has but one move: it must substitute private purposes for public purposes. Leading process federalists thus call on courts to leave substantive federalism issues to Congress so that they can preserve their political capital for securing individual rights.[16] This substitution of private purposes for public purposes implies a negative constitutionalism, to be contrasted with the positive constitutionalism of John Marshall and *The Federalist*. Positive constitutionalism is oriented to public purposes; it seeks to improve public opinion by reconciling it to fairness and the common good. Negative constitutionalism aims at stopping government from violating individual rights. Negative constitutionalism seeks to protect a private sphere and aggregate private preferences in a manner that reduces their collision to tolerable levels. Where positive constitutionalism would educate, negative constitutionalism would coordinate. The contest between Marshallian and process federalism is but part of the broader contest between positive and negative constitutionalism. Elsewhere I have argued for positive constitutionalism on textual, historical, and moral grounds. I apply those arguments to the federalism debate in the concluding chapter of this book. In the present chapter I make the strongest argument I can for process federalism. By book's end I shall propose that Marshallian federalism is the only form of federalism that fits within a defensible view of the Constitution as a whole.

The Rise and Fall of Process Federalism

The story of process federalism in the Supreme Court is the story of *Garcia*. Because *Garcia* overruled *Usery*, we begin with *Usery*. *Usery* held that in 1974 Congress violated the Tenth Amendment by amending the Fair Labor Standards Act (FLSA) to require state and local governments to pay most of their employees the national minimum wage and overtime pay. Rehnquist explained for himself and three other justices that while setting minimum wages and maximum hours for the nation's workforce was "undoubtedly within the scope of the Commerce Clause," Congress could not transgress "affirmative limitations" on the exercise of this power. These limitations included states' rights, which were "akin to" the rights of individuals in the Bill of Rights. Just as the Bill of Rights prevented Congress from regulating commerce in ways that deprived individuals of jury trials and due process, the Tenth Amendment prevented Congress from regulating commerce to disable "States in their capacities as sovereign governments" from "'function[ing] effectively in a federal system.'" Imposing federal employment standards on the states would "displace the States' abilities to structure employer-employee relationships in such areas as fire prevention, police protection, sanitation, public health, and parks and recreation . . . activities typical of those . . . functions . . . which governments are created to provide . . . [and] which the States have traditionally afforded their citizens." Imposed federal standards would leave "little of the States' 'separate and independent existence,'" a result that "does not comport with the federal system of government embodied in the Constitution."[17]

Rehnquist thus tried to (1) elevate state sovereignty (to which he referred at least fifteen times) to the status of constitutionally protected individual rights; (2) resurrect the idea that the Constitution guarantees the states a "separate and independent existence"; and (3) make a state's right to deviate from congressional policy the test of its "separate and independent existence." These steps moved the Court firmly toward Calhoun's understanding of the founding. Contrary to Publius's assertion that the national government was an instrument solely of the people's happiness, Rehnquist implied, as Calhoun had explicitly claimed, that the states established the Constitution to protect their rights as separate sovereign entities, independent of any contrary interests of state residents (like state employees).[18] This reprised Calhoun's view of the antebellum Constitution as a creature of the states. As Calhoun had done, Rehnquist emphasized the separate and independent existence of the states, not their existence as parts of a functioning whole. For Rehnquist as for Calhoun a state demonstrated its existence as a state not by functioning as a part but by standing apart in conflict with the whole—even when the whole was striving for what it was ordained to be. This was "states' rights" in the strict sense: exemptions from acknowledged national power in behalf of sovereign rights to deviate from national policy.

"[N]ot untroubled by certain possible implications of the Court's opinion," Justice Harry Blackmun declined to endorse Rehnquist's argument. He reached Rehnquist's result by balancing Congress's interest in minimally paid workers with the states' interest in lower operating budgets.[19] Justice William Brennan saw the stakes and dissented. He said that a judicial tradition originating in *McCulloch* and *Gibbons* had rejected the idea of Tenth Amendment exemptions from the commerce power and that Rehnquist's opinion to the contrary would "astound scholars of the Constitution" (861–862). To deflect Brennan's criticism by denying its broader implications, Rehnquist claimed *Usery* did not upset the New

Deal Court's overruling of *Hammer v. Dagenhart* and the application of the FLSA to the nation's private workforce (835–836). Nor did *Usery* threaten the Commerce Clause as adequate ground for the Civil Rights Act of 1964.[20] He claimed *Usery* was compatible with a federal freeze on state salaries in the Nixon years as a valid answer to an economic emergency (852–853). A federal tax on a state-operated railroad was permissible under *Usery* because operating a railroad was not a traditional or essential state function (854). A wartime federal price control on a state transaction was permissible under *Usery* (854). And *Usery* did not stop Congress from making federal wage and hour standards for state employees a condition for receiving federal funds (852).

Rehnquist's attempt to domesticate *Usery* failed to explain why a state's control over the pay of its employees was more integral to its existence than its control over the race relations and working conditions of its people or why a state could compromise for federal dollars a prerogative important enough to defeat part of Congress's vision of national prosperity. Rehnquist's rationalization also sat uneasily with the breadth of national power he himself assumed or had to assume to make a majority of the Court. How could a system organized to secure the states' separate and independent existence have evolved a commerce power broad enough to compel the racial integration of Ollie's Barbecue, a family-owned eatery (advertising "homemade pies") located eleven blocks from an interstate highway and even farther from the rail and bus stations of Birmingham, Alabama?[21]

Rehnquist might have answered these objections by resorting to Calhoun's theory that each state of the union continued to enjoy the full and separate sovereignty of the original contracting states. If a state ever was fully sovereign and retained *full* sovereignty, preserving power over its employees while surrendering it over its citizens would be valued just because the state had chosen to do so. No further justification would be necessary. Power over one's employees would not be valued for its role in some scheme for realizing ends like justice, the blessings of liberty, and responsible self-determination. Justifications like these would not work because they would presuppose national standards and corresponding restraints on the states.[22] No such restraint could apply to the fully sovereign entity of Calhoun's theory, for a fully sovereign state (sovereign in both law and fact and over the full range of state activity) would be answerable only to itself. Nor could a charge of inconsistency defeat a policy of power over state employees but not other citizens. This policy might lack mutually compatible parts, to be sure, but "incompatible" here would describe the absence of one principle organizing two different commands, not one command canceling the other. "Power over employees" does not contradict "no power over other citizens" the way "sit down" contradicts "stand up." Incompatible parts would void one or both parts as expressions of sovereignty only if sovereigns as such could issue no command outside a uniformly principled system of commands. Calhoun could have admitted no such requirement, for he claimed sovereignty for political entities that had advanced well beyond the most primitive stage, and uniformly principled command could be no more than a theoretical ideal for such entities.[23] Even if principled uniformity could somehow be a practical requirement, some concrete agent would have to enforce it, and "sovereignty" signifies no higher enforcement agency—no political superior.[24]

In the same year the Court decided *Usery*, the *Texas Law Review* published an article in which Rehnquist exposed the background metaethics of the states' rights position. Notions of "moral rightness or goodness," Rehnquist said, rest solely on the "fact of their enactment" by some authority.[25] So if a sovereign state decided that sovereignty over its employees was more important than sovereignty over its citizens, but not as important as spending other people's tax dollars or evading responsibility for more taxes on one's own people, which is what happens when a state government accepts conditional federal money, no principle of substance or reason other than the will of the fully sovereign state could serve as a standard for assessing this decision. Sovereignty would be sovereignty. It would express itself not in argument, for argument is a practice of mutual submission (of reasons) that assumes fallibility and responsibility to standards of evidence and inference other than the will of either interlocutor. Sovereignty for Rehnquist would express itself as willful assertion, and willful assertion would be in keeping with the inability of states' righters to defend their position with reasons.

Justice Brennan described the distinction between essential and nonessential state functions as unworkable and little more than a mask for judicial policy making.[26] "It is unacceptable that the judicial process should be thought superior to the political process in this area," said Brennan, for "the political branches of our Government are structured to protect the interests of the States, as well as the Nation as a whole, and the States are fully able to protect their own interests in the premises" (876–877). Such was Brennan's claim for process federalism, and to support it he cited passages from *The Federalist* Nos. 45 and 46.[27] He also cited the seminal defense of process federalism, Herbert Wechsler's "The Political Safeguards of Federalism: The Role of the States in the Composition and Selection of the National Government."[28]

A little less than nine years later, in *Garcia*, Justice Blackmun switched to Brennan's position on the distinction between essential and nonessential state functions and the political safeguards of federalism, and a 5-to-4 Court overruled *Usery*. Citing *The Federalist*, Blackmun concluded that "the Framers chose to rely on a federal system in which special restraints on federal power over the States inhered principally in the workings of the National Government itself, rather than in discrete limitations on the objects of federal authority. State sovereign interests, then, are more properly protected by procedural safeguards inherent in the structure of the federal system than by judicially created limitations on federal power."[29] Henceforth, "[a]ny substantive restraint" on the commerce power must find its justification" in "the national political process," not in any judicially declared states' rights (554).

Dissenting in *Garcia*, Justice Lewis Powell cited passages from *The Federalist* congenial to his own position and insisted that by enumerating national powers the framers intended the states to enjoy "'a residuary and inviolable authority over all other objects.'"[30] Powell insisted further that it was the Court's role to decide the intended "balance" between state and national power, and that the balance to be struck was between national power, mostly over foreign affairs and interstate commerce, and "the broad, yet specific areas of sovereignty that the Framers intended the States to retain" (574). These "broad, yet specific powers" were those "traditional functions" that *Usery* sought to protect, like "fire prevention, police protection, sanitation, and public health" (575). Powell criticized the majority's view that, under the Tenth Amendment, "the States retain their sovereign powers 'only to the extent that the Constitution has not divested them of their original powers and transferred those powers to the Federal Government'" (574–575). This, of course, is the defining proposition of Marshall's federalism: that within the ambit of its delegated powers, Congress is supreme. Powell said this view of the Tenth Amendment implies "that Congress is free under the Commerce Clause to assume a State's traditional sovereign power, and to do so without judicial review of its action," a view that "relegate[s] the States to precisely the trivial role that opponents of the Constitution feared they would occupy" (575).

Powell misstated Blackmun's position in *Garcia*. Blackmun did not leave Congress free to seize powers reserved to the states; he denied the existence of powers reserved to the states beyond the rights to participate in national processes. Blackmun's critics have charged that his remaining states' rights are either meaningless or no states' rights at all. They have pointed out that federal standards applicable to the states under the Bill of Rights and the Civil War Amendments have greatly diminished the significance of the structural rights Blackmun would otherwise protect, like the states' right to determine voter qualifications. They have added that rights like the right to representation in Congress were rights not of the states as such but of individuals and interests within the states.[31] The point of these criticisms was to agree with the basic dual federalist assessment of process federalism: its promise of meaningful limits on national power was empty.

Justice Blackmun anticipated this criticism by suggesting that substantive states' rights could be derived from the states' process rights (555). Though Blackmun offered no examples of these substantive rights (556), several come to mind. One would be a state legislature's right to submit an antiwar memorial to Congress, similar to the antislavery memorials that Calhoun persuaded the Senate not to accept.[32] Another example would be a state's right to the seating of its congressional delegation without having to ratify a constitutional amendment, a right that the Reconstruction Congress denied lawful state governments over the objections of President Andrew Johnson.[33] These examples show that what Blackmun saw as the states' process rights and their derivatives are far from meaningless. Yet they also indicate that breaches of the states' rights to participate in national processes occur in crises that prudence places beyond the reach of judicial remedies. For most practical purposes Powell was right about the implications of *Garcia*. The case had virtually denied meaningful limits on national power in behalf of the states.[34] Under the right combination of congressional motives and material circumstances, plenary national power in some areas could mean a trivial role for the states in their traditional areas.

Though Powell offered no example, the trivialization of state powers remains a theoretical possibility in all substantive areas.[35] The Supremacy Clause and the logic of action combine to establish this possibility as a simple matter of practical reason. By seeking to block this possibility Powell implicitly denied that Congress's admitted powers are plenary. He denied that the nation has its choice of means vis-à-vis the states when the nation is doing what it is authorized to do. He moved beyond the strategy of narrowing national power to avoid conflict with states' rights, the method of the Old Court against the Progressive movement and the New Deal. As Rehnquist had done in *Usery*, and as counsel for Maryland had done in *McCulloch*, Powell treated the states' reserved powers as rights in the strong sense—as exemptions even from admitted national responsibilities. Political developments over two centuries had brought matters to the point of ultimate conflict between the Supremacy Clause and a Calhounian understanding of the Tenth Amendment. Powell chose the latter, and since the Civil War had eliminated Calhounian remedies, he asserted a role for the Court as balancer of conflicting state and national interests.

In separate opinions, Rehnquist and O'Connor joined Powell's dissent. Concluding his one-paragraph statement, Rehnquist said he was "confident" that "in time again" the principle of *Usery* would "command the support of a majority of this Court" (580). O'Connor agreed; she predicted that "this Court will, in time, again assume its constitutional responsibility" to prevent "a unitary, centralized government" (589). This was February 1985. Ronald Reagan's reelection as president the previous November and fifty-three Republican senators in the 99th Congress may have contributed to Rehnquist's confidence. He may also have felt with other conservatives of the Reagan era that the old Progressive idea of a national community had given way to small community ideals that traced back to the Antifederalists, Montesquieu, and Aristotle. These ideals, the story went, had reappeared with the New Left in the 1960s and passed, with modifications, to the New Right in the 1980s. William Schambra portrayed these small-republic ideals as foundational to the Reagan Revolution.[36] Rehnquist may also have felt that constitutional logic was on his side, for the Court's long-standing refusal to call pretexts left states' rights in the strong sense as the only meaningful way to redeem the axiomatic promise of limited national power.

Whatever prompted Justice Rehnquist's prediction, it proved right. Seven years after their loss in *Garcia*, Rehnquist and his allies were back carving exemptions from national power. The first "commandeering" case came in 1992; a 6-to-3 Court held in *New York v. United States* that state sovereignty prevented Congress from forcing a state to make arrangements for disposing of its nuclear waste.[37] In 1997 a 5-to-4 Court held in *Printz v. United States* that Congress violated states' rights by temporarily requiring ("commandeering") local law enforcement officers to conduct background checks for handgun purchases.[38]

In 1996 Rehnquist and four of his allies opened a major front against national power under the Eleventh Amendment. The Court had said in 1989 that Congress could authorize private suits against the states under the Commerce Clause if the authorizing statute did so explicitly. Rehnquist and his allies had dissented from that 5-to-4 decision, *Pennsylvania v. Union Gas Co.* (1989).[39] After Clarence Thomas succeeded Thurgood Marshall in late 1991, Rehnquist had a fifth vote for overruling *Union Gas* and declaring, as the Court did in *Seminole Tribe of Florida v. Florida* (1997), that the Eleventh Amendment barred Congress from authorizing private suits against the states under the Commerce Clause or any affirmative grant of power to Congress prior to the adoption of the Eleventh Amendment.[40]

Rehnquist acknowledged that the Eleventh Amendment can be read to bar federal suits against a state only where the plaintiff was an out-of-state citizen or a foreign government suing not under federal law but under state law. That reading was most congenial both to the language of the amendment and to the nationalist view of federalism, for where no federal question is involved, a state declining to be sued claims no exemption from national power. But Rehnquist's theory of the Constitution demanded states' rights not just against private plaintiffs under state laws but private plaintiffs under national laws—states' rights, that is, against Congress's power to authorize private suits against the state governments. "Although the text of the Amendment would appear to restrict only the Article III diversity jurisdiction of the federal courts," Rehnquist said, "'we have understood the Eleventh Amendment to stand not so much for what it says, but for the presupposition . . . which it confirms.'"[41] The putative presupposition was that "each State is a sovereign entity in our federal system."[42] State sovereignty explained the amendment for Rehnquist because "'[i]t is inherent in the nature of sovereignty not to be amenable to the suit of an individual without its consent.'"[43]

Rehnquist thus reasoned that because, as a general matter, a sovereign cannot be sued without its consent, and because the Eleventh Amendment precludes some nonconsensual private suits against the states, the Amendment presupposes state sovereignty against national power. But state sovereignty against national power hardly follows from a premise of state sovereignty against some private suits. State sovereignty against national power can explain the amendment, but there are other explanations. Forrest McDonald (despite his agreement with Calhoun's state sovereignty theory of ratification[44]) suggests an alternative explanation. A concern for state sovereignty against national power "may have . . . moved" supporters of the amendment, says McDonald, "but of equal moment was [the] economic interest" of revenue-strapped states that would avoid actions by British loyalists who sought compensation for property confiscated during the Revolution.[45]

Thus Rehnquist had a choice in *Seminole Tribe*, as did John Marshall when he held that the Eleventh Amendment did not bar personal suits against state officials acting under unconstitutional state laws.[46] Marshall shaped the amendment, as its language permitted, to fit within a nationalist view of the Constitution. Rehnquist shaped the amendment to a dual federalist view of the Constitution. Marshall's interpretation of the amendment was superior because it served a substantive vision that made sense precisely because it was substantive—because it avoided assuming that institutions could be ends in themselves or on a par with the goods for whose sake the institutions were established. No version of the common good was available to Rehnquist. He could not anchor his position in any good other than the unreflective preference of some authority—which is no good at all to anyone other than that authority, if that.[47] Appeals to substantive goods like liberty or even procedural goods like democracy are appeals to general ideas, not their local conceptions, and no such appeal can avoid implying national constraints on the states.

The illogic of Rehnquist's reasoning proved inconsequential, however. Within six years of *Seminole Tribe*, 5-to-4 decisions had applied the principle of sovereign immunity to bar a complaint to the Federal Maritime Commission by a private party against a state[48] and a federal suit by a private party against a state under the federal Patent Remedy Act of 1992.[49] In *Alden v. Maine* (1999) the Court's states' rights block barred a suit in the courts of Maine for overtime pay by state citizens suing under provisions of the FLSA that the Court had upheld in *Garcia*.[50] Congress, it seems, could apply the FLSA to the states *(Garcia)*, but Congress could not choose to enforce the act through private suits against the states *(Alden)*.

State sovereign immunity even came to affect suits under the Fourteenth Amendment, an area to which *Seminole Tribe* had said state sovereign immunity did not apply because the Fourteenth Amendment, unlike the Commerce Clause, was ratified after the Eleventh Amendment. Rehnquist and his allies accomplished this feat through the "congruence and proportionality" test announced in *Boerne v. Flores* (1997).[51] This test permits congressional action under Section 5 of the Fourteenth Amendment only if the legislation satisfies three conditions. Congress must (1) adhere to the judiciary's definitions of rights that are protected by the amendment; (2) show widespread patterns of rights violations, not just isolated or sporadic violations, by the state governments; and (3) tailor legislative remedies that burden the states no more than necessary to correct the violations (520–523, 534–535). With this concern for "the States' traditional prerogatives and general authority to regulate for the health and welfare of their citizens," the Court announced that it would actively scrutinize congressional action under Section 5 (534).

The Court thus slipped into a general presumption against congressional acts under Section 5. Congress failed to rebut this presumption when it authorized suits for patent infringement, essentially because Congress failed to satisfy the Court that it was addressing a problem sufficiently widespread and persistent to warrant national legislation. "Congress appears to have enacted this legislation in response to a handful of instances of state patent infringement that [since the states themselves may provide remedies for patent infringement] do not necessarily violate the Constitution," said Rehnquist in *Florida Prepaid v. College Savings Bank.*[52] In *Kimel v. Florida Board of Regents* (2000), Justice O'Connor wrote for the states' rights bloc that because the "States may discriminate on the basis of age without offending the Fourteenth Amendment if the age classification in question is rationally related to a legitimate state interest," Congress could not act under Section 5 to authorize age discrimination suits against the states.[53] In *Board of Trustees of the University of Alabama v. Garrett* (2001), Rehnquist held for the majority that Congress had failed to show the pattern of unreasonable state discrimination against disabled persons adequate to justify private suits against the states.[54]

The Court went the other way in some later cases. One involved the Family and Medical Leave Act of 1993 (FMLA). In *Nevada Department of Human Resources v. Hibbs* (2003) Rehnquist and O'Connor joined the

6-to-3 majority that upheld the FMLA. Rehnquist argued for the Court that Congress could authorize private law suits to enforce the act against the states because (1) Congress had made the necessary findings of widespread and persistent gender discrimination in the states' family leave policies, and (2) the Court had declared a right against gender discrimination to be a right to be protected by "heightened judicial scrutiny" of governmental policies and practices.[55] In a dissent joined by Justices Scalia and Thomas, Justice Kennedy denied at length that Congress had shown gender discrimination by the states to be sufficiently widespread to justify enforcement by private suits against the states (744–754). Another case involved a section of the Americans with Disabilities Act (ADA). In *Tennessee v. Lane* (2004) O'Connor broke ranks, and a 5-to-4 Court upheld provisions of the ADA as applied to the right of disabled persons to enjoy access to the physical facilities of the state courts.[56] In dissent, Rehnquist said the majority had given mere lip service to the congruence and proportionality test. Beyond scattered "anecdotal evidence," he said, Congress had shown no pattern of states' denying the disabled access to judicial proceedings and facilities (541–546). The justices can thus disagree on whether an act is congruent and proportional, and the states don't win every time. But as of this writing the Court has abandoned *Garcia's* policy of leaving federalism questions to Congress.

Process Federalism: Pros and Cons

Did *Garcia* federalism deserve a short life? The affirmative answer begins with the most salient defect of process federalism: its virtual denial of the federalism axiom. National federalism and states' rights federalism accept the federalism axiom; they agree that national powers are limited. This axiom is an inference from the Constitution's list of specific powers, mostly in Article I, Section 8, the Civil War Amendments, and the Nineteenth Amendment. Where national federalism and states' rights federalism disagree is in the nature of the limits on national power. All three forms of federalism recognize the expressed constitutional powers of the states; these include rights to participate in national electoral and amending processes and limited powers over voter qualifications, congressional elections, and state militias. States' righters derive additional limits on national power from historical facts that enjoy no specific constitutional reference, namely, the categories of social practice (education, public morals, and so forth) historically regulated by the states. Marshallian nationalists oppose pretextual uses of national power, where Congress says that it regulates commerce when all relevant publics, including Congress, understand Congress to be doing something else, like combating partial-birth abortions, school violence, or the indifference of local prosecutors toward some forms of sexual assault and spousal abuse. Marshallian and states' rights federalists thus agree that, in one sense or another, the responsibilities of the national government are "limited." For most practical purposes, process federalism holds otherwise; it all but denies the axiom that the national government is one of limited responsibilities.

Process federalists can easily demure to the dual federalist version of this charge. They can contend against genuine constitutional status for any version of the axiom that protects rights beyond process rights. They can claim, with Marshallian nationalism, and as argued here, that (1) the Supremacy Clause implies the superiority of national ends; (2) these ends include the equal opportunity and physical mobility of individual Americans; (3) narrowing national power to accommodate states' rights offends practical reason by compromising what the Constitution implies are greater goods (security, prosperity, fairness) in behalf of lesser or apparent goods (like racial purity); (4) since exemptions from national power can be defended only by appeal to national standards that would in turn limit states' rights, states' rights beyond process rights are literally indefensible; and (5) as indefensible, state sovereignty offends an aspiration to public reasonableness that is foundational both to the nation's political morality and to political life generally. So process federalists can conclude that if there are states' rights, they can be no more than process rights, inconsequential for most practical purposes though they be.

This response leaves Marshallian federalism as process federalism's only worthy contender. The issue that divides these forms of nationalism is whether constitutionalism in America is committed to any one set of public purposes. This issue can be put in either formal or substantive terms. Formally, the question is whether a constitutional process can be conceived independently of some substantive end. Substantively, the issue is whether the Constitution commits the nation to a secular liberal regime whose people value security, prosperity, fairness, and mobility, or whether the Constitution is neutral between liberal beliefs and attitudes and antiliberal beliefs and attitudes, like those favoring racial supremacy and sectarian solidarity.

The formal question is easy, for no one can name a man-made process that is conceptually independent of any and all substantive ends. "Process" derives from the Latin *procedere*, which means to "go forward," that is, from one place to another. An institutional process in the sense of "method" (from the Greek *hodos*, for road) can exist without a terminus no more than there can be a road to nowhere or to any and everywhere. Processes are named in terms of their ends, like sailing to China or baking corn bread. Civic process are identified in terms of aims like true accounts of what happened (for example, in criminal trials) or a responsiveness to what a population of equals decides is good (in some versions of democracy). So process presupposes substance, and process constitutionalists can describe themselves as such only because they fail to explicate and defend their substantive commitments.[57]

That process federalism might be antiliberal arises from the need to distinguish process federalism from Marshallian federalism and the latter's association with the Large Commercial Republic, a liberal regime. Process federalism as antiliberalism might seem implausible given the opposition of process federalism to dual federalism and the latter's historical associations with antiliberalism. Yet process federalism is no more than a formal doctrine; it opposes a formal relationship between two levels of government. The disfavored relationship is one that either narrows national power to avoid conflict with the states or grants the states subject-matter exemptions from national power. Process federalism as such does not reject substantive values historically associated with states' rights. The pure process federalist has no theory of constitutional ends to deploy against, say, federal aid to parochial schools or federal laws discriminating against same-sex couples.[58] At present, nationally secured individual rights do support arguments against such measures, but these rights are substantive rights, and a process federalist recognizes them only because they can be seen either as conditional to, or the products of, a favored process.[59]

A process constitutionalist would value a freedom from religious establishments not because she, like the framers, found arguments for a regime of secular public reasonableness morally compelling, but chiefly because the freedom from religious establishments was enacted through a favored process or because it performed some procedural function, some "structural or separation of powers function," as Ely described it.[60] A favored process would have to be an arbitrarily favored process, as it turns out, because nothing other than some substantive standard could justify choice between alternative processes, and a process federalist, as such, recognizes no controlling substantive standard.[61] She is officially "neutral" among conceptions of the good; reason cannot tell her that life under a religious establishment, a life of pious submission to ordained authority, is any better or worse than a life of autonomous reflection and choice.[62] Choice between these lives, she avers, must rest on an arbitrary act of commitment or faith.

At bottom, therefore, process federalism is as antirational and antiliberal as states' rights federalism. Neither is rationally defensible. A dual federalist who tries to defend his position appeals to some national standard and thereby vitiates his dual federalism. A process federalist who defends her choice among processes invokes some substantive standard that identifies and thereby limits her favored process. A dual federalist who troubles to defend his position ends up a kind of nationalist, as Calhoun ended up a proslavery nationalist. And a process federalist who defends her choice of process ends up a nationalist who, like Marshall, construes a process to serve the substantive end that justifies the process when it works and justifies disregarding it when it fails, as the framers disregarded the amending process of the Articles of Confederation when it proved dysfunctional to "the exigencies of union."

Yet process constitutionalists may be able to answer this twofold criticism. They can declare, first, that the Constitution's aim is to establish machinery for aggregating and expressing popular preferences, whatever those preferences might be, so long as they avoid violating constitutional rights and processes. This minimalist account of the Constitution's substantive aim—that is, a rights-protecting democracy—might be enough to insulate process federalists from a charge of blindness to the substantive limits they would place on national power. The process federalist could then say that existing constitutional exemptions from national power in the form of individual and minority rights are sufficient to ensure a secular liberal order without the need for holding such an order implicit in the enumeration of powers. The *Garcia* federalist can say, in other words, that judicially enforced constitutional rights obviate the need for a substantive theory of constitutional ends. A liberal order would be guaranteed simply by letting popular beliefs, preferences, and attitudes go where they may as long as they respect the basic rights of individuals and groups. The Constitution would be indifferent to the personal values of the population, including their possible racism and sectarian zeal, as long as the population either restrained its demand for Jim Crow laws and religious establishments or supported politicians and judges who resisted popular demands for such things. Such a constitution would be "made for people with fundamentally different views"—as long as they behaved themselves. The difference between process federalism and Marshallian federalism would thus become largely rhetorical—a matter of how best to rationalize liberal values imposed on antiliberal segments of the country.

Process federalists could then switch to offense. They could claim that if dual federalism and process federalism are ultimately arbitrary, Marshallian federalism is no better, for the bourgeois goods to which Marshallian constitutionalism is committed (security, prosperity, fairness) are themselves rationally groundless. Process federalists could add that Marshall's no-pretext rule is itself pretextual, and in several ways. First, it is dishonest to pretend that power accumulated under the Commerce Clause, the Civil War Amendments, a nationalized Bill of Rights, and the General Welfare Clause permits an isolated state to go its own way in any salient matter of public policy. It is also dishonest to pretend that mutually influential dimensions of lived experience (the economic, the moral, the religious dimensions) can be divided from each other and parceled to different authorities. It is dishonest to pretend that subordinating moral, religious, and aesthetic concerns to growth and profits leaves room for any but moral, religious, and aesthetic commitments consistent with growth and profits—dishonest to deny that God ends up being "The Market" or The Market ends up being "God." And finally, it is dishonest to pretend that there can be a reason—textual, moral, or whatever—for disabling national authority from addressing any problem that confronts the nation as a whole, regardless of the problem's sociological classification.

To all this, process federalists can add that no middle ground exists between process federalism and dual federalism and that process federalism alone can rescue Marshallian federalism from lapsing into dual federalism. Though Marshallians may have no real answers to these objections, I try to answer them in the concluding chapter. They are formidable objections, however, and they deserve a closer look.

Process Federalism and Marshall's No-Pretext Rule

The no-pretext rule separates Marshallian from process federalism; it enables Marshallian federalism to claim consistency with the axiom of limited national powers. The no-pretext rule is also Marshallian federalism's substitute for dual federalism's exemptions from national power. The latter reserves power to the states in categorical terms like education and public morals, while the former would guarantee but one states' right (beyond process rights), namely, a right against pretextual uses of national power. The no-pretext rule would guarantee no more to the states than the honest pursuit of national ends as disclosed by a successful theory of national ends. But this "guarantee" may be practically meaningless and thus pretextual, or so a process federalist can easily maintain. Under the right circumstances, as we have seen, the pursuit of just one national end, like national security, could leave nothing of any consequence to the states. This prospect became vastly more likely after the Civil War and Nineteenth Amendments, the judicial application in the twentieth century of the first nine amendments to the states, the generous interpretation of the Commerce Clause to cover any matter of arguable significance to the nation's economy, and the Supreme Court's acceptance in 1937 of Hamilton's theory of the General Welfare Clause.[63]

This last clause now permits Congress to tax and spend for any purpose, regardless of its connection to an authorized national end. As interpreted, its presence in Article I, Section 8 makes the enumeration of specifics (and thereby a no-pretext rule) relevant only to Congress's direct regulatory power, not to Congress's power to place conditions on the receipt of federal funds.[64] No other power of Congress matches the potency of this clause as a tool for extending Congress's will to areas traditionally handled by the states, including race relations, land use, the drinking age, highway safety, public education, medical care, retirement benefits, unemployment benefits, teen sexual morality, and aid to the disabled. Today, through one legislative instrument or another (regulatory statutes, regulatory taxes, conditional federal spending, and treaties), Congress can foist on unwilling local populations policies that offend otherwise law-abiding elements sometimes to the point of violence (abetted, incidentally, by gun rights recently nationalized by avowed states' righters).[65] Today, the only realistic hope of local majorities is membership in a national coalition that is strong enough to shape the policies of the nation's judicial and elected branches—membership as a part of something national, not a right to live apart. Today, a no-pretext rule would leave the states with little more than *Garcia's* process rights, and it would be pretextual to claim otherwise. *Garcia* federalism can thus claim to perfect Marshallian federalism—perfect it by making it honest.

Garcia federalism can claim to perfect Marshallian federalism in still another way; it may prevent Marshallian federalism from lapsing into dual federalism. Consider again the distinctions between the three kinds of federalism. Marshallian federalism would secure the states' process rights but insists on further limiting national power by a rule against pretexts. Not only must Congress respect rights to participate in national decision, Congress must be honest about what it is doing; it cannot tell reviewing courts that it is regulating commerce when its members see themselves and are seen by their constituents as combating morally, ideologically, or culturally controversial practices like partial-birth abortions, racial discrimination, and antiwar protests. This rule against pretexts implies a states' right: a right against pretexts. This one states' right is Marshall's replacement for dual federalism's indefinite number of subject-matter rights, correlatives of the states' reserved powers. States' rights federalism cannot settle for a general rule against pretexts because such a rule would restrain national power only in the sense of directing it, and properly directed, national authorities could altogether disregard the states' policies. Dual federalists have therefore sought to secure to the dominant political forces in the several states exclusive governmental power over public education, labor relations, race relations, and sexual morality. So Marshallian federalism adds something (a no-pretext rule) to process federalism and subtracts something (categorical states' rights) from dual federalism. Yet by adding something to process federalism it leans toward dual federalism, and by subtracting something from dual federalism it leans toward process federalism.

Lapsing into dual federalism would be the worst of these results because dual federalism is altogether indefensible. To avoid dual federalism, however, Marshallian federalism may have to abandon the no-pretext rule, for, in context, this rule may imply categorical states' rights. As a logical matter a no-pretext rule implies but one right: a right against pretexts. A Marshallian nationalist reads Article I, Section 8 as authorizing Congress to do specified kinds of things.[66] Article I, Section 8, standing alone, need not be read as "do these things, not those things," for "do these things," does not entail "do these things, not those (specified) things." Add the Tenth Amendment, however, and "do these things" becomes "do these things *only*." This is why the Constitution implies no pretexts; a no-pretext rule forbids Congress to use its authorizations as cover for acts beyond its authorization. But in this way the no-pretext rule implies, albeit without specification, the existence of things that Congress is not authorized to do—concerns that Congress is not authorized to express, ends that Congress cannot deliberately seek. In spite of itself, therefore, Marshallian federalism suggests a categorical division of sorts. By acknowledging a state's freedom from congressional pretexts, Marshallian federalism presupposes (again, without specifying) impermissible kinds of congressional motives. A Marshallian would avoid specifying these impermissible motives lest they be construed as affirmative exemptions from national power, types of social practice (education, public safety, family planning) into which Congress cannot intrude, for a Marshallian knows that a grant of plenary national power in just one area may eventually demand displacement of state power in all areas.

Yet Marshall's no-pretext rule would function in a common law culture that aspires to describe singular historical events in terms of a normative tradition that extends from the past into the future. In this culture a judicial decision is more than an event; it is also a "case"—a case of something broader than its singular self. A court's decision usually both instantiates and represents some allegedly preexisting and continually applicable rule or principal. Should the legal question be one of first impression, the court's decision is expected to represent a rule that will apply to "like cases" in a manner consistent with some background principles.

These rule-of-law expectations may not be compatible with reality.[67] Ultimately, there is no predicting what must be done in changing circumstances to defend the nation or secure the welfare of its people.[68] As a matter of practical reasonableness, therefore, the contingent nature of means to national ends precludes the formalistic application of a priori exemptions from national power, however packaged. Practical reasonableness rather requires case-by-case assessments of congressional acts, taking notice of legislative motive and judging the suitability of legislation by at least a moderately deferential standard of reasonableness, a standard that reflects the normative priority of national ends. Authorized national ends did not require displacing local policies in the *Lopez* situation, for example. But we can easily imagine other situations. The local populations of some sections of the country may be hostile to national authority. Congressional regulation of gun possession near military bases in such areas would be consistent with authorized national ends even if gun possession in school zones was not, at least in 1995.

But while a case-by-case approach preserves the discretion that plenary power demands to meet contingencies, it might undermine the values (predictability, equal treatment of like cases) of a legal culture that attaches precedential status to decided cases. In this culture a called pretext on one occasion will turn up in arguments against future acts independently of circumstances and motivations. *Lopez* could thus suggest a constitutional presumption of state sovereignty over the local possession of firearms. Opponents of our hypothetical federal regulation of guns near military bases might thus claim *Lopez* as a precedent. In common law context, therefore, and in spite of itself, Marshallian federalism inclines toward a categorical division of responsibilities between nation and state, a dual federalist division admissible by no defensible constitutional theory. One could cure this problem by dropping the no-pretext rule. But without a rule against pretexts, Marshallian federalism graduates to process federalism.

With a rule against pretexts, Marshall's federalism risks repeating another mistake of dual federalism: an artificial view of the way people understand themselves. This mistake would offend the very principle of responsible government that the no-pretext rule seeks to represent. Before the Civil War, Marshall's no-pretext rule would have directed Congress to act chiefly for economic or security reasons. The Civil War Amendments broadened the nation's responsibilities. They charged Congress and the federal courts with a duty to ensure fairness at the hands of the states for persons liberated from slavery. Because there was no moral difference either between blacks and whites or among varieties of injustice, the courts eventually extended the protection of the Civil War Amendments to whites, ethnic and religious minorities, political dissidents, women, the handicapped, homosexuals, and others. The courts thus construed the amendments as a promise to the nation's people that their state and local governments would govern them in ways they could respect as members of a national community.

This assurance was destined to affect, and did affect, the nation's private morality, for the nation's people included interracial couples, parents and children who resented official school prayers, couples who wanted to practice birth control, women who sought to end early pregnancies, and same-sex couples. By virtue of the Court's actions, the rights of these people were now officially worth the costs they imposed on the community at large, and that fact helped to change people's attitudes toward themselves and others. As a matter of private attitudes, Americans are not as racist, homophobic, or bigoted as they used to be.

The Civil War Amendments worked no fundamental change in one respect, however, for no meaningful line ever separated security and economic concerns from moral concerns, of either a public or private nature. Concrete actions have multiple dimensions. People do not act for purely economic as separate from noneconomic purposes. People typically seek wealth to live well and/or do good, and their moral and religious beliefs shape their conceptions of living well and doing good. Even if economic and noneconomic beliefs were separable for analytic purposes, empowering the national government to facilitate economic prosperity *and* granting its economic policies supremacy over conflicting state policies, economic and noneconomic, would effectively outlaw or marginalize beliefs or practices that obstructed national objectives, no matter the importance to affected groups of the interests sacrificed. Thus, in 1988 the Supreme Court upheld a decision of the U.S. Forest Service to build a six-mile road and permit timber harvesting on federal land near sites sacred to the Yurok, Karok, and Tolowa peoples of northern California.[69] A study commissioned by the Forest Service recommended against the road because an alternative route was available and the planned route "'would cause serious and irreparable damage to the sacred areas which are an integral and necessary part of the belief systems and lifeway of Northwest California Indian peoples.'"[70] For a 6-to-3 majority Justice O'Connor held for the Forest Service against a free-exercise challenge by the tribes. "Even if we assume that . . . the . . . road will 'virtually destroy the . . . Indians' ability to practice their religion,'" she said, "government simply could not operate if it were required to satisfy every citizen's religious needs and desires. A broad range of government activities—from social welfare programs to foreign aid to conservation projects—will always be considered essential to the spiritual wellbeing of some citizens, often on the basis of sincerely held religious beliefs."[71] As a constitutional matter, in other words, ends served by "a broad range of governmental activities" are simply more important to the constituent people for whom the Constitution speaks than conformity to "sincerely held religious beliefs."

O'Connor's statement effectively depreciates at least some, if not all, "sincerely held religious beliefs." It fits comfortably within a theory of the Constitution and Lockean liberalism generally that subordinates religious pursuits to economic pursuits and cultivates, by rewarding, virtues that are useful to the regime's ends. Diamond called these virtues the "bourgeois virtues" of a commercial republic; they include economy, sobriety, moderation, work, honesty, and prudence.[72] These virtues serve commodious life on earth free initially of sectarian and class war and subsequently also race war. Diamond's point was that the Large Commercial Republic reflected the Enlightenment's theory of "men at their very best."[73] This theory had economic and moral dimensions, and the integrated character of these dimensions in the lives of real people would make it irrational to vest a government with responsibility for some dimensions and not all. We can see this by asking how a government charged with advancing the peaceful life of industrious and prosperous men and women in a world market could be indifferent to the education of its people, their knowledge of and attitudes toward other cultures, their growing chemical and electronic addictions, the sexual morality of their formative years, and the racist, sexist, homophobic, and economic barriers to their equal opportunity.

Process federalism transcends the schizoid view of human reality by ignoring artificial lines between the inseparable dimensions of human life. By contrast, Marshallian federalism falsifies reality by pretending to separate what cannot be separated and fostering the myth that plenary national power over the economy and federal responsibility for civil rights and civil liberties leaves meaningful areas of autonomy for the states. And as it cultivates this myth, Marshallian federalism comes into conflict with its own interpretive method. If Marshall could reason from the specific powers of Congress and the president in foreign and military affairs to a general power of national security, and if later Marshallians could reason from Congress's specific economic powers to a general power over the nation's economy, nationalists can take these two general responsibilities (for the nation's security and economic health) as evincing an even more comprehensive responsibility: power to address all matters of national concern.

Though dual federalists deny any such power, history offers impressive testimony for it. Lincoln saw federalism as "the principle of generality and locality" (Message to Congress, July 4, 1861), and Publius suggested much the same in several places (2:8, 3:13, 9:55, 10:63, 12:78, 22:143, 27:171–172).[74] In the Constitutional Convention, the Virginia Plan would have granted Congress power "to legislate in all cases to which the separate States are incompetent, or in which the harmony of the United States may be interrupted by the exercise of individual Legislation." (May 29, 1786) This language remained in the draft document until it went to the Committee of Detail on July 24. When the committee reported to the Convention on August 6, it had replaced a general power with an enumeration of specifics. But the enumeration in Article I, Section 8 can be and apparently was seen as the framers' conception of what, in 1787, were matters of general concern. No less a present-day dual federalist than Randy Barnett acknowledges this point, albeit after an initial effort to deny it.[75] And the original reason for granting Congress any powers—the states' incompetence to deal with problems that concerned the whole—would support other powers as moral and technological change elevated other matters (like working conditions, education, race relations, the treatment of women, the civil rights and personal liberties of a mobile population, and treatment of the disabled) from local to national concern.

The remaining step to process federalism would be conceiving "national problem" to include whatever the national government recognized as worthy of the nation's attention. A dual federalist must reject this proposal, of course. She would seek a line between national and subnational problems that replicates her line between state and national spheres of authority. She would hold that even if violence against women or gun possession in school zones or partial-birth abortions or teen pregnancies may appear or actually be national problems in fact, problems in fact do not have to be problems in law—that just because something is a national problem does not mean that it must fall within the regulatory competence of the national government. On one interpretation of this proposition, it is beyond dispute. As a logical matter, a government does not have to have the authority it needs to address the problems of its people. The inadequacy of the Continental Congress to the nation's problems was what motivated the constitution of 1789, and the amending provisions of this constitution presuppose the possibility of future constitutional inadequacy. Yet if a constitution can be interpreted as adequate to the real problems of its people, why interpret it any other way? No one denies that constitutional language and history *can* be read to express a "principle of generality and locality." The only question is why not read constitutional language and history that way. What good would a states' rights definition of "national problem" serve?

This is the same question whether an argument from goodness or rightness can justify dual federalism generally. That argument has yet to appear because it cannot appear. Bear in mind that the dual federalist needs more than a policy argument; the question is not whether a particular social or economic problem might best be handled locally. Refusing to question this possibility would be tantamount to holding Congress infallible, and no one does that. The question is who finally decides between centralized and decentralized policy responses. Our dual federalist cannot rest with the thesis that it is unwise to centralize the response to a given problem, like partial-birth abortions. Such a thesis turns on whether a national program will achieve a balance of results that the nation will approve. This is a question whether national power ought to be exercised, not whether it constitutionally exists.

Our dual federalist would have to argue that a national program would be unlawful regardless of its material prospects, even if a multistate approach will fail, and notwithstanding the ambiguity of constitutional text and history. Her argument would be that although the relevant constitutional materials (history, text, precedent) admit different interpretations, and while interpretation *x* enables the government to ameliorate real national problems and interpretation *y* does not, the courts should choose *y*. The absurdity of this argument flows from the forum's requirement of a public reason and a connection between reason and good that disables what is admittedly bad for the country as a reason for its conduct. Thus there seems no good reason to deny that the Constitution embodies Lincoln's "principle of generality and locality." Marshall's interpretive method justifies this principal, and a process federalist can claim that this principle makes Marshall's no-pretext rule dysfunctional or pointless.

Process Federalism and the Constitution's Deepest Commitment

Finally, a process federalist can point to what we have seen as the implication of the Constitution's amendability coupled with humanity's inability to reject thinking for one's self on the basis of experience sharable in principle by humankind generally: the Constitution's ultimate commitment to a secular public reasonableness. A process federalist can claim that the object of this commitment is a process, not a substantive state of affairs, because fallible humanity can never be sure that what it thinks is good really is good.

We must now see whether Marshallian federalism can answer these objections.

7

WHY MARSHALLIANS SHOULD (BUT PROBABLY WON'T) WIN THE FEDERALISM DEBATE

We have examined different theories of what questions judges should ask when deciding state-federal controversies. Marshallian federalism asks whether Congress is pursuing authorized ends. Dual federalism asks whether and why Congress is substituting its policies for those of the states. Process federalism asks virtually no questions about state-federal boundaries. The ambiguities of the nation's constitutional text and history make responsible choice among these theories depend on an argument—a showing that one theory is best for the country. The formal requirements of a good argument eliminate dual federalism. The requisite argument must take place in a national forum and follow the principles of practical reason, and dual federalism cannot meet these tests. We must choose between the two kinds of national federalism. This chapter contends that Marshallian federalism should win this contest because Marshallian federalism belongs to an ends-oriented or welfarist understanding of the Constitution, an understanding that is superior to the rights orientation of process federalism.

The argument of this chapter is a theoretical argument, however, and whatever the theoretical merits of Marshallian federalism, widespread preoccupation with constitutional ends may cause more harm than good to the nation's politics. Those who see risks in an ends-oriented constitutionalism are in good company. They can cite Aristotle's suggestion that doubt about a constitution's ends can be a good thing. Doubts about a regime's ends can serve political unity by enabling different factions to pledge loyalty to the same regime.[1] At a time of deepening division in America, common possessions should be treated as gift horses, and clarity about the Constitution could destroy it as something all Americans would want to claim as their own. Critics of an ends-oriented constitutionalism can add that an ends orientation is itself anticonstitutional in view of the American founding's leading operational tenet: that between checking and balancing private interests and fostering patriotic self-sacrifice, the former is the better strategy for pursuing public purposes. This "better strategy" emphasizes individual rights conceived as exemptions from governmental power; it demphasizes desirable states of society (security, prosperity, fairness) that constitutional powers envision.

Positive constitutionalists have their own arguments, however. Two centuries of one culture war after another make it increasingly harder to believe that political conflict in America can be confined to negotiable economic interests. Nor can anyone deny the regime-level stakes in the current struggle between hidden-hand faiths (in God and The Market) and the Enlightenment faith in experiential reason. Clarity about constitutional ends could be a bad idea if it precipitated or worsened a regime-level struggle. But where such a struggle is irreversible, the quest for clarity offends no obligation of citizenship. I proceed to the case for Marshallian federalism.

Theories of Federalism and the Constitution's Character

Marshallian federalism belongs to a positive or ends-oriented view of the Constitution. It deals with state-federal controversies by asking not what rights the states might have but whether Congress is pursuing authorized national ends. Marshallian federalism thus presupposes a theory of national ends, a theory of "the kind of country the United States was intended to be." One theory of national ends is the Large Commercial Republic, a vision that Martin Diamond and Walter Berns derived from their reading of the constitutional text, the founding debate, *The Federalist*, and the philosophic tradition of which *The Federalist* is a part. This chapter returns to the suggestion of Chapter 3 that the Constitution's deepest commitment is a "politics of secular public reasonableness." My account of the Constitution is continuous with, not opposed to, that of Diamond and Berns. I contend, in other words, that while a secular public reasonableness does not entail the Large Commercial Republic, the latter's economic and cultural commitments (security, equal opportunity, fairness, mobility, moderate religiosity, experiential science, reasonable cultural pluralism) conform more closely to reason's demands than its various faith-based and social Darwinist alternatives. Most importantly, I agree with Diamond and Berns that the Constitution is much more than a constitution of government. A Marshallian views the Constitution as a set of institutional means to a desirable state of society, including the kinds of people who are at home in that kind of society. Because the Constitution would establish and ordain institutional means to good things—good government, to be sure, but chiefly a good way of life—the Marshallian constitution is a positive constitution.

By contrast, process federalism, with process constitutionalism generally, separates the Constitution from any specific way of life or any specific set of human qualities. Process constitutionalism sees the Constitution chiefly as an arrangement of governmental offices and functions. The rights of process constitutionalism are either rights to participate in the processes of government or rights against government. These rights against government are restraints on government's pursuit of security, prosperity, well-being, and other public purposes. Process federalism thus expresses a negative constitutionalism. Though process federalism would secure the rights of state functionaries (like state electorates and legislatures) to participate in the nation's governmental processes, and though the right to participate is a positive right, these rights are rarely abridged, and the academic founders of process federalism aimed chiefly at preserving judicial resources for protecting individual and minority rights from popular majorities. For the process federalist, the Constitution is "made for people with fundamentally different views." Process federalism classifies no specific social result as an object of constitutional duty; it views no social situation as an unconstitutional state of affairs. It assumes that conditions like the income gap, the rise of the Religious Right, the surge of antigovernment populism, and the segregation of public schools via "free private choice" are matters of constitutional indifference.

Marshall's rule against pretexts manifests the difference between Marshallian and process federalism. The former holds that the several powers of the national government envision specific public goods (the commerce power and allied powers envisioning economic prosperity, for example), and that when Congress uses these powers for other ends it acts unconstitutionally. The no-pretext rule assumes that Congress can misuse its powers even when acting in ways that threaten no protected individual right, no right of another national branch, and no state's right to participate in the nation's government. The only situation left to fall under a no-pretext rule would be Congress's seeking an unauthorized state of society—

formally, any state other than that adumbrated by powers enumerated in Article I and elsewhere, including the Civil War Amendments and the Nineteenth Amendment. Following Diamond and Berns, I have contended that these authorized goods are the benefits of the Large Commercial Republic (like prosperity and equal opportunity) and its associated personal virtues (like personal responsibility, honesty, religious moderation, and racial indifference). Process constitutionalism denies this or any range of substantive commitments. By dispensing with the no-pretext rule, process federalism implies that constitutional government can seek any state of affairs that does not violate protected individual rights and structural principles, and that constitutional government is concerned with people's behavior, not their attitudes or their character. The contest between process federalism and Marshallian federalism involves two sets of issues: the relative merits of positive and negative constitutionalism and whether process federalism perfects Marshallian federalism.

For Positive Constitutionalism

Process federalism represents negative constitutionalism; Marshallian federalism represents positive constitutionalism. Prove the superiority of one model of the Constitution as a whole, and you have an argument for the superiority of one theory of federalism.

The case for positive constitutionalism is complicated by cultural factors external to its merits. Positive constitutionalism emphasizes public purposes and relies on the virtue of public purposefulness among politicians and ultimately among voters. Though this kind of constitutionalism demands much of voters and politicians, public purposefulness is not altogether absent in America's consumer and rights-oriented culture; politicians, academics, and opinion leaders regularly profess it. But a sense of fallibility, a habit of self-criticism, and reluctance to impose on others are hallmarks of a genuine concern for doing the right thing (as opposed to doing one's own thing), and the increasingly doctrinaire character of the nation's political leadership exposes its avowed public purposefulness as more rhetorical than genuine. Moreover, an orientation to public purposes is essentially the prudential orientation of institutional planners and reformers ("framers," if you will), and, clearly, the nation has lost the capacity to produce and support institutional planners and reformers. One cause of this loss is the public purposelessness fostered by the founding's reliance on private economic incentives as integral to its solution to the problem of majority faction. A related factor is the profound interdependencies of a global economy that pressure the world's several peoples to surrender their self-directedness to a global oligarchy.

Positive constitutionalism also goes against dominant intellectual currents. Despite their long decline in modern metaethics, orthodox varieties of moral skepticism in academic law and the social sciences handicap any effort to channel intellectual effort from theories of negative rights to theories of constitutional ends. Thus, progressives and libertarians alike fear that orienting the Constitution to substantive public purposes will drain support from constitutional rights, especially rights associated with "free private choice" in matters that range from abortion to segregated schools. And a court-centered constitutional discourse associates things constitutional with rights instead of ends because American courts vindicate rights; for the most part, they do not order or exhort politicians to pursue constitutional ends.[2] Though I touch on these and related factors as I proceed, I shall not revisit all that I have said about them elsewhere, for they affect the political feasibility of a Marshallian approach, not its merits as constitutional theory. I can concede that the nation's political culture favors process federalism and negative constitutionalism and still argue that Marshallian federalism and positive constitutionalism are theoretically superior and even crucial to the Constitution's ultimate survival.

The case for positive constitutionalism can begin by noting that some rights are conceptually linked to governmental power while others are conceptually independent of governmental power. The First Amendment freedom of speech assumes governmental power as part of its meaning because the First Amendment says Congress shall make no law abridging speech. The Fifth and Fourteenth Amendments prohibit not loss of liberty but loss of liberty at the hands of government without due process of law. Rights whose meaning (not whose actual enjoyment) is independent of governmental power include rights to life, liberty, and the pursuit of happiness. These rights are conceptually independent of government because they make sense as normative for human conduct in a state of nature. You can believe that it is wrong to steal what others have worked for whether formal state institutions exist or not. The Declaration of Independence conflates rights to life and liberty with the goods that they are rights to and holds that "Governments are instituted among men" to secure these rights—these rights in their positive aspects; these rights understood as goods. Thus, government would not secure the *right* to life; the right is secured by God or Nature. Government would secure *life*, the good thing that the right is the right to.

The upshot of the distinction between rights conceptually linked to and rights conceptually independent of governmental power is that governments would not be instituted solely to secure the former. Governments would not be instituted to secure *constitutional* rights. Constitutional rights are rights against government, and no rational actor would establish a government solely or even chiefly for the sake of restraining it. No sane actor would make a government, a machine, or anything else for the sole or the chief purpose of restraining its operation or use. A chair that is hard to sit in may be good for laughs, but it would be a bad chair, and no craftsman as such would deliberately make a useless or dangerous chair just to be making one. While the enjoyment of goods like life and liberty can be an end of government, constitutional rights cannot be ends of government. I do not deny that a practice of "debate on public issues . . . [that is] uninhibited, robust, and wide-open" can be an end of government. For free speech is essential to the pursuit of public purposes by fallible actors, and where private forces would restrain public debate, government could secure public debate by restraining the forces that threaten it. But no one would establish a government solely or chiefly to stop *the government* from restraining debate. If stopping the government were the sole or the chief end in view, or if the risk of harm from government outweighed the prospects of benefits from government, no rational person would establish government in the first place.[3]

Those who deny the priority of ends over rights and the positive over the negative dimension of rights might shift from a conceptual to a historical claim. The claim would be that because the founding of the American Constitution was motivated largely by abuses of power in the states, the move to a limited national government was a move from more government to less government. This is Randy Barnett's understanding of the founding,[4] a view that is hard to square with the great emphasis in *The Federalist* on "energy in Government" and Publius's theory that responsible government educates the public to its true interests, contrary to the public's initial inclination if need be.[5] But even if we grant Barnett's thesis arguendo and say the framers transferred power from the states to the nation with libertarian intentions, an expectation of less actual government would not imply less constitutional authority to govern. The distinction here is between what actually happens and what legally can happen—what government actually *does* and what government is *authorized* to do. Less actual government (aside from what that might mean) is compatible with as much authority to govern as anyone would want. An expectation of less government would not conclude the question of constitutional authority—authority to govern more or govern less as contingencies demanded.

Barnett cannot successfully contend that the framers sought not only less government as a matter of national policy but also less government as a matter of constitutional authority. For to the extent that the framers intended less constitutional authority for the nation, they left more constitutional authority for the states, contrary to what Barnett describes as the framers' main intention: to cure state abuses of private rights by taking constitutional authority from the states. Yet even if the framers sought, for liberty's sake, to diminish all authority, national as well as state (a policy whose rationality I have denied in a critique of Barnett's thesis[6]), the founding was a move from one government to another, not from government to anarchy, and it would remain true that no sane actor would establish a government solely or mainly to limit it. A diminished government would still have some affirmative social good as its *chief* purpose, for if restraining the pursuit of that good were valued over the good pursued, establishing the government would be irrational. Move from the abusive state governments to the most modest of nightwatchman national governments, and an oft-quoted proposition of *The Federalist* would still hold: framers of "a government which is to be administered by men over men" should "first enable the government to controul the governed; and in the next place, oblige it to controul itself" (51:349). Powers and ends would come first; restraints and rights would come later.

Other critics of ends-oriented constitutionalism could claim that, as a historical matter, liberal thinkers from Locke to the authors of *The Federalist* conceived the protection of private rights as the end of government, and that since the rights in question were negative rights, like the right to be left alone in the enjoyment of one's property, liberal constitutionalism is negative constitutionalism.[7] This conclusion is arbitrary in several ways, as I have shown in a critique of Michael Zuckert's constitutionalism.[8] To begin with, so-called negative rights have a positive aspect, namely, the good to which a right is a right and from which a right derives its value to the person who claims the right. Thus, the right to life is valuable because life is valuable, and the enjoyment of life is the good envisioned by claiming the right. Moreover, honoring some rights means dishonoring claims to other rights, a fact that guarantees that all governments are redistributive governments, that all governments represent some background conception of both the good life and the good person, and that no government is open to "people with fundamentally different views." Thus, government must employ coercive taxation to fund the courts, police, prosecutors, and other agents of a rights-protecting regime. Government must take the property of latecomers (namely, their opportunities in nature and their natural liberty to preserve themselves as they see fit) in order to protect the property of first possessors. And a regime that purports to separate church and state and honor the freedom of religious exercise must discriminate against those religions that hear God demanding active efforts, including violence, to establish God's kingdom on earth right now. The faux separationist regime in the United States effectively establishes a range of those religions whose teachings either support or coexist with the worldview of the regime.[9] This establishment takes the form of tax subsidies and tax-funded services to domesticated religions and criminal sanctions against such undomesticated religious practices as polygamy, snake handling, and the ritual use of controlled substances.

In view of these realities, references to "negative constitution" or "constitution of negative liberties" flow either from moral skepticism, a failure of thought, or ulterior motives. The negative constitutionalist who is also a moral skeptic avoids talk of constitutional ends because, as a skeptic, she holds that ultimate ends are arbitrary. Yet she works in a field of discourse that must assume that some ends and corresponding practices and attitudes are, in reason, better than others; as a negative constitutionalist she herself assumes the superiority of a rights-protective regime. The liberal who holds that liberalism is committed to genuine diversity and open to fundamentally different views lacks reasons for preferring liberalism to antiliberalism; she also ignores the limits on toleration manifest in the criminal laws of liberal regimes. And normative theorists who know, yet refuse to acknowledge, that all government is redistributive are trying (albeit perhaps with public-spirited intent) to mask either their inability or their unwillingness to defend tax-funded services and benefits ("welfare") for some people but not all.[10]

Beyond the Large Commercial Republic:
A Politics of Public Reasonableness

Yet even if positive constitutionalism were superior to negative constitutionalism process federalists could claim, first, that their position is the logical culmination and thus the perfection of Marshallian federalism, and second, that a nationalist who stops short of process federalism lapses into dual federalism, an altogether indefensible position. To answer these challenges to Marshallian federalism, I remind the reader of what Marshallian federalism represents.

Chapter 3 of this book outlines Martin Diamond's argument for the Large Commercial Republic as the state of affairs that constitutional government in the United States was designed to achieve and maintain. Diamond derived his theory partly from his understanding of what a good society is, partly from historical sources like Locke and the founding debate, and especially from his view of the social conditions and attitudes requisite for the system to function as described in *The Federalist*. Thus, a legislature in which many different interests regularly formed shifting coalitions would be an unlikely reflection of an agricultural people divided by hostile religious commitments. Accordingly, Diamond reasoned, the Constitution presupposes an urban-industrial society whose people are religiously moderate—a society, as Berns was to put it, where people typically subordinate their religious beliefs to their economic interests.[11] In addition to religious moderation, this people, at its best, would display the "bourgeois virtues" of honesty, reliability, and initiative. Their conception of lawful gain would reflect the value they placed on voluntary exchange. They would find gratification in the discipline of, and take pride in the talent for, acquiring property. In this way they would display the virtue of "acquisitiveness," a socially responsible and beneficial disposition that Diamond distinguished from the vice of "greed," the desire merely to hold property with no purpose other than the exclusion of others.[12]

Diamond's was a Hamiltonian view of constitutional ends. Hamilton's view has been controversial since the founding, and it can hardly be more than one of several conceptions of the American Way. The controversial nature of any conception of constitutional ends imposes a special burden on positive constitutionalists: they must find an end of government that (1) can claim constitutional provenance and (2) is rationally imperative under any circumstances where choice is materially possible. A "secular public reasonableness" meets these requirements. This secular public reasonableness is a quality of a people's political psychology, conceived as a virtue. A people would possess this virtue to the extent that the public generally or some trusted leadership stratum habitually formulated and justified policy on the basis of experiences about ends and means that are sharable in principle by human beings as such, without need of divine revelation, and regardless of special inherited characteristics like race, gender, and sexual preference.[13]

At least four sources attest the constitutional provenance of this secular public reasonableness: the Declaration of Independence, the nation's founding experience, *The Federalist*, and the constitutional text.[14] *The Federalist* No. 1 appeals to this virtue when it calls on Americans to rise above "accident and force" and demonstrate mankind's capacity for "establishing good government from reflection and choice." The Declaration of Independence manifests this virtue when, from "a decent respect to the opinions of mankind," it declares the causes of the revolution by submitting "facts . . . to a candid world." With its guarantees for speech and press and its proscription of a national religion, the First Amendment would secure key conditions for a politics of public reasonableness. Article VI would do the same by banning religious tests for public office. The Fourteenth and Nineteenth Amendments extend the sphere of public reasonableness to all races and genders—and arguably, therefore, to any other inherited characteristic that does not affect the capacity for reflection and socially responsible choice. The conceptual connection between law and reason and the instrumental nature of American law combine to make the due process clauses of the Fifth and Fourteenth Amendments general guarantees that all laws in the United States will satisfy some level of public reasonableness.[15] Article V, the amending provision, establishes lawful ways to exercise a right that the Declaration of Independence infers from a premise of human equality: the right of people to alter or abolish government that "becomes destructive of ends" for which government is established.

Article V warrants further comment. Article XIII of the Articles of Confederation was the precursor of Article V, and the fate of Article XIII reveals a crucial relationship between public reasonableness and established institutional forms. In *The Federalist* No. 40 Madison showed how public reasonableness can dissolve a legal procedure designed to institutionalize public reasonableness itself. Here Madison tried to justify the decision of the Constitutional Convention and the Continental Congress to establish a new constitution through a ratification process that bypassed Article XIII. This decision was no small matter, for Article XIII was the law of the land, and its message was clear and emphatic. It declared that "the articles of this confederation shall be inviolably observed by every State" and that no changes be made "at any time . . . in any of them" save by agreement of Congress and "the legislature of every State." Though Congress had initially charged the Convention with "revising the articles," implicitly in a manner consistent with Article XIII, which called for action by every state legislature, Congress later acted on the Convention's recommendation to ratify the new constitution not through Article XIII but through ad hoc constitutional conventions in as few as nine states. Here was a clear violation of the prevailing constitution, and the Antifederalists were quick to charge that it incorporated a principle of lawlessness in the very founding of the new system.[16]

Madison disagreed; he denied that proposing the new ratification procedure was a lawless departure from Congress's charge to the Convention. He emphasized the part of Congress's charge that called for a constitution "'adequate to the exigencies of government and the preservation of the Union,'" the very union that Article XIII declared "perpetual." The Articles had proved inadequate to the exigencies of government and the preservation of the Union. The old constitution had failed; the people had a right to alter or abolish it; and Article XIII had proved altogether unworkable as a way to exercise this right. The Confederation's principle of unanimity was an "absurdity," said Madison, an absurdity that would have subjected "the fate of 12 states to the perverseness or corruption of a thirteenth," as little as "1/60th of the people of America" as a whole (40:262–263). Here Madison assumed that he was referring to one people, not thirteen, and that a rule that allowed a small fraction of the whole to veto a large majority denied the very principle of equality that justified government by consent of the governed.

Madison also assumed a connection between law and experiential reason when he refused to follow a rule that experience had proved to have absurd consequences. He went on to say that "in all great changes of established government, forms ought to give way to substance" because "a rigid adherence" to institutional forms that fail to work as intended negates "the transcendent and precious right of the people 'to alter or abolish their governments as to them shall seem most likely to effect their safety and happiness.'" He added that when institutions break down, "it is impossible for the people spontaneously and universally, to move toward their object," and that "it is therefore essential, that such changes be instituted by some *informal and unauthorized propositions*, made by some patriotic and respectable citizen or number of citizens" (40:265; his emphasis).

Both common sense and the Constitution support Madison's position. The Constitution's amendability presupposes the fallibility of the authority (We the People) for whom the Constitution speaks. Yet the Constitution's claim to supremacy in Article VI implies no higher authority than the constituent sovereign. If this sovereign is fallible, therefore, it must be fallible relative not to higher political authority but with respect to its objects—justice, the common defense, the general welfare, and so on. The sovereign authority may have erred regarding the means to these ends or in its conception of these ends or both. Either way, the Constitution, by allowing amendments, implies that sovereignty can't guarantee success. Madison thus assumed (1) that constitutional ends are real goods about whose meaning and whose means established authority can be wrong; (2) the sovereign wants real goods, not apparent goods; and (3) if experience suggests better conceptions of constitutional ends or means, the sovereign wants appropriate institutional change.

Madison's justification for bypassing Article XIII thus indicates that the fallibility that calls for a path to constitutional change extends to the legally established procedures for constitutional change. These procedures are as fallible as any other constitutional provisions, and when they fail, as Article XIII clearly had failed, they cease to be legally binding. Madison's position was a matter of common sense, "plain reason," he called it: "where the several parts [of a lawful order, like Congress's charge to the Convention] cannot be made to coincide, the less important should give way to the more important part: the means should be sacrificed to the end, rather than the end to the means" (40:259–260). From the ends-oriented and nationalist position that Madison assumed in *The Federalist* No. 40 (and which one could reasonably impute to the generation of 1789), Article XIII was intended to function as a way to change the established constitution if and when the established constitution ceased to be an instrument of the national interest. Madison assumed an audience that saw the established constitution as more than a way for each of several contracting parties to protect its own separate interests. This assumption was evident in Madison's judgment that it would be absurd to follow Article XIII and allow Rhode Island to veto change that was good for everyone else. What made this course an "absurdity" was the national interest—not the interests of Rhode Island as a separate entity.

If anyone was guilty of "lawlessness," therefore, it was the Antifederalist who assumed that what was "absurd" was to be determined by standards that were entirely local. This assumption would have degraded the law by rendering it fundamentally arbitrary. It would also have degraded the people of Rhode Island as "perverse[]," to use Madison's word. For had they been fully conscious of their position, they would have believed what no one can coherently claim: that one can rightly serve one's perceived good at the expense of others since what is good and right are solely matters of local opinion.[17]

Plain reason notwithstanding, Madison's position raises difficult questions. If a constitutional prescription can cease to be law when it proves inadequate to reasonable conceptions of its function, what one promises when swearing to "preserve, protect, and defend the Constitution" becomes unclear. Can one, in strictness, preserve a constitution (all of it?) that allows its own amendment? Can one preserve a constitution that incorporates principles (moral and prudential) that, under the right circumstances, allow for, if not demand, wholesale change by means other than its formal procedures? These questions implicate the further question of just what the Constitution might be. To an ends-oriented constitutionalist this question involves what the Constitution's essential commitment might be. And since the Constitution's amendability prompts this question, an ends-oriented constitutionalist would be seeking an end that is in some sense an unamendable institution—a practice or a virtue that an observer cannot understand a people as having abolished or abandoned. I contend here that this unamendable institution is a secular public reasonableness—the disposition to establish and maintain "government from reflection and choice" that the *The Federalist* No. 1 treats as the nation's distinguishing virtue (1:3).

Whether the Constitution's essential aim is a secular public reasonableness depends in part on whether an actor (individual or collective) can choose to live without reflection and choice about ends and means on the basis of what is evident (evidently good and feasible) in principal to everyman at all times where reflection and choice are physically possible. (I say where physically possible because few would talk about reflection and choice on a rack, or shackled at the bottom of a cave, or under the gun.) This question has many elements, two of which press immediately: (1) whether an actor can choose to live without reflection and choice; and (2) whether the object of public choice can be some good other than what is generally evident independently both of God's revelation (to some, not all) and inheritances that all persons do not share, like specific race, gender, or sexual orientation.

Of course, a society can lack the capacity to establish and maintain government by reflection and choice. A community that has this capacity at one stage of its history can lose it to any number of forces. An enlightened people need not remain enlightened. It can suffer foreign military, economic, and cultural domination. It can suffer the ruinous consequences of constitutional and policy mistakes, like the framers' over reliance on a strategy of private incentives that played its part in killing chances for the trusted leadership community that, as we have seen, Madison saw essential to a people's capacity for constitutional reform. Both an individual and a group can commit suicide or simply run out of steam. But whether government from reflection and choice survives, a people that has a choice cannot actively choose to live under any other government. The reason lies in the logic of action that I outlined in Chapter 3.[18]

Aristotle observed that people act for what they think is some good. Desired goods, coupled with beliefs about means, constitute the "reasons for action," and to describe someone's conduct as an act an observer would have to have sufficient empathy with the putative agent to appreciate how he could believe that the result of his conduct was a good thing for him. Consider a happy three-year-old who drank antifreeze because, youngster that he was, he associated the liquid's pleasing color with sweetness, and he confounded what is good with what he liked. We could not accurately say the child committed suicide, for we normally assume that life is better than death and because the child (being happy ex hypothesi) would have no reason to believe otherwise. Generalizing from this example, we would not describe an event as an act unless we had reason to believe that the bodily motions of the prospective actor were calculated to cause a change in the world that the actor regarded as a good. In short: no perceived and desired good, no reason; no reason, no action. If one could abandon reason—which abandoning would be an act to which the logic of action applied—one would have a reason for abandoning reason. But this would be absurd: if one has a reason for doing something one doesn't abandon reason by doing it, notwithstanding further consequences that no one would choose.

Suicide might seem a counterexample to this conclusion, for abandoning life would be abandoning reason, and I concede, arguendo, that suicide may sometimes be choiceworthy—or at least that, at a modest level of analytic refinement, we can see some events called suicides as "acts." But prospective suicides (the persons) choose not to live—not to live at all. They choose not to live lives of any description, including lives without reason. So choosing suicide is choosing to end life, not to live without reason. Another counterexample might be a choice to destroy one's frontal lobes. I admit arguendo that one could describe this event as a choice. Such a choice would result in one's living without the capacity to think and choose. But even if we could call the event that resulted in the loss of frontal lobes an act (as opposed to a suffering, an event caused by mental illness), we could not say, after this act was completed, that "the actor" chooses to live without the capacity to think. Because choice implies thought, and because "the actor" in our example can think no longer, we cannot say that he chooses to live without thinking. So, I submit, choosing to live without thinking and choosing is impossible. See someone who is "living" without reflection and choice and you see a victim of accident and force, a person who is suffering, not acting, even if he is suffering the consequences of his own past acts.

Something similar holds for an act of submitting to authority—I mean a total submission, to any authority, including the authority of those who claim to speak for God. Total submission to God's authority would be living without reflection and choice; God's will, however known, would suffice as a reason for action. But, as Adam's story indicates, human beings cannot see obedience to God, standing alone, without more, as an unquestioned good. Because the human mind is fallible and because bad things happen or seem to happen to human beings as a result of forces beyond their control or expectations—but not beyond God's—the human beings cannot avoid thinking that God is capable of willing things that, standing alone, without more, are bad. This fact of human thought about God is reflected in the hymn that says "God moves in mysterious ways his wonders to perform." Had sacrificing Isaac not seemed a bad thing both to Abraham and the readers of Genesis, or had Abraham thought God incapable of following through with the sacrifice, no one could understand obedience to God's command as a test of Abraham's piety. To count as an act, therefore, submitting to God would have to be seen as a means to some additional result, which result would be a good apparent to human beings independent of God's special revelation. Abraham's obedience is best seen as a test of Abraham's faith in God—that is, his belief that God would reward his obedience with a good, something good or apparently good for Abraham, something other than the fact of God's satisfaction with an obedient subject. And, indeed, God had promised Abraham such a good. For Abraham's obedience, God had promised Abraham fame as the father of a great nation (Genesis 12:1–3). God did not have to tell Abraham that fame as a great founder (or the inherent value of being a great founder) was a good thing. Had Abraham assumed otherwise, he could have made no sense of God's offer. God promised Abraham something that Abraham and the readers of Genesis believed good on the basis of their worldly experience. And when Abraham met the test involving Isaac, God reiterated the promise (Genesis 22:15–18).

The same principle applies to God's later promise of everlasting life: its status as a good depends on worldly experiences of man as man independent of special revelation. Though life after death is not a worldly good, its value to mortals presupposes that they experience some good in their worldly existence, such that they can believe that life is a good. Because people are generally attracted to life and pleasure and averse to pain and death, we can understand why people would be attracted to a pleasant life after death. So even though life after death would be an otherworldly good, its intelligibility as a good depends on worldly experiences.

Where submission to authority makes sense as an act, therefore, the actor must appreciate the goodness of the promised or expected result. Yet *total* submission—submission without reservation—precludes relying on one's own judgment about what is good; total submission precludes thinking for oneself about anything, means or promised end. If when people act they act for the sake of what they think is some good, one cannot actively decide to submit totally to any authority, including God's authority. This is not to say that one cannot submit, for one can be forced to submit. Perhaps some people can live totally submissive lives, a possibility I deny but that I need not question here. My contention here is that one cannot *actively choose* a life of total submission, and the reason one cannot do this lies in what it means actively to choose.

Thus, people cannot choose to live without thinking about how to live. An individual cannot willingly abandon a life of thinking for oneself, and a community cannot willingly abandon a life of deliberation among its fully franchised members, however small the membership circle. American constitutional history, the American constitutional text, and the nature of action converge upon the conclusion that a commitment to an experiential or secular public reasonableness is the nation's essential institutional commitment. This is the one constitutional institution, in a capacious sense of "constitutional institution," that cannot actively be amended out of existence. Though this commitment has an antiauthoritarian aspect that favors a democracy of some kind, democracy need not preclude an electorally accountable elite of a kind that the American framers claimed to be.[19] It does preclude a nobility that rules by hereditary entitlement, as indicated by Article I, Section 9 and Article IV, Section 4. It also precludes a theocracy, as confirmed by the ban in Article VI on religious tests for office.

Because a regime of public reasonableness is practicable only to the extent that its physical environment includes periods of respite from life-threatening emergencies that leave no time for reflection and no options for choice, its many conditions include manageable if not more-or-less peaceful international and domestic environments, along with natural conditions and levels of technology that permit life without predation and exploitation at home and abroad. Because a regime of public reasonableness presupposes human fallibility about ends and means, it presupposes the possibility of scientific and moral error, and therewith the possibility of progress toward scientific and moral truth. Because this regime presupposes that humans can interrupt the natural course of things in accordance with their intentions, it assumes a measure of autonomy for human thought from the commands of forces like God, History, and The Market. It also assumes psychological mechanisms (individual and collective) that enable thought to determine physical movement (of the body and the body politic). Whether these conditions actually do or can obtain are matters of controversy that I leave aside. It suffices here that constitutional discourse presupposes them.

How then is the Large Commercial Republic related to the regime of secular public reasonableness? The Constitution's essential commitment to public reasonableness places the Hamiltonian constitution in a larger context, a context of reflection and choice about the meaning of, and the means to, the common good. And the norms of this larger context shape the Hamiltonian constitution. In this larger context, for example, individual rights are conceived as functional to public purposes.[20] Property rights make sense because property is a secular good that responds to needs (essentially of the human body or the body-centered self) that transcend cultural, sexual, racial, and other differences, and (where people are moral equals) because property is supposed to be exchanged on a voluntary basis, as reasons are supposed to be. Yet property is protected not on the theory that property is whatever one successfully appropriates, that property precedes justice, and that justice means protecting property.

In this larger context defined by the requirements of reason, property does not precede justice; justice precedes property. That justice precedes property is indicated by the fact that no one claims that justice demands protection for everything that anyone might successfully appropriate; that the labor of persons held in slavery is "successfully appropriated" does not make slavery just. Some prior sense of justice shapes what counts as property because claims must be justified claims to count as rights.[21] Since justified means publicly justified, property is protected on the basis of assumptions about what is good for the community: that taxing and spending to maintain the many institutions for protecting property (including criminal sanctions that deprive latecomers of their natural rights) increases the wealth of the community as a whole and expands the opportunities for all of the community's responsible members.[22]

Something similar would hold for speech. Because speech can impose burdens on the community and its members, speech would be protected not because it feels good to "express yourself," but because deviant and critical speech can serve a function crucial to the community's hopes for objectively better conceptions of, and means to, public purposes.[23] The community in question would be one of people who admit that they can be mistaken both in their conception of the common good and the means thereto. The fallibility of these people would commit them less to any particular view of the good life than to an attitude and a process of inquiry: collective reflection (public giving and testing of reasons) and choice.

Yet this process would be more than a mere process. It would be seen and valued as a truth-seeking process, a process for getting closer to a true understanding of the common good. It would be valued also as a disposition or a virtue—an admirable way for both a community and an individual to be. Thus, in the beginning of the The Federalist No. 1 Hamilton can take pride in this alleged disposition of his readers, and to clarify the meaning of this disposition, he contrasts it with local prejudices and attachments "little favorable to the discovery of truth" (1:4–5). This view of the scope of free speech parallels the previous argument here against states' rights. The main reason substantive states' rights are hard to accept is that they serve no national end. They impose costs on the nation that no one can justify to the nation. For justifying something to the nation involves linking it to a national end, and substantive states' rights, unlike speech and property rights, play no role in the pursuit of national ends.

If the Large Commercial Republic serves the larger end of a secular public reasonableness, then the latter is the ultimate constitutional end. This would make a secular public reasonableness the end of Marshallian federalism, that kind of federalism which is committed the ends of constitutional government. Constitutionally speaking, therefore, the Large Commercial Republic is a national commitment only insofar as secular public reason can reaffirm it as the best feasible version of the good life.

Does Process Federalism Perfect Marshallian Federalism?

We have seen that one argument for process federalism flows from Marshall's interpretive method in *McCulloch*. Here Marshall understood enumerated specifics to authorize general aims. No one doubts Marshall's way of thinking when it comes to national security. Nor has anyone shown why Marshall's way of thinking should not apply to national prosperity, especially since no one claims that the several enumerated powers signify ends in themselves. No one claims, for example, that the activity of regulating commerce is a good thing, independently of results like good order and prosperity. But just as specific powers make sense in light of national security and national prosperity, authorizations to pursue these ends evince a still more general authorization. We have seen that Lincoln understood this more general authorization as a "principle of generality and locality." By this principle, state and local governments handle state and local matters, the national government handles national concerns, and no a priori categories separate state and local matters from national concerns.

On all these points, Marshallian federalism would have to agree with process federalism. Process federalism goes on to insist, however, that in concrete cases courts should defer to Congress on what constitutes national concerns and that the states have rights only to participate in the processes of national decision. Marshallian federalists hold for an additional right: a right against pretextual uses of national power. This would be a judicially enforceable right. Process federalism responds that under the principle of generality and locality, no rule against pretexts applies to Congress because the fact that Congress addresses a problem makes that problem a national problem. If process federalists are right about this last point—that Congress's concern suffices to establish a problem as a national problem—Marshallian federalism would evolve into process federalism by virtue of Marshall's own approach to constitutional interpretation.

We saw in Chapter 6 that another argument for process federalism is premised on the General Welfare Clause of Article I, Section 8. Under the Supreme Court's Hamiltonian reading of this clause, Congress can tax and spend for any purpose that respects the separation of powers, the states' process rights, and protected individual rights. So even where Congress might lack authority to regulate directly (regarding school curricula, drinking age in the several states, and the sexual morality of the nation's teens, for example), Congress can regulate indirectly by attaching regulatory conditions to the receipt of federal funds by state and local governments. Add what Congress can do through taxing and spending to what it can do through direct regulation, and nothing remains for a ban on pretexts to do. So, on this account, restraints on Congress's aims can take no constitutional form other than structural rules and the constitutional rights of individuals and minorities.

Our process federalist could claim further that her position makes more sense than Marshallian federalism even from a concern for a restricted set of substantive national ends. For if the Constitution's essential institutional commitment is a politics of secular public reasonableness, the Constitution is committed to a process—secular public reason. This end, our process federalist would say, is adequately served by judicial enforcement of structural rights that secure the fora and processes of decision, rights to participate in these fora and processes, and substantive rights that elevate reason over other authorities, like rights against religious tests and establishments, against abridgment of speech and press, against racial discrimination, against arbitrary laws, and against prejudicial adjudication.

Finally, we saw in Chapter 6 that another argument for process federalism amounts to a prediction that a common law culture will eventually make Marshall's no-pretext rule practically meaningless. Because stare decisis requires judges to describe decided cases as evincing rules that apply to future cases, stare decisis will transform past findings of pretextual conduct into fixed categories of pretextual acts. And since fixed categories of pretextual acts would be equivalent to fixed categories of substantive states' rights, Marshallian federalism would lapse into dual federalism, an irrational outcome. Process federalists can thus argue that the Constitution is best served by eschewing a theory of constitutional ends and enforcing individual constitutional rights, the separation of powers, and the states' process rights.

A Marshallian Response

A Marshallian's way of thinking about the enumeration of powers would incline him to describe American federalism as Lincoln did: a "principle of generality and locality." But a Marshallian will disagree that whatever any congressional majority might call a national problem is, in fact, a national problem. As an expression of ends-oriented constitutionalism, Marshallian federalism attaches substantive content to the idea of the American nation. By "national problem" a Marshallian will mean a state of affairs that is problematic in view of the kind of country the Constitution committed the nation to be—problematic to people who aspire to that ideal state of affairs. This ideal is the Large Commercial Republic, as long as reason continues to affirm its supremacy among affordable ways of life. Citizens of this ideal republic value security and prosperity over racial, religious, and ideological purity. They favor eyewitness testimony over hearsay and therewith science over tradition, and they reject notions of privileged evidence of either scientific or moral truth. As we have seen, these people are committed ultimately to a politics of secular public reasonableness. But this cannot mean that Congress has unrestrained power to declare a national problem. For a politics of secular public reasonableness entails many restraints on power; it excludes appeals to racist, sexist, and other antiliberal values, as we have seen. If the U.S. Congress sees gay marriages in Massachusetts as problematic on religious grounds, acknowledged or not, a Marshallian court should disagree, for gay marriages pose no evident threat to the wealth of people taken at random or to the disposition of people to reason with each other on the basis of goods that all can appreciate. What is problematic to a Marshallian are threats to a regime of secular public reasonableness, like the rise of the Religious Right, faith in "market forces" that is blind to the lessons of experience, unreflective moral skepticism in the social sciences and law, populist depreciation of science and scientific "elites," racism masked as color-blindness, homophobia masked as tradition, and dogmatism of all varieties—moralistic and scientistic.

Accordingly, a Marshallian would disagree that, under the General Welfare Clause, Congress can tax and spend for anything it might want. The scope of the General Welfare Clause was the subject of a post-ratification debate between James Madison and Alexander Hamilton. The received view of Hamilton's position is that of our process federalist: the general welfare means what Congress wants it to mean, and Congress can tax or spend for any purpose that does not violate structural norms and protected individual rights. Madison charged that Hamilton's reading would render the national government one of unlimited powers. He claimed that the general welfare should comprise no more than ends connected to the specifics of Article I, Section 8.[24] In *United States v. Butler* (1936),[25] the Supreme Court seemed to accept Hamilton's position, and this theory survives to the present. But Hamilton's position need not be read as it has been received. From the spending he proposed in his Report on Manufactures, he could have agreed to link the spending power to the remaining provisions of Article I, Section 8, *if* those provisions had been seen as justifying broad powers over the nation's economy and defense. Thus, he spoke of spending for "whatever concerns the general interests of learning, of agriculture, of manufacturers, and of commerce." From these applications one could deny that Hamilton supported a power to spend for any and every one of Congress's possible aims.[26]

An excessively broad power would find no necessary support even in the received view of Hamilton's position. Any power to spend for the general welfare would still require that Congress act on a reasonable view of the general welfare, and no theory could count as reasonable that refuses a reason to any segment of the responsible adult population. This requirement would rule out spending for racist, sectarian, and other antiliberal purposes. For there could be no reason a socially responsible black, female, or gay American could see for excluding him or her from the benefits and protection that the state extends to persons generally. Finally, the fact that Hamilton and Madison disagreed creates the need for choice among their theories. A responsible choice must flow from a coherent argument in the national interest, and an ends-oriented argument is the only kind that could fit this description—for, once again, rational actors establish governments not to limit them but for the sake of substantive goods.

An admissible theory of the general welfare would conceive the general welfare as a state of affairs in which each responsible citizen had the capacity to pursue his or her reasonable wants in reasonable ways. Reasonable wants pursued in reasonable ways would mean goods and methods that appeared or could appear reasonable to people generally, not just to the isolated individual or to some closed racial or religious group. The Aryan Nation, the Caliphate, and the Christian Commonwealth would therefore be out as versions of the general welfare, while the Large Commercial Republic could be in. This is so because human beings typically share the material needs that the Large Commercial Republic elevates over spiritual and aesthetic needs specific to particular races and religions.[27]

I say the Large Commercial Republic "could be in," not "definitely is in." I emphasize this because elevating material over spiritual and aesthetic needs can be defended only by a comprehensive theory of the human condition, which theory would in turn need defending. This effort would begin by treating liberalism as one worldview among many, including worldviews grounded in specific racial and religious identities, like the Aryan Nation, the Caliphate, and the Christian Commonwealth. A defense of comprehensive liberalism would have to show its superiority to any and all forms of comprehensive antiliberalism. Such a showing is possible even if we can question it after the showing is made. Let me explain in terms of the difference between bourgeois liberalism and its present competitors: the difference is the value that liberalism aspires to place on experiential reason in public affairs.

This difference is decisive if it is indeed true that (1) people act (when acting in an unequivocal sense) for the sake of what they think is some good; (2) actors believe that the goods for which they act are real goods; and (3) human actors are fallible both in their conceptions of real goods and the means thereto.[28] If these propositions are true, it follows that (4) no mature and fully aware person can actively choose to abandon a life of self-critical thought about (a) what is good and (b) how to pursue it. Thus, no reasonable person could define the general welfare in a manner that subordinated experiential reason to other authority. Nor, in light of her fallibility and her resulting need to test her views by other opinions, could any reasonable person subordinate everyone else's reason either to her preferences or even to her reasoned conclusions. Authorities other than reason include such argument stoppers as the imperatives of racial purity and the putative commands of God, History, The Market, and The Volk. They even include the authority of reasoned conclusions themselves. Because reasoned conclusions can always be wrong, they cannot reasonably achieve axiomatic status or avoid the need for continuing reaffirmation.

Reasoned conclusions in behalf of bourgeois liberalism can be wrong even if we cannot affirm their error. Liberalism's fallibility justifies that regime's continuing self-criticism and openness to antiliberalism. And though no regime is fully open to its antithesis (liberalism is open to anti-liberal thought and speech, not action), liberalism's openness to antiliberal thought and speech does take risks that antiliberal regimes are unwilling to take.

The Constitution's commitment to secular public reasonableness means Congress cannot legitimately tax and spend in ways designed to subordinate experiential reason to religious and racist commitments. Nor could Congress tax and spend in ways that had the subordination of reason as an unintended but foreseen effect. This last point follows from the Constitution's instrumental nature. The Constitution seeks more than government that behaves by the letter of the rules; it seeks a quality of life centered on a willingness to justify public policy to all who seek justification. Government has an affirmative duty to pursue this quality of life, and government can fail in this duty either intentionally or unintentionally. Thus, Congress could not lawfully fund school voucher programs whose purpose or effect was teaching children that their most important consideration in the voting booth, the business transaction, or their dealings with others generally was their race, their religion, their sexual orientation, or anything other than their capacity to exchange reasons about what to believe and how to live. Whether particular fiscal measures will have such effect or are so motivated are questions of fact that courts must decide. The Constitution cannot guarantee good-faith answers to these questions. But in situations where following the Constitution is possible (I won't pause here to discuss the problem of constitutional emergencies), the Constitution requires that the questions of motive and effect be asked and answered honestly, or as honestly as conditions permit without doing more harm than good.

At this point process federalists can return to their claim that if the Constitution's ultimate end is a politics of public reasonableness then the Constitution is committed ultimately to a process, not to a specific substantive state of affairs. A Marshallian could respond that this argument for process federalism separates reasoning from its objects, and in so doing it overlooks key presuppositions of practical thought. Man-made processes are identified by the ends that they are widely expected to serve, as we can see by the relationship between open windows (states of affairs) and the process of opening windows. Because the physical steps requisite to opening windows are indeterminate, the procedural component of window opening can always be described by the name of the action-type itself, which incorporates the teleological component of the action type. Thus, "window opening" can describe the procedures of pushing a button, lifting a sash, turning a crank, and even tossing a chair. Accordingly, being committed to a specific process (a process with a name) is being committed to the end or ends to which the process is means. Public reasonableness, a virtue, manifests itself in the practice or the process of public reasoning; concrete instances of public reasoning must always be about something; and public figures, including judges, typically claim that what they are reasoning about is some aspect of the common good (justice, the common defense, the general welfare). American judges cannot claim to be faithful to the Constitution at the same time that they affect an interest solely in "the law," to the exclusion of justice and the general welfare, for if the Preamble has any meaning at all, the Constitution authorizes only those enactments that aim at reasonable conceptions of ends like justice and the general welfare.

To a Marshallian, constitutional processes seek ends like national security and prosperity as real goods; constitutional processes are ways to improve chances that government will serve the true interests of its people, as opposed to the people's immediate and unreflective inclinations.[29] The same holds for secular public reasoning, the process that manifests the virtue of secular public reasonableness. This virtue is itself a good way to be, an essential element of human well-being, conceived as the capacity (the skills, the energy, the inclination) and the opportunity to act on what reason discloses as probably good for one's self.[30] As a process, self-critical reasoning with others on the basis of generally shared and shareable experiences is a means to better conceptions of preambular ends and scientifically sounder means to those ends. Commitment to this process reflects an appreciation of human fallibility, a desire for real goods as opposed to apparent goods, and an aversion to illusions regarding a good life and how to approximate it in practice.

Unable to conceive an aimless (man-made) process, the process federalist must find some end or ends that her processes serve. She has three options: (1) national ends conceived as real goods to which public opinion must be reconciled, ends of the kind served by Marshallian federalism; (2) the separate ends of individual states of the union, conceived either as state governments or the people of each state in its sovereign capacity; or (3) the more-or-less immediate wants of the individual persons who constitute the nation's population, wants conceived as demands that must be reconciled to each other through bargaining, not to good-faith conceptions of real public goods, arrived at through reflection and deliberation.

If process federalism were aimed at preambular ends, process federalism would be Marshallian federalism. Process federalists must therefore reject the first option: a concern for public purposes. Process federalism, a nationalist position, must also reject its processes as means to the interests of the states as separate political communities. Nor can a nationalist who is also a democrat allow that government can justly possess rights that are separable from the interests of its citizens, persons who are free to move from their home state to any other state. A nationalist believes further that the most important interests of individual citizens are best represented by the national government. Three reasons support this belief. First, people who think for themselves cannot choose to abandon their capacity to examine locally prevalent beliefs against standards that they assume have more than local content. Second, because people who do think for themselves cannot knowingly and deliberately choose to surrender their capacity to think for themselves, they cannot surrender their capacity to act on what they think best, including their right to leave home for some part of the country where they think they can live better, a right presently guaranteed to Americans by Article IV, Section 1 and the Fifth, Ninth, and Fourteenth Amendments. And third, the Supremacy Clause implies that reflective and mobile individuals are better represented by the national government than by the government of any state.

This leaves the third option for our process federalist. From her position within a general view of the Constitution as a set of processes, she must say that the affirmative ends served by those processes are the several ends of the nation's individual citizens. Yet a Marshallian agrees with a version of the same proposition: that government should serve the interests of the nation's individual citizens. All forms of nationalism respect the individual. The Thirteenth Amendment promises that the national government will secure a limited right of the individual to her own body. And Sections 1 and 5 of the Fourteenth Amendment promise that the national government will secure the individual's right to move from place to place. Because this right includes the right to leave what would otherwise have been the place of the individual's formative years, the right to move implies a further right of the individual to define herself in terms not of this or that local conception of justice and well-being, but of justice and well-being themselves. And since the civil right to move is a right to move within the territorial jurisdiction of the national government, the right to move suggests ultimately that the United States is a place, perhaps the place, where the individual can seek and act on true conceptions of justice and well-being themselves. Our question thus becomes what marks the difference between these two versions of the same proposition: that government should serve the interests of the nation's individual citizens.

The Marshallian, following *The Federalist*, holds that government should serve the *true* interests of individuals, as opposed to their unreflective inclinations, and therefore that a fully responsible government—a government responsible *to* the public *for* doing the right thing—will lead the public to appreciate an approximation of the public's true interest. If our process federalist is to distinguish herself from our Marshallian, she must implicitly deny the distinction between the public's true interests and the public's momentary inclinations and say that government can aggregate and perhaps redirect private preferences from one apparent good to another but not elevate them toward some real good. This move would raise two questions: whether process constitutionalists can justify their unavoidable discrimination among apparent goods, and whether they can avoid supposing a difference between real and apparent goods.

Process and Substance

Whether goods are apparent or real, the process constitutionalist will discriminate among them. No one holds that constitutional government can accommodate whatever ends any and all individuals might seek. At present, the Constitution can serve only those individual ends that are compatible with constitutional processes and reasonable versions of the civil rights and civil liberties that the Constitution promises to all. As any number of zealously antiliberal groups in the United States can testify, a constitution that requires respect for liberal rights is a constitution that discriminates against antiliberalism.[31] This constitution denies the right of antiliberals to live in exclusively black or white or Christian or Jewish or straight or gay communities, with the legal power to remain as they are—forcing them all the while (through taxation and conscription) to support lives they may detest. To this the process federalist can reply that while the Constitution presently excludes some communities, the Constitution's amendability makes present limitations on admissible preferences a contingent matter—and that, in principle, therefore, constitutional government includes all possibilities, even antiliberal ones. This conclusion, if true, would excuse the process federalist from the burden of developing a substantive theory of constitutional ends.

But this conclusion would be false. Whether retail, as when the nation ratified the Bill of Rights, or wholesale, as in the shift from the Articles of Confederation to the Constitution, amending a constitution either leaves some institutions in force or moves from one set of institutions to another, and no identifiable institution can be open to all ends, no matter how important the given ends may be to some. Thus, no end seems more important to billions of people worldwide and may objectively be more important to everyone than favor in God's eyes. Yet we have seen that because men and women cannot actively cease thinking for themselves, they cannot voluntarily submit to clerical authority in all things. No man-made constitution could be compatible with God's will in all things. The limited and fallible mind of human being's puts the course of God's will beyond their ability to know. And human fallibility guarantees that the beliefs and expectations embodied either in written laws or in informal patterns of behavior will eventually prove inadequate to the course that God wills. The same holds for humanity's ability to cope with the contingencies of an unmanageable material reality. Sooner or later, man-made processes will fail the test of what is compellingly right or good—unless the test were radically subjective, in which case we could not talk about either a "test," or the reflective process called "testing," or human kind (the reflective kind) itself.

The Constitution's amendability has no effect on this conclusion (inevitable institutional failure), for we have seen limitations in the principle of amendability itself. We have seen that the Constitution's amendability represents an awareness of fallibility, a desire for progress away from opinion and toward knowledge (of ends and means), and corresponding commitments to both the virtue and the practice of secular public reasonableness in public affairs. This is an unamendable commitment, yet it is far from innocuous. It excludes racist and sectarian ends to which billions of people worldwide and many millions of Americans seem profoundly committed. Secular reason may even doubt that secular reasonableness can be the controlling virtue of any viable regime.

Though a politics of secular public reasonableness might tame religion and subordinate it to commerce, it could not ignore the unintended consequences of a life dominated by the pursuit of wealth. It would have to acknowledge that while the quest for unlimited economic growth fosters industry and science, it also fosters self-indulgence, a sense of self-importance, the myth that each is the best judge of his or her own interest, the reduction of public reason to a mask for self-serving calculation, and a moral skepticism that displaces self-critical reason with the Scylla of nihilism and the Charybdis of dogmatism. Responses to these unintended consequences have included calls for government support of religious institutions and activities (especially in education) that foster the private morality requisite for the decency of a commercial society. Because this support would be less than strictly consonant with liberal principles, it would take the form of what Berns once described as "indirect aid that has the effect of supporting religion without raising it above the subordinate position to which . . . [liberalism] consigns it."[32]

Such secular use of religion would raise a further concern, however: the viability of liberalism itself. To be effective, the use of religion for secular ends must be disguised as respect for religion, for while a true believer could accept a divine command to render unto Caesar that which is Caesar's, no true believer could let Caesar decide the question. No true believer could accept Caesar's command to "render[] unto Caesar whatever Caesar demands and to God whatever Caesar permits," which was Berns's pithy summation of liberalism's relationship to religion.[33] The use of religion for secular ends thus implies a society of a benighted and observant many and an enlightened and secular few. The few, moreover, would have to be invisible to the many. The regime of secular public reasonableness would thus depend on a hidden and manipulative elite and the effectiveness of what an impolitic candor could only describe as a lie.

Unable either to accept this outcome in principle or to administer it in practice, we would be left with daunting questions. How can a social order that encourages production for the sake of consumption keep self-serving calculation from destroying public reasonableness? Or, to put it differently, how can a regime that liberates all-too-common pursuits maintain a focus on the common good? On the other hand, what alternative is there to the bourgeois society? How could a regime that restrained common pursuits avoid falsifying reality—a dangerous thing for those who hope to cope with reality? We can tell someone to sacrifice for the common good or resist exploiting others only if doing the right thing is itself a means to what she can see as a greater good, like glory or salvation. But our experience with these alternative ends is very ugly (the religious wars of the sixteenth and seven-teenth centuries, for example), and, in any event, we cannot help doubting the real bases for these alternatives (things like glory and salvation) and therewith their true value.

I mention these difficulties here not to explore them but to point out that a process of secular public reasonableness is fraught with problems and far from open to all outcomes or open only to uncontroversial ones. Because it enables some ends and precludes others, it is unavailable to the theorist who would avoid formulating a substantive theory of constitu-tional ends. The question for our process theorist would be how she can justify her inevitable choice among ends. She cannot find a process that accommodates all wants; she cannot justify excluding wants that her cho-sen process excludes unless she can justify the process; and she cannot justify the process unless she can defend it as means to some good that is either momentarily unquestioned (like prosperity in America) or unques-tionable (like the truth about the best feasible way of life).[34] But if she did see her favored process as means to some specific public good or range of public goods, she would be an ends-oriented theorist, and her jurispru-dence would contain a rule against pretexts.

A process constitutionalist might then respond that for most of Ameri-can history national federalism has served liberal ends and states' rights federalism has served antiliberal ends, and that enforcing the Bill of Rights and the Civil War Amendments serves the same result without a theory of substantive ends that might defeat the Constitution as a sym-bol of national unity in an era of ideological division. Though prudence may well recommend this rights-protective strategy under some condi-tions, treating process federalism as a strategy for pursuing constitu-tional ends concedes the theoretical superiority of ends-oriented consti-tutionalism. Process federalism as a strategy also concedes the superiority of Marshallian federalism, if only as the position of an elite that shifts from the language of ends to the language of rights when addressing the uninitiated. Once again, as with the secular use of religion mentioned above, we would have a solution that involved a public-spirited and enlightened elite and a self-interested, benighted mass. The few (like Washington, Hamilton, and Marshall) would be ends oriented, and the rest of us would be rights oriented. How the rights-protective society of the many could regularly produce, recruit, and support an ends-oriented leadership stratum—and why the deserving few would willingly serve the many—would remain the preeminent constitutional problems they have always been.[35]

Two further points must be made here. Securing participatory rights and negative liberties cannot substitute for affirming substantive constitutional ends, and securing negative liberties and process rights is impossible without an active concern for substantive constitutional ends. Unconnected to public purposes, rights to have one's wants represented and to exempt one's beliefs and activities from public power assume that each person is the best judge of what he wants and that government exists to aggregate people's wants. The belief that each person is the best judge would be true only for persons who had no contradictory wants and could have no contradictory wants. And since every conscious want presupposes the real as opposed to the apparent goodness of what is wanted, one who claims to be an authority for his wants would also have to claim final and perfect knowledge of the difference between real and apparent goods. That no minimally reflective person claims such final knowledge and consistency of wants falsifies a claim that is all too common in a consumer culture, the claim to know what one wants. Consumers usually just pursue (apparent) wants without self-conscious claims that their wants belong to sets of coherent wants that correspond to what is truly worth wanting. In sum, people cannot be assumed to know what they want, for they can want contradictory things, and they lack what their actions presuppose: final knowledge of what is best for themselves.

Sensitivity to this fallibility of wants marks the difference between what Madison called "a scheme of representation" that "refine[s] and enlarge[s] the public views" and a system that aggregates apparent individual preferences—the difference between government as responsible for reconciling public opinion to its true interests and government as merely responsive to public opinion.[36] Because no one knowingly seeks merely apparent goods, everyone who reflected on that fact would want to know the difference between real and apparent goods. Since this knowledge would be pursued through dialectical and self-critical processes, people need good-faith debate with others, and all such debate implicates common goods. Thus, I cannot say in dialogue with others (real or imagined others) what I might propose privately (and falsely) to myself: that the good is my dominion over others. By submitting my beliefs to the criticism of others I switch from goods that I enjoy at the expense of others to goods that I can enjoy in community with others. I switch from purely private to legitimately private and thus to public purposes—from standing apart to being a part.[37] This dialectical progression from a state of isolation and assertiveness to a state of membership and quest may not occur in the history of any given individual or community save by aspiration, for people do not inevitably live lives that reflect the logical structure of their wants. But the corresponding civic orders are different orders, and they cannot substitute for each other. If there could be a regime of infallible creatures pursuing their unreflective wants, it would be different from a regime of fallible creatures seeking what is worth wanting. A rights-securing regime is no substitute for an ends-oriented regime.

Even if a practice of securing rights were fit for fallible creatures, its survival would depend on its embrace by an ends-oriented regime. Domestic protests can prolong wars; security for first possessors can destroy opportunities for deserving latecomers; due process can free killers who kill again. Securing rights is a costly practice. This practice is administered by judges and elected executive officials and paid for by taxes. The representatives of the people appoint these judges and impose these taxes. Ultimately, therefore, no matter what "fine declarations may be inserted in any constitution," "the only solid basis for all our rights" is "the general spirit of the people and of the government," as Hamilton said.[38] Equal opportunity is a pipe dream in a society of racists, sexists, and homophobes. Crime-ridden communities will not respect the rights of criminal defendants. So a regime that is committed to securing rights will pursue the social conditions favorable to public support for the rights secured. Social conditions hospitable to rights are pursued not through the rights themselves, but through the powers to regulate and to tax and spend. These powers are expressly dedicated to public purposes. So equal opportunity and the attitudes requisite to realizing it as a state of society have to be conceived as aspects of preambular ends like justice and the general welfare. The practice of honoring rights depends on whether securing rights serves public purposes that include pride in sacrificing for rights that display our interest in truth and our capacity for reflection and choice.[39] Whether rights are positive or negative, a constitution that actually secures their enjoyment will be a positive constitution.

As it happens, the U.S. Constitution itself, as written, compels no clean separation between rights as exemptions from power and rights as provisions of power. For at least a thirty-year period beginning in 1966, the Supreme Court read the Fourteenth Amendment as empowering Congress to enact laws that maintained the social conditions for respecting individual and minority rights.[40] This was an apt reading of the Constitution, for the Civil War taught or should have taught Americans that honoring rights is a practice whose maintenance can require unvarnished governmental power. Notwithstanding the Supreme Court's dual federalist opinions in the *Civil Rights Cases*[41] and *Boerne v. Flores*,[42] a positive constitutionalist would read the Civil War Amendments as empowering the nation's policy-making branches to disregard states' rights as needed to achieve and maintain a national political culture that values each individual on the basis of his or her contribution or potential contribution to national security and prosperity. I turn to this point in connection with our final problem: whether Marshallian federalism risks dual federalism.

Marshallian Federalism and Dual Federalism

The process federalist claims that, in practice, Marshall's no-pretext rule amounts to dual federalism. If proved, this charge would sink Marshallian federalism, for dual federalism is indefensible in a national forum. We have seen that three related arguments support the charge that Marshallian federalism amounts to dual federalism. The first contends that a no-pretext rule would be a form of dual federalism, for the rule would do more than direct the national government to its proper ends. The rule would imply that the states can pursue ends that the nation cannot pursue, and though Marshallians would avoid specifying ends reserved to the states (lest they ossify into exemptions from national power), a category of ends "reserved to the states" would remain a genuine concept of constitutional law. The second argument holds that, like dual federalism, Marshallian federalism separates the economic, moral, religious, and other dimensions of human self-understanding that are united in lived experience, and that this artificial dispersion of unified elements serves only to mask, and thus avoid responsibility for, the moral implications of all judicial decisions. Finally, *Garcia* federalists can claim that in a common law culture Marshall's no-pretext rule would lead to a body of precedents that would eventually amount to categorical restraints on national power.

The answers to these charges involve Marshall's interpretive method and the Constitution's commitment beyond the Large Commercial Republic to a secular public reasonableness. Marshall's interpretive method justifies viewing federalism as a principle of generality and locality that leaves the national government responsible for all national problems. National problems are conditions—material and attitudinal—that undermine constitutional ends. And a secular public reasonableness is the Constitution's ultimate end. This end is a republic of mutually responsible persons—persons who try to answer requests for reasons with submissions about what is good and what works that seem reasonable to all on the basis of common experience. This test excludes racism, sexism, homophobia, and dogmatic zeal of all forms: ideological, religious, and antireligious. Acts that fall into these categories defeat the nation that the framers described as rising above accident and force and acting from reflection and choice. We can reject this claim of the framers as a human possibility no more than we ourselves can choose to live without reflection and choice.[43] Congress cannot tax, spend, or regulate, if either the purposes or the foreseeable effects of its acts fall into antiliberal categories. Antiliberal measures are unconstitutional not just because they offend constitutional rights but also because they defeat an end (secular public reasonableness) that national authorities are, in reason and implicitly by oath, compelled to pursue.

A no-pretext rule should function to keep Congress faithful to its proper ends, not to reserve power to the states. Consequently, a no-pretext rule need not imply that the states can do things that Congress cannot do. A no-pretext rule would exist in a context that includes the Civil War Amendments and the Nineteenth Amendment, and the ends promised by these amendments and their enforcement provisions should preclude antiliberal state policies. From an ends-oriented view, a grant of constitutional power imposes a duty to exercise that power as needed to secure the end for which the power was granted.[44] Even if the ends promised by the Civil War Amendments were merely negative liberties, the material and attitudinal conditions for honoring those liberties could be approximated and maintained only by exercises of government's regulatory and fiscal powers. So even if *Lopez* should be read to reserve school discipline to the states, both Congress and the Court would have a duty to stop the states from achieving this or any other end through measures that manifested racism, sexism, religious (or antireligious) bigotry, and other forms of antiliberalism. Though dual federalists might choose to read *Lopez* as "reserving school discipline to the states," no one will contend that *Lopez* must be read that way, and a nationalist judge will not read *Lopez* that way.

We come finally to the question whether a no-pretext rule in a common law system would produce precedents that functioned as categorical states' rights. The force of a case as a precedent case is offset by the fact that different judges can and regularly do interpret precedent cases differently.[45]

Justice Thomas reads *Brown v. Board of Education* as barring racial classifications whose sole aim is either to prevent or to promote black and white children being educated together.[46] Justice Stephen Breyer sees a racially integrated education as the promise of *Brown*.[47] In *Whitney v. California*,[48] Justices Edward Sanford and Louis Brandeis held importantly different views of the "clear and present danger test" announced in *Schenck v. United States*[49] And Chapter 3, above, discusses the dual federalist and nationalist readings of *Gibbons v. Ogden*. Compounding differences over how to describe the rule of a precedent case are differences over the weight to accord the rule in constitutional litigation where, after all, the touchstone of authority should be the constitutional text, not what judges have said about the text.

But because "Justice" and the "blessings of Liberty" are ends of constitutional government, and since stare decisis can serve justice and liberty only sometimes (for no one claims old courts are infallible), normative status and weight should attach only to cases that can be construed to advance justice and liberty. The Court in *Lawrence v. Texas* (2003)[50] would hardly have advanced anyone's liberty in standing by *Bowers v. Hardwick* (1986).[51] Moreover, since the rule of a case is typically debatable, the rule of a case should be formulated to advance justice and liberty. Justice Breyer's formulation of the rule in *Brown* is demonstrably better than that of Justice Thomas because the undoubted influence of private attitudes on electoral behavior and therewith ultimately all governmental behavior precludes hope for color-blind government where political power is in race-conscious private hands. In sum, since no real good can possibly be served by fabricating a priori categories of states' rights, a rule of precedent that flowed from a concern for justice and liberty could not produce a corpus that functioned as categorical states' rights. Though categorical states' rights can easily emerge from the practice of stare decisis, they cannot do so consistently with the values (justice and liberty) that justify that practice. Sometimes the only way to avoid unwanted consequences is to be aware that they can easily materialize.

What Lies Ahead?

Neither the Constitution nor its history sends a clear message regarding the meaning of American federalism. Whether the American union is one of separate political sovereigns or one united people, whether national

powers should be broadly or narrowly construed, whether states' rights restrain national power—answers to these questions call for an argument.
This argument must be submitted to a national forum, and it must invoke
a nationally recognized good whose best conception would apply to the
states through a national agency. The forum thus condemns states' right
federalism before its argument even begins. The current political success
of states' rights federalism therefore has nothing to do with its intellectual
merits, for it has none. If common sense governed constitutional debate,
Marshallian federalists and process federalists would be the only contes-
tants in the arena. And if victory depended solely on theoretical considerations, Marshallian federalism would win, for it alone is consistent with
the Constitution's assumptions regarding the pursuit of real goods by fallible actors.

Yet the pursuit of public goods by fallible actors involves a relationship
between leaders and followers that may have obtained at the American
founding but now seems utopian. Madison describes the founding situation
as one in which "patriotic leaders" enjoyed the "enthusiastic confidence of
the people" as external danger and "a universal ardor for new and opposite
forms" repressed "the spirit of party" and "stifled the ordinary diversity of
opinions on great national questions" (49:340–341). Madison's reference to
the ardor for new forms echoes Hamilton's famous observation in *The Federalist* No. 1 that "it seems to have been reserved to the people of this
country . . . to decide whether societies of men" can rise above "accident
and force" and establish "good government from reflection and choice" (1:3).
Madison's reference to patriotic framers is complemented by Hamilton's
boast in *The Federalist* No. 9 that American constitution makers are more
competent than the lawmakers of old. Ancient democracies "were kept in a
state of perpetual vibration between tyranny and anarchy," he says, while
our salvation lies in a new "science of politics" that includes "balances and
checks," independent courts, and the enlarged orbit of government that
Madison elaborates in *The Federalist* No. 10 (9:50–51). Madison predicts that
the founding's coincidence of patriotism, trust, and competence will fade to
be replaced by the new system of checks and balences as foreign threats re-
cede and the nation lapses into politics as usual (49:41). Though Marshall
accepted the new science of politics, his ends-oriented approach to states'
rights and his promise against pretexts assume that some policy makers and
judges will be actively concerned with the public purposes that national

powers envision. Today the leadership situation that Madison attributed to the founding is far beyond realistic hopes. And it is Marshallian federalism's great misfortune that it presupposes a relationship of trust between the general public and a leadership community that pursues the public's true interests in a civil and self-critical way.

I have argued what I set out to argue: that states' rights federalism is indefensible, that the only real debate is between Marshallian and *Garcia* federalism, and that Marshallian federalism deserves to win the debate. I have conceded throughout, however, that Marshallian federalism would be hard to maintain, especially against the multiple fallacies of the rights-oriented constitutionalism that the framers themselves installed as central to their hopes for a politics of reason. This negative constitutionalism makes the practice of Marshallian federalism all but impossible today. Although the only intellectual issue is between the two forms of nationalism, the only likely debate is between process federalism and states' rights federalism. I conclude this book with a prediction of what will come if states' righters win this debate—a prediction that builds on what Michael Greve and Erwin Chemerinsky have said about what motivates today's states' righters.[52]

States' rights federalism in our time will not mean what it meant in the nineteenth century. Because the states cannot hope to govern business corporations gone global on the shoulders of modern technology, states' rights in our time will achieve what the original states' righters feared most: rule by a monied elite. This monied power will become a government unto itself whose logic precludes the idea of social justice and makes government an agent of those who were lucky enough to get there first. These lucky ones are called "first possessors." What they control is called "property." Official coercion to secure property from third parties is called "justice." And social justice, including equal opportunity, by the visible hand of public-spirited authority, is called "theft." The new power denies that its distinctions merely rationalize government by accident and force (government by accident because first possessors were first by chance, and government by force because government forcibly restrains late comers from the holdings of first possessors). The new power forgets its property-securing theory of justice long enough to justify itself by appealing to what's good for all, including latecomers. The theory is that protecting the property of first possessors creates more opportunities for latecomers who, if they have better ideas or work harder, will overtake those ahead of them, as impersonal markets determine. When this theory fails in practice, however, government will be powerless to ensure opportunities for latecomers, for the new monied power will have crippled the nation's old governments.

I say governments, not just the national government. States' rights federalism will weaken all of the nation's governments, state and federal. As the global oligarchy expands beyond the control of the old American governments, new governments will emerge, for oligarchy, like all forms of government, claims whatever power it needs to realize its aims. The new governments will have an international reach, as do such of its forerunners as the World Trade Organization and the European Central Bank. This will be the Large Commercial Republic globalized—the Large Commercial Republic become an axiom and as such finally separated from and destructive of the deepest commitment of its founding, a politics of public reflection and choice. Thus does states' rights federalism prepare for power far removed from what Judge Vinson calls "our federalist system." And thus will the American population finally lose what little remains of its capacity for rational self-examination and meaningful constitutional reform.

NOTES

Introduction

1. William S. Livingston, "A Note on the Nature of Federalism," *Political Science Quarterly* 67, no. 1 (March 1952): 81–82.
2. This statement will be qualified later, but not withdrawn. I note also that "We the People," a preambular phrase, need not imply democracy, a form of government, for history provides many examples of peoples' installing nondemocratic rule.
3. Alexander Hamilton, James Madison, and John Jay, *The Federalist*, Jacob E. Cooke, ed. (Middletown, CT: Wesleyan University Press, 1961), No. 45, p. 309. References to *The Federalist* hereinafter will be designated with the paper number followed by a colon and the page numbers of Cooke's edition. Thus, No. 45, p. 309 will be "45:309."
4. *The Federalist*, 1:5–6. Hamilton says that critics of the proposed constitution are apt to forget "that the vigour of government is essential to the security of liberty; that in the contemplation of a sound and well informed judgment, their interest can never be separated; and that a dangerous ambition more often lurks behind the specious mask of zeal for the rights of the people, than under the forbidding appearance of zeal for the firmness and efficiency of government."
5. See Sotirios A. Barber and James E. Fleming, *Constitutional Interpretation: The Basic Questions* (New York: Oxford University Press, 2007).
6. See Walter Berns, "The Meaning of the Tenth Amendment," in Robert A. Goldwin, ed. *A Nation of States: Essays on the American Federal System* (Chicago: Rand McNally, 1961), 130–131; Malcolm M. Feeley and Edward Rubin, *Federalism: Political Identity and Tragic Compromises* (Ann Arbor: University of Michigan Press, 2008), 25–26.
7. See The Declaration of Independence; see also Justice Holmes, dissenting in Lochner v. New York, 198 U.S. 45, 76 (1905).
8. See esp. Walter Berns, *The First Amendment and the Future of American Democracy* (New York: Basic Books, 1976), chap. 1, esp. 9–15, 21–28.

9. I.e., "private" lives that society and the public authorities recognize as lawful and worth supporting by the institutions of civil society, institutions that depend on taxes.

10. Robert K. Faulkner, *The Jurisprudence of John Marshall* (Princeton, NJ: Princeton University Press, 1968), 5–6, 20–24, 134–147.

11. Sotirios A. Barber, *Welfare and the Constitution* (Princeton, NJ: Princeton University Press, 2003), 44–46, 53–55, 106–117. 146–147. See also Stephen Holmes and Cass R. Sunstein, *The Cost of Rights: Why Liberty Depends on Taxes* (New York: Norton, 1999), 113–116, 139–147, 152–158, 183–188.

12. See William H. Rehnquist, "The Notion of a Living Constitution," *Texas Law Review* 54 (1976): 704–706.

13. See Barber, *Welfare and the Constitution*, 113–114, 122–124.

14. For a suggestion that this was the aim of Rehnquist's federalism revival, see Erwin Chemerinsky, *Enhancing Government: Federalism for the 21st Century* (Stanford, CA: Stanford University Press, 2008), 227.

15. Berns, "The Meaning of the Tenth Amendment," 141.

1. Why the States Can't Check National Power

1. Florida v. Department of Health and Human Services, 2011 WL 285683 (N.D. Fla.), at 10. Upheld in relevant part by the U.S. Court of Appeals for the 11th Circuit, August 12, 2011; see http://www.uscourts.gov/uscourts/courts/ca11 /201111021.pdf (accessed 10/11/11), esp. 166–171.

2. *The Federalist*, 45:309.

3. 2011 WL 285683 (N.D. Fla.), at 10, 38.

4. Id., at 39.

5. See id., at 33–34.

6. Id., at 44 n.30.

7. He could propose, equivalently, that upholding states' rights is an element of the general welfare, and a more important one than goods like security and prosperity.

8. 2011 WL 285683 (N.D. Fla.), at 33–34.

9. See William S. Livingston, "A Note on the Nature of Federalism," 81–82; for a recent confirmation of Livingston's account of federalism as a juridical concept, see Feeley and Rubin, *Federalism*, 12, 16.

10. 426 U.S. 833.

11. Special Message to Congress, July 4, 1861, in Roy P. Basler, ed., *Abraham Lincoln: His Speeches and Writings* (New York: Grosset & Dunlap, 1946), 604.

12. The Court overruled *Usery* a decade later, in *Garcia v. San Antonio Metropolitan Transit Authority*, 469 U.S. 528 (1986). But the states' rights logic of *Usery*— states' rights as *exemptions* from otherwise plenary national power—reappeared in the so-called commandeering cases, New York v. United States, 505 U.S. 144

(1992) and Printz v. United States, 521 U.S. 898 (1997). Chapter 4 will distinguish properly termed "states' rights" cases, like *Usery* and *Printz*, from cases that serve dual federalist ends not by carving exemptions from national power but by defining national power narrowly to minimize encroachments on the states' reserved powers. Cases that exhibit the definitionist strain of dual federalism make up all but a handful of dual federalist cases and include famous cases like *Dred Scott v. Sanford*, 60 U.S. 393 (1857), *Hammer v. Dagenhart*, 247 U.S. 251 (1918), and *United States v. Lopez*, 514 U.S. 549 (1995).

13. Gonzales v. Raich, 545 U.S. 1.

14. For another opinion that the act exceeds the commerce power, see Commonwealth of Virginia v. Sebelius, Civil Action No. 3:10CV188, U.S. District Court for the Eastern District of Virginia, Memorandum Opinion, by Judge Henry E. Hudson, esp. 21–24 (Dec. 13, 2010).

15. See Justice Thomas's dissent in *U.S. Term Limits, Inc. v. Thornton*, 514 U.S. 779, 846–850 (1995).

16. Gary Wills, *A Necessary Evil: A History of American Distrust of Government* (New York: Simon & Schuster, 1999), 68–69.

17. Id., 209–218.

18. Texas v. White, 74 U.S. 700, 724–726 (1869).

19. Joseph Story, *Commentaries on the Constitution of the United States* (Durham, NC: Carolina Academic Press, 1987), 708 [Bk. 3, chap. 44, sec. 1001].

20. See James E. Fleming, *Securing Constitutional Democracy: The Case of Autonomy* (Chicago: University of Chicago Press, 2006), 200–205.

21. For a discussion of constitutional emergencies that replays the debate between ancient and modern constitutionalism, see Clement Fatovic, *Outside the Law: Emergency and Executive Power* (Baltimore: Johns Hopkins University Press, 2009), esp. 253–276.

22. Robert Barnwell Rhett was a leader of the secessionists (the "fire eaters") in South Carolina for the three decades prior to the Civil War. A six-term member of the U.S. House of Representatives, he was elected to the U.S. Senate on Calhoun's death in 1850. He resigned from the Senate in 1852 to protest his state's refusal to secede from the union in that year. Rhett's influence in South Carolina politics is largely credited with forcing Calhoun to move to the right on the states' rights question in the late 1820s. For his version of the contract theory, see William C. Davis, *Rhett: The Turbulent Life and Times of a Fire-Eater* (Columbia: University of South Carolina Press, 2001), 39–42, 53–54.

23. See Smith v. Allwright, 321 U.S. 649 (1944).

24. The nation is a collectivity. Its voice can't be an aggregate of the voices of its members. It can only be what its most authoritative statements, usually its official documents, say. If most Americans are racists, they are unwilling to say so in the nation's most authoritative documents. This fact suggests that what

Lincoln called "the better angels of our nature" (Basler, *Lincoln's Speeches and Writings*, 588) is a real dimension of the way people actually understand themselves.

25. 17 U.S. 316, 421.

26. Id, at 403–405.

27. Id., at 405, 408, 415–417; Faulkner, *Jurisprudence of John Marshall*, 194–195.

28. 17 U.S. 316, 408–409; see also Barber, *Welfare and the Constitution*, 96–100, 132.

29. 17 U.S. 316, 421.

30. See Gerald Gunther, ed., *John Marshall's Defense of McCulloch v. Maryland* (Stanford, CA: Stanford University Press, 1969), 18–19; Mark R. Killenbeck, *M'Culloch v. Maryland: Securing a Nation* (Lawrence: University Press of Kansas, 2006), 141–158 (quoting from Madison's letter to Spencer Roane of Sept. 2, 1819, at 154–155); Ernest A. Young, "Just Blowing Smoke? Politics, Doctrine, and the 'Federalism Revival' after Gonzales v. Raich," *2005 Supreme Court Review* (Chicago: University of Chicago Press, 2006), 30–31; Robert F. Nagel, *The Implosion of American Federalism* (New York: Oxford University Press, 2001), 75.

31. Letter to Spencer Roane, Sept. 2, 1819, in Gaillard Hunt, ed., *The Writings of James Madison* (New York: Putnam's, 1908), 8:450–451.

32. 17 U.S. 316, 421.

33. See Hoke v. United States, 227 U.S. 308 (1913); Gonzalez v. Carhart, 550 U.S. 124 (2007).

34. See Ronald Dworkin, *A Matter of Principle* (Cambridge, MA; Harvard University Press, 1985), 34–57; Michael S. Moore, "A Natural Law Theory of Interpretation," *Southern California Law Review* 58 (1985): 338–349, 352–358; Barber and Fleming, *Constitutional Interpretation*, Chaps. 6–7.

35. Moore, "A Natural Law Theory of Interpretation," 291–294.

36. Ronald Dworkin, *Taking Rights Seriously* (Cambridge, MA: Harvard University Press, 1977), 132–137.

37. For this interpretation of Dworkin's criticism of concrete originalism, see Barber and Fleming, *Constitutional Interpretation*, 79–98.

38. See id., 105–107.

39. Faulkner, *Jurisprudence of John Marshall*, 194–195.

40. See Garcia v. San Antonio Metropolitan Transit Authority, 469 U.S. 528, 550–551, 554 (1985); Jesse H. Choper, *Judicial Review and the National Political Process: A Functional Reconsideration of the Role of the Supreme Court* (Chicago: University of Chicago Press, 1980), 171–179; Herbert Wechsler, "The Political Safeguards of Federalism: The Role of the States in the Composition and Selection of the National Government," *Columbia Law Review* 54 (1954): 553, 559.

41. See John Hart Ely, *Democracy and Distrust: A Theory of Judicial Review* (Cambridge, MA: Harvard University Press, 1980), 48–54.

2. John Marshall and a Constitution for National Security and Prosperity

1. 17 U.S. 316.

2. A commercial or economic purpose for enactments under the Commerce Clause is presently a requirement under *United States v. Lopez*, 514 U.S. 549 (1995). Consistently with *Planned Parenthood v. Casey*, 505 U.S. 833 (1992) Congress could protect late-term fetuses under a theory of Section 1 of the Fourteenth Amendment rejected by the Rehnquist Court in *DeShaney v. Winnebago*, 489 U.S. 189 (1989) and a theory of Section 5 of the Fourteenth Amendment rejected by the Rehnquist Court in *City of Boerne v. Flores*, 521 U.S. 507 (1997). Members of the states' rights block joined the majority in both *DeShaney* and *Boerne*.

3. United States v. Morrison, 529 U.S. 598.

4. United States v. Darby Lumber Co., 312 U.S. 100 (1941).

5. Garcia v. San Antonio Metropolitan Transit Authority, 469 U.S. 528 (1985).

6. 60 U.S. 293 (1856).

7. 247 U.S. 251 (1918).

8. Barber, *Welfare and the Constitution*, 38–41; Wills, *A Necessary Evil*, 75–82.

9. 198 U.S. 45.

10. 17 U.S. 316, 407–408, 416; Faulkner, *Jurisprudence of John Marshall*, 33–38, 134–147.

11. 17 U.S. 316, 407.

12. David N. Mayer, "'Necessary and Proper': West Point and Thomas Jefferson's Constitutionalism," in Robert M. S. McDonald and Theodore J. Crackel, eds., *Thomas Jefferson's Military Academy: Founding West Point* (Charlottesville: University of Virginia Press, 2004), 56–59, 63–66.

13. Writing in the popular press on June 30, 1819, under a pseudonym, Marshall said the Jeffersonian critics of his *McCulloch* opinion were attempting "by construction, essentially to reinstate that miserable confederation whose incompetence to the preservation of our union" was demonstrated by "the short interval between the treaty of Paris and the meeting of the general convention at Philadelphia." See Gunther, *Marshall's Defense of McCulloch v. Maryland*, 155.

14. 17 U.S. 316, 423.

15. Letter from John Marshall to James Monroe, June 13, 1822, quoted by Faulkner, *The Jurisprudence of John Marshall*, 83.

16. 22 U.S. 1, 194 (1824).

17. See Wickard v. Filburn, 317 U.S. 11 (1942).

18. 17 U.S. 316, 423.

19. 521 U.S. 898, 918–922, 923–924 (1997).
20. See Gary Lawson, Geoffrey P. Miller, Robert G. Natelson, and Gary I. Seidman, *The Origins of the Necessary and Proper Clause* (New York: Cambridge University Press, 2010), 142, n.19. At 521 U.S. 898, 924, Scalia cites Gary Lawson and Patricia P. Granger, "The 'Proper' Scope of Federal Power: A Jurisdictional Interpretation of the Sweeping Clause," *Duke Law Journal* 43 (1993): 297–326, 330–333.
21. See Forrest McDonald, *Alexander Hamilton: A Biography* (New York: Norton, 1979), 256–257. In 1825 the Kentucky legislature asked the state's governor "'whether it might be advisable to call forth the physical power of the State'" to resist the Supreme Court's decisions favoring the national bank; see Forrest McDonald, *States' Rights and the Union: Imperium in Imperio, 1776–1876* (Lawrence: University Press of Kansas, 2000), 54.
22. 17 U.S. 316, 431–432, 435–436
23. See Gunther, *Marshall's Defense of McCulloch v. Maryland*, 54–55, 110. See also Killenbeck, *M'Culloch v. Maryland*, 154–155.
24. See Herbert J. Storing, *What the Anti-Federalists Were For* (Chicago: University of Chicago Press, 1981), 43–47; see also Gunther, *Marshall's Defense of McCulloch v. Maryland*, 71–72, 112–113.
25. Faulkner, *Jurisprudence of John Marshall*, 20–33.

3. The Implications of Marshallian Federalism

1. Wickard v. Filburn, 317 U.S. 111 (1942).
2. Gonzales v. Raich, 545 U.S. 1 (2005).
3. See Employment Division v. Smith, 494 U.S. 872 (1990).
4. See Barber, *Welfare and the Constitution*, 126–129.
5. 403 U.S. 217 (1971).
6. Id., at 224, citing Fletcher v. Peck, 6 Cranch 87, 130 (1810).
7. 403 U.S. 217, 224–225.
8. 247 U.S. 251 (1918).
9. Lochner v. New York, 198 U.S. 45 (1905).
10. Ely, *Democracy and Distrust*, 139–145. See also the review of cases in Justice White's dissent in *Palmer*, 403 U.S. 217, 241–243.
11. Ely, *Democracy and Distrust*, 136–137, citing Village of Arlington Heights v. Metropolitan Housing Development Corp., 429 U.S. 252 (1977) (racially disproportionate impact of a village zoning policy was not enough to violate the Equal Protection Clause without evidence of discriminatory intent); and Washington v. Davis, 426 U.S. 229 (1976) (a pattern of failing test scores for black applicants is not sufficient to prove racial discrimination without showing the tests were prepared with an intent to discriminate).

12. See Ely, *Democracy and Distrust*, 136–148.
13. Thomas M. Cooley, *Treatise on Constitutional Limitations* (Boston: Little, Brown, 1908), 829.
14. Id., at 11.
15. 28 Stat. at L. 963 (1895).
16. 188 U.S. 321, 357.
17. Hipolite Egg Co. v. United States, 220 U.S. 45 (1911).
18. 227 U.S. 308.
19. Caminetti v. United States, 242 U.S. 470, 491.
20. 247 U.S. 251, 276.
21. Id., at 272, 273.
22. Id., at 272.
23. Id., at 270–272.
24. Id., at 280.
25. William F. Swindler, *The Constitution and Chief Justice Marshall* (New York: Dodd, Mead, 1978), 57–58; C. Herman Pritchett, *The American Constitution* (New York: McGraw-Hill, 1968), 691.
26. 110 U.S. 87, 132 (1810).
27. Id., at 130.
28. Id., at 133–34.
29. Faulkner, *Jurisprudence of John Marshall*, 20–33.
30. 403 U.S. 217, 224–225.
31. Ely, *Democracy and Distrust*, 137.
32. 403 U.S. 217, 224–225, 258–260.
33. One reason Black might have pretended the city had more evidence can be found in the separate concurrences of Chief Justice Warren Burger and Justice Harry Blackmun. Both noted that in recent years the pools had operated at a loss, and both felt that the evidence of a racial motive was speculative and circumstantial. The city said it was closing the pools not simply because of the court order to integrate, but because integration would make operating the pools an even greater financial drain than before. What both justices wanted to avoid was locking the city into operating the pools "for an indefinite time in the future, despite financial loss of whatever amount, just because, at one time, the pools . . . had been segregated." See 403 U.S. 217, 227–230. No one successfully answered a point suggested by both Justice White and Justice Thurgood Marshall: the city had no good evidence that the pools would continue to lose money, and the city's refusal to wait and see was itself evidence of racial intent. Id., at 258–259, 273.
34. See Georg H. von Wright, *Norm and Action: A Logical Inquiry* (London: Routledge & Kegan Paul, 1963), 35–41.

35. Id., at 27–28, 36–37.
36. See generally Sotirios A. Barber *The Constitution of Judicial Power* (Baltimore: Johns Hopkins University Press, 1993), esp. chaps. 2, 7.
37. For recognition of this point by a professed skeptic, see Stanley Fish, "Almost Pragmatism: Richard Posner's Jurisprudence," *University of Chicago Law Review* 57 (1990): 1474. For further discussion see Sotirios A. Barber, "Stanley Fish and the Future of Pragmatism in Legal Theory," *University of Chicago Law Review* 58 (1991): 1036–43.
38. The Court used states' rights grounds to strike down this law in *Bailey v. Drexel Furniture Co.*, 259 U.S. 20 (1922). Congress passed the tax law in 1919 in an attempt to do through the taxing power what the Court said a year before, in *Hammer v. Dagenhart*, Congress couldn't do through the commerce power.
39. Here I leave aside important questions. One is whether Congress can lawfully act through administrative and executive agents to whom it has delegated broad authority. Another is whether Congress can be held responsible when emergencies justify congressional acquiescence to executive initiatives. I omit comment on these problems here because they do not involve federalism and because I have addressed them elsewhere.
40. 379 U.S. 241.
41. Martin Diamond, *The Founding of the Democratic Republic* (Belmont, CA: Wadsworth, 1981), chap. 3, esp. 70–78. The leading recent critic of Diamond is Alan Gibson. Gibson attacks Diamond's theory as a derivative of the Tenth Federalist and as an attribution to James Madison. Gibson accepts Diamond's theory as an attribution to Hamilton and Marshall. Gibson would also accept a Hamiltonian reading of *The Federalist* as a whole for readers who would impart one coherent message to that work. Yet Gibson rejects this last ambition on historical grounds. Gibson finds that Hamilton (the industrialist) and Madison (ever the agrarian) had different visions of the nation, and that this rules out a coherent Publius. See Alan Gibson, "The Commercial Republic and the Pluralist Critique of Marxism: An Analysis of Martin Diamond's Interpretation of Federalist 10," *Polity* 60 (1993): 487, esp. 501, 511, 515, 526.

4. Why States' Rights Federalism Is Impossible to Defend

1. On March 9, 2009, the *Wall Street Journal* reported on p. A6 ("California Marijuana Dispensaries Cheer U.S. Shift on Raids") that a "'quasi-legal' marijuana culture" had developed in California, one of thirteen states that permitted medicinal use of the drug. "Californians who seek out certain doctors can easily obtain prescriptions for marijuana use," said the report, and "some high-school students do this as soon as they turn 18."
2. The idea that the Fourteenth Amendment seeks merely a color-blind government, not a color-blind society, ignores historical facts and implies a negative

constitutionalism that makes no sense. Unaddressed "private" violence against Southern blacks motivated the amendment, and rational actors would establish governments for the sake of social results, not just to limit the governments. If limiting government were the chief end of constitution makers, they wouldn't establish governments in the first place. See Barber, *Welfare and the Constitution*, 8–12, 22–29, 36–40.

3. Pritchett, *The American Constitution*, 355.

4. 299 U.S. 304.

5. Id., at 315–318.

6. Id., at 318.

7. See William Schambra, "Progressive Liberalism and American Community," *The Public Interest*, no. 8 (Summer, 1985).

8. 501 U.S. 452, 458–459 (1991). Feeley and Rubin (*Federalism*, 22) call this "[a]n extensive catalog of pseudofederalism arguments."

9. *The Federalist*, 28:179. (O'Connor cited Clinton Rossiter, ed., *The Federalist Papers* (New York: Mentor, 1961), 180–81; The Cooke and Rossiter editions are identical, except for Cooke's retention of the original spelling and capitalization, including the capitalization of "General Government," which occurs twice in the quoted passage.

10. Cooke, ed., *The Federalist*, 51:350–351. (O'Connor quotes from the Rossiter edition, 323, which is identical to the passage in Cooke.)

11. Edward Purcell, *Originalism, Federalism, and the American Constitutional Enterprise* (New Haven, CT: Yale University Press, 2007), 51.

12. Id., at 51–52.

13. See "Declaration of the Immediate Causes Which Induce and Justify the Secession of South Carolina from the Federal Union," Dec. 24, 1861.

14. John C. Calhoun, *The Papers of John C. Calhoun*, Clyde N. Wilson, ed. (Columbia: University of South Carolina Press, 1959–2003), 13: 395.

15. Sotirios A. Barber, *The Constitution of Judicial Power* (Baltimore: Johns Hopkins University Press, 1993), chap 2.

16. Alan Wolfe describes a public whose ideological divisions, ignorance of public policy, and cynicism toward politics figure as causal factors in current institutional ills like the collapse of civil deliberation in Congress. See his *Does American Democracy Still Work?* (New Haven, CT: Yale University Press, 2006), 40–49, 53–56.

17. Feeley and Rubin, *Federalism*, 26–27.

18. *See* Randy E. Barnett, *Restoring the Lost Constitution: The Presumption of Liberty* (Princeton, NJ: Princeton University Press, 2004), 278–291, 302–312; Richard A. Epstein, *How Progressives Rewrote the Constitution* (Washington, DC: Cato, 2006), 52–77; Michael S. Greve, *Real Federalism: Why It Matters, How It Could Happen* (Washington, DC: AEI Press, 1999), 11–19, 25–33, 79–84.

This book takes up arguments by Epstein and Greve. For a discussion of Barnett, see my "Fallacies of Negative Constitutionalism," *Fordham Law Review* 75 (2006): 651, 663–666 .

19. Greve, *Real Federalism*, 2–3.

20. For an overview of the most salient issues, see Purcell, *Originalism*, 179–181.

21. Feeley and Rubin reserve "federalism" for what I'm calling "dual federalism." They deny that competitive federalism (their "fiscal federalism") is federalism at all. They see it as a policy of decentralization by a utilitarian regime that values efficiency over other goods, like environmental protection and religious salvation. See Feeley and Rubin, *Federalism*, 16, 24, 80–85. For a similar assessment, see Purcell, *Originalism*, 279–281.

22. Greve, *Real Federalism*, 2.

23. Id. In December 2008 the Pew Research Center reported that 43 percent of Americans resided in states other than their home states. See http://pewsocial trends.org/assets/pdf/Movers-and-Stayers.pdf, accessed on September 29, 2010.

24. See Saenz v. Roe, 526 U.S. 489, 500–504 (1999).

25. Greve, *Real Federalism*, 4.

26. Id.

27. I explore the implications of constitutional amendability in "Constitutional Failure: Ultimately Attitudinal," in Jeffrey Tulis and Stephen Macedo, eds., *The Limits of Constitutional Democracy* (Princeton, NJ: Princeton University Press, 2010), 25–27.

28. See Stephen Macedo, *Liberal Virtues: Citizenship, Virtue, and Community in Liberal Constitutionalism* (Oxford: Clarendon Press, 1990), 10–12, 19–20, 40–50. To the objection that a "rational kind" exceeds nationalistic identities, one can respond by citing Hamilton in *The Federalist* No.1 that "It has been frequently remarked, that it seems to have been reserved to the people of this country, by their conduct and example, to decide the important question, whether societies of men are really capable or not, of establishing good government from reflection and choice, or whether they are forever destined to depend, for their political constitution, on accident and force" (1:3). This passage is of a piece with Jefferson's assumption in the Declaration of Independence that "the causes which impel" the American Revolution were consonant with, or would ultimately prove consonant with, "the opinions of mankind." No metaethical objection to these claims can succeed. A moral realist would allow the possibility of moral truths applicable in principle to all of humankind. Moral conventionalists and moral subjectivists could not object to the application of what Hamilton and Jefferson believed unless they had evidence that Americans actually believed otherwise. And whatever Hamilton and Jefferson might have said about anything at all, a moral skeptic could cite no reason why anyone ought to believe otherwise, for a moral

skeptic denies that there can be a real reason why anyone ought to do or believe anything.

29. Against my contention that true believers and skeptics have no place to go, one can claim that the Constitution permits enclaves from which believers can persuade others to reject a liberal order. Assuming that "persuade" excludes force and fraud, I would deny this possibility on the theory that reason cannot reject reason. I argue on conceptual and historical grounds in Chapter 7 that there can be no reasonable rejection of a life of secular public reasonableness; that a secular public reasonableness is the one firm commitment of a liberal order; that it constitutes the principle of constitutional amendability itself; and that it is beyond the process of constitutional amendment, correctly understood. Should a life of secular public reasonableness be lost through one or another form of force or fraud, the Constitution itself would be lost, not just amended. According to this argument, the Constitution does secure a place for true believers as individuals in larger communities that recognize their rights of speech and even voluntary association—but not their right to government's coercive power. They cannot have coercive states of their own. This may seem regrettable to those who value an unrestricted self-determination. But Chapter 7 argues that it is undeniable in any case. The value placed on choice cannot justify a coercive state for true believers, for such a state would replace government by reflection and choice with pious submission to an inscrutable will or to those who truly speak for that will, whoever they might be.

30. Richard A. Epstein, *Takings: Private Property and the Power of Eminent Domain* (Cambridge, MA: Harvard University Press, 1985), 57–62, 93–96.

31. Greve, *Real Federalism*, 4; Epstein, *How Progressives Rewrote the Constitution*, 114.

32. 163 U.S. 567 (1896).

33. Epstein, *How Progressives Rewrote the Constitution*, 103.

34. 198 U.S. 45 (1905).

35. 247 U.S. 200 (1927); Epstein, *How Progressives Rewrote the Constitution*, 107–108.

36. Id., at 106–108, citing Minersville School District v. Gobitis, 310 U.S. 586 (1940).

37. Epstein, *How Progressives Rewrote the Constitution*, 108–109.

38. Id., at 110.

39. Greve, *Real Federalism*, 18.

40. Epstein, *How Progressives Rewrote the Constitution*, 19–25.

41. Id., at 22.

42. Id., at 129.

43. Id., at 117–137.

44. Epstein, *How Progressives Rewrote the Constitution*, 33–35, citing Addyston Pipe & Steel v. United States, 175 U.S. 211 (1899) and Swift & Co. v. United States, 196 U.S. 375 (1905).

45. 156 U.S. 1 (1895).

46. Epstein, *How Progressives Rewrote the Constitution*, 34–35.

47. Id., at 35.

48. Id., at 142 n.59.

49. Id., at 53.

50. The claim that no one thought to regulate manufacturing before 1937 overlooks the Thirteenth Amendment. When the Thirteenth Amendment gave Congress power to enforce its ban on slavery, it gave Congress some authority over the incidents of production, and Congress exercised this authority in ways indifferent to race in an 1867 statute banning peonage (compulsory service based on indebtedness) and an 1874 statute banning the "padrone system," in which unscrupulous adults imported children to work without pay as street beggars, bootblacks, and musicians. See United States v. Kosminski, 487 U.S. 931 (1988).

51. Epstein, *How Progressives Rewrote the Constitution*, 52.

52. I assume here that it is at least possible for Congress to be a forum of rational decision in the public interest, an assumption Epstein could well deny. Epstein assumes that the federal judiciary is a better forum for rational decision in the public interest. I will not ask whether Epstein's preference for courts over legislatures suggests that the public interest is better served by a deliberative process that purports to represent principle than by a process of bargaining among self-serving actors or their representatives. The issue addressed in this chapter is states' rights federalism, not invisible-hand economics or invisible-hand constitutionalism or how Epstein can embrace one but not the other.

53. 9 Wheat. 1 (1824).

54. For a partial summary, see Maurice G. Baxter, *The Steamboat Monopoly: Gibbons v. Ogden, 1824* (New York: Knopf, 1972), 61–62.

55. Epstein, *How Progressives Rewrote the Constitution*, 27, 69.

56. Quoted in Pritchett, *The American Constitution*, 253.

57. 22 U.S. 1, 194.

58. Id.

59. Epstein, *How the Progressives Rewrote the Constitution*, 69–70 (his emphasis).

60. Pritchett, *The American Constitution*, 254–255.

61. Epstein, *How Progressives Rewrote the Constitution*, 71.

62. Id., at 69 (his italics omitted).

63. Randy Barnett, one of Epstein's intellectual allies, concludes after an extensive lexicographical inquiry into the eighteenth-century use of "commerce" that a "possible original meaning" of the Commerce Clause would be a general power over the nation's economy. Barnett concedes this despite his interest in

limiting "commerce," as Epstein does, to little more than interstate transportation. See Barnett, *Restoring the Lost Constitution*, 313; cf. 278–291, 302–312.

64. Richard A. Epstein, "The Federalism Decisions of Justices Rehnquist and O'Connor: Is Half a Loaf Enough?" *Stanford Law Review* 58 (2006): 1793, 1801.

65. Baxter, *Steamboat Monopoly*, 56–57.

66. Epstein, *How Progressives Rewrote the Constitution*, 71.

67. The Rehnquist Court achieved this reversal in *Boerne*, which held inter alia that Congress cannot remedy a state's violation of the Fourteenth Amendment unless it fashions a remedy whose scope is "congruent" with the violation and whose cost to the states is "proportional" to the harm suffered by the victims of state action. This test works as a presumption against congressional action under the Fourteenth Amendment. See City of Boerne v. Flores 521 U.S. 507, 527–534 (1997).

68. 22 U.S. 1, 195.

69. Message to Congress, July 4, 1861, in Basler, *Lincoln's Speeches and Writings*, 604 (Lincoln's italics).

70. Terri Schiavo was a comatose Florida woman whose withdrawal from life support by permission of state courts provoked a law of Congress signed by President George W. Bush in March 2005. Acting under Section 5 of the Fourteenth Amendment, Congress sought to direct the federal courts to reopen a state court's permission to withdraw life support. The federal courts refused to cooperate with the law on separation of powers grounds. For the story from a supporter of the law, see Steven G. Calabresi, "The Terri Schiavo Case: In Defense of the Special Law Enacted by Congress and President Bush, *Northwestern University Law Review* 100 (2006): 151, esp. 164–167.

71. Larry Kramer, "Understanding Federalism," *Vanderbilt Law Review* 47 (1994): 1485, 1502.

72. 17 U.S. 407, 415.

73. Epstein, *How Progressives Rewrote the Constitution*, 27.

74. See Richard A. Epstein, "An Outline of Takings," *University of Miami Law Review* 41 (1986): 3.

75. See Sotirios A. Barber, "Congress and Responsible Government," *Boston University Law Review* 89 (2009): 689, 702–705.

76. Compare Feeley and Rubin, *Federalism*, 25–26: "[T]rue federalism cannot be regarded as a means of favoring any specific, first-order norm, because its essence is to permit a multiplicity of norms. It favors only the second-order norm that no first-order norm should dominate the polity." My point, or my way of putting the point, is that states' righters cannot defend themselves in a national forum without invoking a controlling national standard whose existence states' righters cannot admit and remain states' righters. I put the point this way because I am not sure what is meant by second-order norms.

As I understand the distinction between first- and second-order *propositions*, only first-order propositions have prescriptive counterparts. The proposal that "no first-order norm should dominate the polity" is prescriptive in form, and for this reason I would call it a first-order norm. As I see it, therefore, it is incoherent to say "no first-order norm should dominate the polity." I contend, in any case, that no one can give a reason of any kind—first-order, second-order, or whatever—for states' rights beyond process rights and a right against pretexts.

5. John C. Calhoun's False Theory of the Union

1. For the moral realist (objectivist) assumptions of everyday political discourse, see David O. Brink, *Moral Realism and the Foundations of Ethics* (Cambridge: Cambridge University Press, 1989), 23–24.
2. For a counterargument, see Michael Blake, "Defending Dual Federalism: A Bad Idea, but Not Self-Defeating," *NOMOS* 50, forthcoming, 2013.
3. James H. Read, *Majority Rule versus Consensus: The Political Thought of John C. Calhoun* (Lawrence University Press of Kansas, 2009), 83–89.
4. See John C. Calhoun, *The Papers of John C. Calhoun*, Clyde N. Wilson, ed. (Columbia: University of South Carolina Press, 1959–2003), 13:59–60.
5. Compare the Anti-Riot Act of 1968, 18 U.S.C. §§ 2101, 2102.
6. See Calhoun, *Papers*, 14:42.
7. Id., at 14:46; 14:11; 14:13–14; 14:31–34.
8. Read, *Majority Rule versus Consensus*, 106.
9. Calhoun, *Papers*, 28:7, 11–12, 37–40.
10. Read, *Majority Rule versus Consensus*, 35–36, 39–51.
11. Calhoun, *Papers*, 28:80–82.
12. Id., at 28:84–86.
13. Id., at 28:165–167.
14. Id., at 28:100.
15. Id., at 28:83–84.
16. Id., at 28:77.
17. See The Virginia Commission on Constitutional Government, *We The States* (Richmond, VA: William Byrd Press, 1964), 322.
18. 514 U.S. 779, 846–848.
19. Schambra, "Progressive Liberalism and American Community," 38–42, 46–48.
20. *The Federalist*, 43:296–297.
21. James Madison, *The Papers of James Madison*, David B. Mattern, ed. (Charlottesville: University Press of Virginia, 1991), 17:308–309.
22. 17 U.S. 316, 404.
23. See Patrick Henry's speech to the Virginia Ratifying Convention of June 5, 1788, reprinted in Herbert J. Storing, ed. *The Anti-Federalist* (Chicago: University of Chicago Press, 1981), 299, 301, 305.

24. Virginia Commission on Constitutional Government, *We The States*, 152–154.

25. *Congressional Debates*, 21 Cong. 1st sess., 72 (1829–30), Jan. 26, 1830.

26. David Franklin Houston, *A Critical Study of Nullification in South Carolina* (Cambridge, MA: Harvard University Press, 1896), 108–110.

27. For this formulation of the question, see Pritchett, *The American Constitution*, 64–65. The soundness of the states' rights position also depends on the soundness of the legal-moral and interpretive theories it embodies; these theories converge to form what is now called an "originalist" approach to constitutional meaning and obligation. With many other writers over the past forty years, especially Ronald Dworkin and Michael S. Moore, James Fleming and I have argued against all forms of originalism except the one rejected by most self-styled originalists. See Barber and Fleming, *Constitutional Interpretation*, Chaps. 6–7.

28. Basler, *Lincoln's Speeches and Writings*, 603–604.

29. Storing, "The Problem of Big Government," in Robert A. Goldwin, ed. *A Nation of States* (Chicago: Rand McNally, 1961), 71–73.

30. Calhoun, *Papers*, 28:77.

31. Id., 28:85–86. Calhoun quotes from Washington's letter of September 17, 1787, transmitting to Congress in his capacity as presiding officer of the Constitutional Convention "that Constitution which has appeared to us the most advisable." Read shows that Calhoun misrepresented the transmission letter: *Majority Rule versus Consensus*, 91–92.

32. Calhoun, *Papers*, 28:87.

33. Id., 152–157. See also Read, *Majority Rule versus Consensus*, 93–94. In *McCulloch*, Marshall read the Necessary and Proper Clause as enhancing congressional power by permitting Congress a wide choice of means. Maryland saw the clause as restricting Congress's choice of means to those absolutely necessary. A second way to read the clause restrictively is to focus on the word *proper* and to claim, as Calhoun does here, that a congressional act that conflicts with background principles of state sovereignty is improper for that reason alone. Justice Scalia echoed Calhoun's reading of the Necessary and Proper Clause in *Printz v. United States*, 521 U.S. 898, 923–924 (1997). For a discussion, see above, 61–62.

34. Calhoun, *Papers*, 28:82–83.

35. Read, *Majority Rule versus Consensus*, 90–91.

36. Calhoun, *Papers*, 28:74.

37. Feeley and Rubin, *Federalism*, 101–102.

38. See Calvin H. Johnson, *Righteous Anger at the Wicked States: The Meaning of the Founders' Constitution* (New York: Cambridge University Press, 2005), Chap. 1.

39. Calhoun, *Papers*, 28:8.

40. Read, *Majority Rule versus Consensus*, 55–56.
41. Senate speech of April 4, 1816 on the Tariff of 1816, reprinted in Ross M. Lence, ed. *Union and Liberty, The Political Philosophy of John C. Calhoun* (Indianapolis, IN: Liberty Fund, 1992), 303.
42. Read, *Majority Rule versus Consensus*, 62–65.
43. Feeley and Rubin, *Federalism*, 101.
44. Calhoun, *Papers*, 28:100.
45. Read, *Majority Rule versus Consensus*, 63.
46. Calhoun, *Papers*, 28:230.
47. Id. 28:233.
48. Letter to Humphrey Marshall, May 7, 1833, quoted in full in Faulkner, *The Jurisprudence of John Marshall*, 99–100.
49. Read, *Majority Rule versus Consensus*, 88–89.
50. Reasoning from the pattern of federalism decisions by the Rehnquist Court, Erwin Chemerinsky suggests the Court was concerned less with empowering the states than with crippling federal protection for minority rights and freeing business corporations from federal regulation, See Chemerinsky, *Enhancing Government*, 225–227.

6. States' Rights as Rights Only to Participate in National Processes

1. Berns, "The Meaning of the Tenth Amendment," 141, 141–143, 145–148.
2. See Martin Diamond, "Ethics and Politics: The American Way," in Robert H. Horwitz, ed. *The Moral Foundations of the American Republic* (Charlottesville, VA: University Press of Virginia, 1986), 75–76.
3. Barber and Fleming, *Constitutional Interpretation*, 36–38.
4. Purcell, *Originalism*, 51.
5. See *The Federalist* 45:309. See also Johnson, *Righteous Anger at the Wicked States*, 1–2, 16–29.
6. One might claim, as Calhoun did, that the nation did not really abandon the Articles because the principles of the Articles are the controlling principles of the Constitution (*Papers*, 28:80–82). But no contemporary dual federalist known to me would admit that her position implies that the Constitution ordains a confederation. That is, no dual federalist today would contend that "*if* states' rights federalism, *then* no fundamental change from the Articles to the Constitution." The only thing that could be proved by such an argument would be the absurdity of the if-clause (states' rights federalism), for the historical and textual evidence against the then-clause (no fundamental structural change) is overwhelming. This evidence includes the testimony of *The Federalist*: that the Constitution altered "the first principles and main pillars" of the Confederation (15:93). This is not to deny continuity and common ground, however. It is not to deny that despite structural differences

the Articles and the Constitution share the political morality of the Declaration of Independence; see Diamond, *Founding of the Democratic Republic*, 61–70. Nor is it to deny overlap of structural features or a genetic continuity between the Confederation and the new union; see *The Federalist* 39:253–257; 40:260–262; see also Barber, "Constitutional Failure," 26. What is denied is what was important to Calhoun: that the Constitution's new government is an agent of the states, designed by them to secure their independence and well-being as separate political entities, and ultimately dependent on the voluntary subscription of each of the ever-separate entities. This may have been the Confederation; no one is left to claim that it is the Constitution. To deduce otherwise from a given proposition is to condemn that proposition.

7. For a recent discussion, see Fatovic, *Outside the Law*, 204–205.

8. Anticipating a charge of hypocrisy in *Gonzales v. Carhart*—and thereby highlighting the fact—Justice Thomas (joined by Justice Scalia) said that "whether the [Partial Birth Abortion Ban] Act of 2003 constitutes a permissible exercise of Congress' power under the Commerce Clause is not before the Court. The parties did not raise or brief that issue; it is outside the question presented; and the lower courts did not address it." With this, Thomas voted to uphold the act. 550 U.S. 124, 169 (2007).

9. See *The Federalist* 45:309.

10. See id., 1:3. Discursive, as opposed to physical, defenses of the local involve measurement by nonlocal standards—"higher [than local] standards."

11. See George Lewis, "Virginia's Northern Strategy: Southern Segregationists and the Route to National Conservatism," *Journal of Southern History* (February 2006) 72:1: 115–118.

12. 426 U.S. 833 (1976).

13. 469 U.S. 526 (1986).

14. 488 U.S. 1041 (1992).

15. See Chemerinsky, *Enhancing Government*, 48–49.

16. Choper, *Judicial Review and the National Political Process*, 175–176, 201–203.

17. 426 U.S. 833, 851–852, quoting from Coyle v. Smith, 221 U.S. 559, 580 (1911).

18. I.e., independently of the interests of individuals (1) who saw themselves as free to relocate to another state without losing their identity, and (2) who valued either (a) their freedom to relocate more than their existing state of residence or (b) their present place of residence *plus* their freedom to relocate more than their present place of residence *minus* their freedom to relocate. Though Calhoun clearly presupposed individuals with one such view of themselves, none of these individuals could have endorsed Calhoun's theory of state sovereignty. The individual implicit in Calhoun's theory of state sovereignty could have no sense of self more authoritative than his state's general will. His state's general will would have to define the content of his higher self. His

awareness of other wills would be assumed by his awareness of other states. But he would have to see these other wills as altogether alien and inimical to his own. He would therefore place no value on a freedom to relocate out of state (except for hostile purposes). That the original Constitution presupposed individuals with a larger sense of self is indicated by the Preamble, the Full Faith and Credit Clause, the Privileges and Immunities Clause, and even the Fugitive Slave Clause. Indeed, this larger-than-local self was assumed even by the Articles of Confederation, which entitled "the free inhabitants of each of these states . . . all privileges and immunities of free citizens in the several states," together with "free ingress and regress to and from any other state" and the same "privileges of trade and commerce" as citizens of the several states (Article IV). All these provisions presuppose that individual identity survives changes in residence from one state to the next—that leaving home is not in itself a form of suicide. Calhoun himself attended Yale and studied law in Litchfield, Connecticut. He served three terms in the U.S. House of Representatives, he served as a U.S. secretary of war, he twice sought the presidency, he was elected to the U.S. Senate three times, and he died in Washington, D.C. while a U.S. senator. Nothing in his life suggests a self-understanding remotely like that presupposed by the theory of the union he began to defend in the late 1820s.

19. 426 U.S. 833, 856.

20. Or so Rehnquist indicated at 841 n17, by favorably citing *Heart of Atlanta Motel v. United States,* 379 U.S. 241 (1964).

21. See Katzenbach v. McClung, 379 U.S. 294, 301–307 (1964).

22. See Sotirios A. Barber, "National League of Cities v. Usery: New Meaning for the Tenth Amendment?" in Philip B Kurland, ed., *1976 Supreme Court Review* (Chicago: University of Chicago Press, 1977), 180–181.

23. See Ronald J. Alan, "Constitutional Adjudication: The Demands of Knowledge and Epistemological Modesty," *Northwestern University Law Review* 88 (1983): 432–435.

24. See Wills, *A Necessary Evil,* 62, 67–68.

25. See Rehnquist, "The Notion of a Living Constitution," 702. For commentary on Rehnquist's moral skepticism, see Barber and Fleming, *Constitutional Interpretation,* 23–25, 30–32, 39–40.

26. 426 U.S. 833, 864–865, 867–869.

27. 45:311–312; 46:317–318.

28. *Columbia Law Review* 54 (1954): 543.

29. 469 U.S. 528, 553–554.

30. 469 U.S. 528, 470, citing *The Federalist,* 39:256.

31. See Kramer, "Understanding Federalism," 1510–11; Erwin Chemerinsky, *Enhancing Government,* 27, 59–60.

32. See Read, *Majority Rule versus Consensus,* 154–155.

33. Alfred H. Kelley, Wilfred A. Harbison, and Herman Belz, *The American Constitution: Its Origins and Development* (New York: Norton, 1983), 339.

34. See Kramer, "Understanding Federalism," 1506–14.

35. An aspect of foreign affairs in which the states' role is not trivial as a matter of national policy (not as a matter of states' rights) is relations with the Indian tribes. See generally, David E. Wilkins and K. Tsianina Lomawaima, *Uneven Ground: American Indian Sovereignty and Federal Law* (Norman: Oklahoma University Press, 2005), chap. 6.

36. See Schambra, "Progressive Liberalism and American Community," 46–47.

37. New York v. United States, 505 U.S. 144.

38. Printz v. United States, 521 U.S. 898.

39. 491 U.S. 1.

40. 517 U.S. 44 (1997).

41. Id., at 54, citing Blatchford v. Native Village of Noatak, 501 U.S. 775, 779 (1991).

42. Id., citing passages from Hans v. Louisiana, 134 U.S. 1, 13 (1890), and *The Federalist*, No. 81.

43. Id., quoting from Hans v. Louisiana.

44. Forrest McDonald, *States Rights and the Union: Imperium in Imperio, 1776–1876* (Lawrence: University Press of Kansas, 2000), 19–22. 105–106, 109.

45. Id., at 36.

46. Osborn v. Bank of the United States, 9 Wheat. 738 (1824).

47. An author (the maker of something) may feel good on seeing her will manifest in something else. But if the author is a human author whose act is to be understood by other observers, she cannot call her results good without trading on some conception of goodness that her observers understand as independent of her will—and that she on reflection understands as independent of her will. An actor who reflects on her act takes the position of an outside observer of her act. To describe an event as an act an observer must be able to see the actor as pursuing what she thinks is a good, for as Aristotle says, an actor acts for what she thinks is some good. If a subject suddenly gulps down a fluid clearly labeled "kerosene" and proclaims "I like it," an observer would have doubts about whether she was acting or suffering—i.e., suffering some mental disorder. The putative actor could not explain "her" behavior to an observer by saying "I like it" because usage indicates a difference in meaning between "I like it" and "it's good," and the observer would have to empathize to some extent with the prospective actor in order to see how she could say "it's good." We can therefore doubt that the unreflective preference of an authority is good even to the authority. See Barber and Fleming, *Constitutional Interpretation*, 180–185.

48. Federal Maritime Commission v. South Carolina State Ports Authority, 535 U.S. 743 (2002).

49. Florida Prepaid Postsecondary Education Expense Board v. College Savings Bank, 527 U.S. 627 (1999).

50. 527 U.S. 706 (1999).

51. 521 U.S. 528.

52. 527 U.S. 627, 645–646.

53. 528 U.S. 62, 83.

54. 531 U.S. 356, 370.

55. 538 U.S. 721, 730–736.

56. 541 U.S. 509.

57. The exemplar of this difficulty in postwar constitutional theory is John Hart Ely, who was widely criticized for failing to acknowledge his substantive commitments. For a recent statement, see Fleming, *Securing Constitutional Democracy*, 29–35.

58. For an example of the former, see the Bush-era pilot school voucher program for the District of Columbia, The D.C. School Choice Incentive Act of 2003 (Title III of Division C of the Consolidated Approriations Act, 2004); P.L. 108-199 Stat. 3 (2004). An example of discrimination against same-sex couples is Section 3 of the Defense of Marriage Act (P.L. 104-199, 110 Stat. (1996).

59. See Ely, *Democracy and Distrust*, chap. 5.

60. Id., 94.

61. Laurence Tribe, "The Puzzling Persistence of Process-Based Constitutional Theories," *Yale Law Review* 89 (1980): 1070–71.

62. See Ely, *Democracy and Distrust*, 62, 70, 95, 99, 100, 102.

63. See Steward Machine Co. v. Davis, 301 U.S. 548 (1937).

64. For a discussion see Barber, *Welfare and the Constitution*, 137–143.

65. McDonald v. City of Chicago, 561 U.S. 3025 (2010).

66. For an argument that delegated powers imply constitutional duties, see Sotirios A. Barber, *The Constitution and the Delegation of Congressional Power* (Chicago: University of Chicago Press, 1975), 37–41.

67. See Barber and Fleming, *Constitutional Interpretation*, 135–140.

68. For a recent demonstration that this fact was fully appreciated by the authors of *The Federalist* and the philosophic tradition of which they were a part, see generally Fatovic, *Outside the Law*, chaps. 2–5.

69. See Lyng v. Northwest Indian Cemetery Protective Association, 485 U.S. 439 (1988).

70. Quoted at 485 U.S. 439, 442 (1988).

71. Id., at 451–452.

72. See Martin Diamond, "Ethics and Politics: The American Way," in Robert H. Horwitz, ed. *The Moral Foundations of the American Republic* (Charlettosville, VA: University Press of Virginia, 1986), 83–85, 101–102; see also Walter Berns, "Religion and the Founding Principle," in Robert H. Horwitz, ed. *The Moral*

Foundations of the American Republic (Charlettosville, VA: University Press of Virginia, 1986), 210–217, 223–228; Macedo, *Liberal Virtues*, 265–277.

73. Diamond, "Ethics and Politics," 75.

74. For passages in *The Federalist* that support dual federalism, see 10:63, 52:358–359, 55:356, 83:560.

75. See Barnett, *Restoring the Lost Constitution*, 351, cf. 155–157. For an analysis of Barnett's position on the scope of the commerce power, see Sotirios A. Barber, "Fallacies of Negative Constitutionalism," Fordham Law Review 75 (2006): 663–666.

7. Why Marshallians Should (But Probably Won't) Win the Federalism Debate

1. See Aristotle, *Politics*, 1294b.

2. The exception to this rule is use of the judiciary's equity powers to reform state-operated institutions like officially segregated schools and overcrowded prisons. This use of the equity power may seem merely an apparent exception because, in constitutional cases, federal courts employ equity not to secure desirable states of affairs per se but to remedy violations of individual rights. But dual federalists have long seen the practice as more than the vindication of negative liberties. They have criticized the practice for crossing a line that separates judicial from legislative power. See Gary L. McDowell, *Equity and the Constitution: The Supreme Court, Equitable Relief and Public Policy* (Chicago: University of Chicago Press, 1982), chaps. 6–7. The practice illustrates a point I shall repeat at the conclusion of this book: A serious concern for vindicating negative liberties will secure the social conditions for the actual enjoyment of negative liberties. (Who will contend with a straight face that a racist society can support a "color-blind" government?) These conditions include a public willing to pay the costs of supporting negative liberties, which in turn depends on some measure of responsibility to others in the exercise of negative liberties. As with any social state of affairs, its pursuit and maintenance depend on governmental power, not on governmental forbearance.

3. See Sotirios A. Barber, "Liberalism and the Constitution," *Social Philosophy and Policy* 24 (2007): 256–261.

4. Barnett, *Restoring the Lost Constitution*, 33–38, 64–66, 192–195.

5. Storing, "The Problem of Big Government," 66–74, 79–85; Barber, "Congress and Responsible Government," 691–92, 703–10.

6. What might be meant by less government is complicated by the fact that any given regime will try to exert itself as needed for its ends. A free-market regime can demand a robust national security state, upward redistribution through regressive taxation, a conception of justice that favors first possessors over

latecomers, and extensive and expensive systems of domestic police, courts, and prisons. See Barber, "Fallacies of Negative Constitutionalism," 651–667.

7. James W. Ceaser, "What Kind of Government Do We Have to Fear?" in Arthur M. Melzer, Jerry Weinberger, and M. Richard Zinman, eds., *Politics at the Turn of the Century* (Lanham, MD: Rowman & Littlefield, 2001), 87–92; Michael P. Zuckert, *Launching Liberalism: On Lockean Political Philosophy* (Lawrence: University Press of Kansas, 2002), 313–317, 324–328.

8. Barber, "Liberalism and the Constitution," esp. 256–262.

9. Macedo, *Liberal Virtues*, 53–55, 260–263.

10. Barber, *Welfare and the Constitution*, 8–22.

11. Diamond, *The Founding of the Democratic Republic*, 71–78; Berns, "Religion and the Founding Principle," 214, 223.

12. Diamond, "Ethics and Politics: The American Way," 76–83.

13. See Macedo, *Liberal Virtues*, 54–64.

14. Barber, "Congress and Responsible Government," 698–703.

15. I argue for a meaningful standard of reasonableness, reasonableness "with [at least] a bite," for all legislation, state and national in *On What the Constitution Means* (Baltimore: Johns Hopkins University Press, 1984), 123–131.

16. Storing, *What the Anti-Federalists Were For*, 7–8.

17. A citizen of Rhode Island who asserted this proposition silently to himself could not (coherently) have expressed it publicly, for it is absurd to say in a practical context that "*it is true that* there's no truth about what's right." Aside from whether an individual can believe what he cannot publicly express, a collectivity can be said to believe only what can be publicly expressed. Rhode Island therefore cannot have believed that it could *rightfully* determine what was right. Rhode Island, a collectivity, had to assume objective standards of right conduct—that is, more than merely local standards of right conduct.

18. This part of my argument borrows from the following works: Barber and Fleming, *Constitutional Interpretation*, 179–184; Michael S. Moore, *Law and Psychiatry: Rethinking the Relationship* (Cambridge: Cambridge University Press, 1984), 71–74 ; Georg H. von Wright, *Norm and Action* (London: Routledge & Kegan Paul, 1963), 35–39.

19. See *The Federalist*, 40:265; 49:341. See also, Gordon S. Wood, *The Creation of the American Republic: 1776–1787* (New York: Norton, 1969), 483–499.

20. See Holmes and Sunstein, *The Cost of Rights*, 58–62, 115–117, 123, 149–151, 152–155.

21. Barber, "Liberalism and the Constitution," 257–258.

22. Holmes and Sunstein, *The Cost of Rights*, 115–116, 229–230; Barber, *Welfare and the Constitution*, 49–50, 103; see also Diamond's anticipation of Rawls's "difference principle" in "The Federalist," in Leo Strauss and Joseph Cropsey,

eds. *The History of Political Philosophy* (Chicago: Rand McNally, 1972), 649–650.

23. Holmes and Sunstein, *The Cost of Rights*, 107–108.

24. See Pritchett, *The American Constitution*, 245–247.

25. 297 U.S. 1.

26. Barber, *Welfare and the Constitution*, 139–142. For the "Report on Manufacturers," see Harold C. Syrett and Patricia Syrett, eds., *The Papers of Alexander Hamilton* (New York: Columbia University Press, 1961–79), 10:302–304.

27. Martha Nussbaum thus defends liberalism on the basis of universal experiences relating to the human body (hunger, physical pain, etc.); human mortality; the dependency of children; cognitive mental functions; the ability to recognize other persons; and the separate physical and psychological identity of persons. See "Aristotelian Social Democracy," in Bruce Douglas, Gerald Mara, and Henry Richardson, *Liberalism and the Good* (New York: Routledge, 1990), 217–226.

28. Fallibility presupposes moral and scientific realism, and the evidence for fallibility lies in disagreement and disappointed expectations. Discursive disagreement (as opposed to silent disagreement and violent disagreement) does not prove antirealism, since persons in discursive disagreement assume they're doing more than just asserting their beliefs; they're claiming that their beliefs are *true*, and they're submitting their claims to a truth-seeking process, namely, discursive disagreement. Because this process relies essentially on eyewitness evidence (or credible reportage of eyewitnesses), the process itself seems biased against sectarian forms of antiliberalism. (I leave aside forms of antiliberalism based on the Socratic thesis that only a very few human beings if any can seriously aspire to substitute truth for prejudice and that only these few are fit to rule themselves and others.) Liberals can defend themselves against this charge by pointing out that religionists themselves assume the superiority of eyewitness to verbal report, for reportage is graded by its distance from eyewitnessed events, and believers themselves demand credible eyewitnessed testimony for the occurrence of miracles. Even though believers have to take the word of scripture for the Creation, scripture takes the form of eyewitnessed testimony. Genesis says God created the world, not that some say God created the world.

29. See *The Federalist*, 10:62; 49:342; 51:349, 352; 57:384; 63:423–424; 71:482–483. See also, Barber, "Congress and Responsible Government," 691–692.

30. See Nussbaum, "Aristotelian Social Democracy," 208–214.

31. See Stephen Macedo, *Diversity and Distrust: Civic Education in a Multicultural Democracy* (Cambridge, MA: Harvard University Press, 2000), 84–87.

32. Walter Berns, *The First Amendment and the Future of American Democracy*, 69–71; see also Berns, "Religion and the Founding Principle," 226–227.

33. Berns, *The First Amendment and the Future of American Democracy*, 44.

34. This good would be ultimately unquestionable because secular public reasonableness (the virtue) is ultimately unquestionable and because the ultimate objects of secular public reasoning (the practice) are the best life under ideal conditions and the best feasible life under existing or reasonably foreseeable conditions; see Barber, *Welfare and the Constitution*, 107–110. Secular public reasonableness is unquestionable because questioning something (as distinguished from inarticulate wonder or doubt) involves a speaker addressing full sentences to an audience, and hence a public, however small. Even introspective questioning presupposes a public, as evinced in the expression "I asked myself"; this reflective self is a public of two. In addition to its public nature, the practice of questioning something involves the principles of grammar, inference, and evidence, which principles constitute the practice of reasoning. Questioning is thus a form of reasoning. Because we can't question something save through the practice of reasoning itself, we can't question either reasoning or our ambition to be reasoning beings. This is a layered ambition. "I am a reasoning creature" means "It is true that I am a reasoning creature." But my fallibility makes it unclear that I can ever say that something is true. The only way I believe I can approximate truth is by testing my opinions against the opinions of others. The desire to be reasonable thus includes the desire to appear reasonable, to others and to one's self as another. Thus, we can't really question the desire to be and appear to be reasonable. And because appearing reasonable is appearing reasonable to others who are like ourselves, we can't really deny our status as social beings. That is, we can't *articulately* deny our sociality, although we may have reason to pretend to do so to others when we believe that doing so serves a common end.

35. See Storing, "The Problem of Big Government," 80–85; *The Federalist*, 57:384; Fatovic, *Outside the Law*, 223–244.

36. *The Federalist*, 10:62; compare 71:482–483. For the change in views about the nature of responsible government since the founding, see Jeffrey K. Tulis, *The Rhetorical President* (Princeton, NJ: Princeton University Press, 1985).

37. See Barber, "Fallacies of Negative Constitutionalism," 657–659.

38. *The Federalist*, 84:580.

39. See Holmes and Sunstein, *The Cost of Rights*, esp. 61–62, 115–117; Barber, "Liberalism and the Constitution," 260–261. As Hamilton indicates in *The Federalist* No. 1, the pride would be that of self-directed beings. The practice of rights would protect individuals and groups who stand against conventional beliefs about the good, which, as conventional, are mere opinions. Thus, the nation as a whole may believe prosperity is a good worth the sacrifice of other goods, like salvation or long-term ecological survival, and this opinion may be wrong. If it is wrong, no one who believes it wrong can really want it, for

people who are not suffering some mental illness or chemical addiction want only what they think is good. Since no one really wants merely apparent goods, apparent desire for the latter must be seen not as freely chosen but imposed, typically by social convention, peer pressure, etc. Those who aspire to freedom therefore aspire to replace convention with truth about the good. This is why the practice of some liberal rights can be a true source of pride. True pride is justified by a willingness to institutionalize self-criticism, which the community does when it honors rights integral to truth-seeking processes, like freedom of responsible political speech.

40. See Katzenbach v. Morgan, 384 U.S. 641 (1966).

41. 109 U.S. 3 (1883).

42. 521 U.S. 507 (1997).

43. An observer who contends that (*p*) "no one can be devoted to truth beyond his versions of the truth" contradicts himself by submitting (*p*) as true, not just his version of the truth. And if he offers (*p*) to an anonymous audience, he assumes that people generally want to and can conform their opinions to the truth, not just their versions of the truth. Our observer therefore can't deny the possibility that the framers were interested in justice, not just their versions of justice, and that their interest in justice, if genuine, would have caused them to change their opinions about the treatment of women and racial and other minorities. As Dworkin suggested in his famous thought experiment, no framer would admit to being committed to his personal conception of justice, not justice itself; see *Taking Rights Seriously*, 134–135.

44. See Barber, *The Constitution and the Delegation of Congressional Power*, 37–41.

45. This discussion of the rule of precedent relies on Moore, "A Natural Law Theory of Interpretation," 352–371.

46. See Parents Involved in Community Schools v. Seattle School Dist. No. 1, 551 U.S. 701, 746–748 (2007).

47. Id., at 801–803

48. 274 U.S. 357, 371–372, 372–380 (1927).

49. 249 U.S. 47, 52 (1919).

50. 539 U.S. 558 (voiding a state law that criminalized homosexual conduct).

51. 478 U.S. 186 (upholding a state law that criminalized homosexual conduct; overruled by Lawrence v. Texas, 539 U.S. 558).

52. See Greve, *Real Federalism*, 2; Chemerinsky, *Enhancing Government*, 227.

ACKNOWLEDGMENTS

This book would not have been possible without the support of the American Council of Learned Societies and Notre Dame's College of Arts and Letters. I received generous help from the staff of the Charleston Library Society and from Nicole Tolbert, who prepared several "final" drafts of the manuscript. I'm grateful for the criticisms and advice of Elizabeth Knoll, Gary Lawson, and an anonymous reviewer for the Harvard University Press. I've profited from the criticism of participants of various conferences at which I presented parts of my argument over the last several years. These include Michael Blake, Alan Gibson, Stephen Macedo, James Read, Frank Slade, Robin West, and Ernest Young. I'm especially grateful for the criticisms and advice of Karen Flax, James Fleming, Jeffrey Tulis, and our departed friend, Walter Murphy.

Sotirios A. Barber
Notre Dame, IN

INDEX

and positive constitutionalism, 54; on states
as checks on national power, 95–96; on
priority of public goods over negative
liberties, 177–178; and public reasonableness,
181; on responsible government, 198. *See also*
Hamilton, Alexander; Madison, James

Federalism axiom: as inference from
enumeration of powers, 28, 35, 159;
Marshallian view of, 44; as denying the
multiple dimensions of human conduct,
84; process federalism's denial of, 159;
different versions of, 160. *See also*
Federalism

Feeley, Malcolm: on faux states' rights
arguments, 100, 142; on political identity,
142; on competitive federalism, 220n21; on
futility of defending states' rights federalism,
223n76

Fleming, James, 39

Fletcher v. Peck (1810), 45, 70, 73, 74–78

*Florida Prepaid Postsecondary Education
Expense Board v. College Savings Bank*
(1999), 158

Frankfurter, Felix, 106

Fugitive Slave Act (1793), 37, 136

Garcia federalism: *See* Process federalism

*Garcia v. San Antonio Metropolitan Transit
Authority* (1985), 20–22, 53, 61,148, 149,
153–156

"Generality and locality," principle of: as the
principle of American federalism, 33, 112,
118; Abraham Lincoln's statement of, 33, 116,
169, 190; and competitive federalism, 101;
John Marshall's statement of, 116–117; logic
of, 117–118; Larry Kramer on, 118; and the
Virginia Plan (Constitutional Convention of
1787), 169–170; criticism of, 170; and process
federalism, 170; and Marshallian federalism,
192, 204

General Welfare Clause, 191, 193–195

Gibbons v. Ogden (1824), 59–60, 111–115

Gibson, Alan, 218n41

Gonzales V. Carhart (2007), 227n8

Gregory v. Ashcroft (1991), 94–95, 100

Greve, Michael, 41, 101–105, 208

Gun Free School Zones Act (1990), 89, 100

Hamilton, Alexander: on need for strong
government, 4; on practical reason, 4–5; as
positive constitutionalist, 32; on war powers,
34; on states as checks on national power,
37–38, 95–96; on ends of government,
180–181; on public attitudes as basis for
securing private rights, 203; on government
by reflection and choice, 208

Hammer v. Dagenhart (1918), 40, 61, 70

Hayne, Robert Y., 137

Heart of Atlanta Motel v. United States (1964),
83

Holmes, Oliver Wendell, Jr., 55, 72, 106

Identity, personal: and states' rights, 13, and
right to travel, 104–105, 227n18; and public
reasonableness, 105, 213n24, and practical
reason, 147. *See also* Identity, political;
National community

Identity, political, 137–138, 140–144. *See also*
Identity, personal; National community

Internal improvements, 58–59. *See also*
General Welfare Clause

Interposition. *See* Nullification

Jefferson, Thomas: as states' righter, 8, 40, 131;
on nullification, 57–58; and compact theory
of union, 94, 130–131; on slavery as necessary
evil, 126

Johnson, Andrew, 154

Kennedy, Anthony, 159

Kentucky Resolution (1798), 57–58, 94, 130. *See
also* Jefferson, Thomas

Kimel v. Florida Board of Regents (2000), 158

Kramer, Larry, 118

"Large Commercial Republic": as comprehensive Constitutional end, 85–87, 169, 173, 180,
209; values of, 175, 188, 190–192; and public
reasonableness, 193–195; and Martha
Nussbaum's defense of liberalism, 223n27.
See also: Berns, Walter; Diamond, Martin

Lawrence v. Texas (2003), 206

Lawson, Gary, 62

Leadership, political: 16, 18–19, 32–33, 87, 175,
201–202, 207–208